D0499615

"*Mama Can't Remember Anymore is [...]* that is also highly readable... Wexler's con[...] wisdom are empowering, and will go far to help assuage the guilt and frustration that caregivers often feel when confronted with elder care.*"

Jeanne Gordon, writer and Newsweek
contributor, in GCM JOURNAL

"*Mama Can't Remember Anymore offers a comforting, practical yet compassionate approach to this challenging experience. As a Geriatric Care Manager, I have recommended it as required reading to family members, many of whom borrow my well-worn copy! We also have your books in the lending library of our church's Parish Nurse Program. All three copies are usually checked out!*

So many people have commented to me that Mama Can't Remember Anymore is one of the most helpful resources that they have encountered. Thank you for creating this wonderful book."

Paula P. Tchirkow, LSW, ACSW, President,
Allegheny Geriatric Consultants, Pittsburgh, PA

"*I'm happy to tell you that I am using the second edition of Mama Can't Remember Anymore: Care Management of Aging Parents and Loved Ones as a supplementary text in my teaching.*

In the Economics of Aging, we emphasize issues of health and long-term care. The book is especially valuable in giving students your unique practitioner-based perspective on assisted living, nursing homes, Alzheimer's Disease, and the profession of geriatric care management. It provides the human, professional, and geriatric perspective to which all of these students should be exposed."

Neal E. Cutler, University of Pennsylvania
Adjunct Professor of Gerontology and Social Policy

"*Your book <u>Mama Can't Remember Anymore</u> has been a helpful tool in my practice. I recommend the book to clients so that they won't feel so alone. It gives an overview of how to handle an aging parent. The adult child can learn how different professions coordinate their efforts and what resources are available.*"

Ruth Phelps, Esq., President
Southern California Chapter of
National Academy of Elder Law Attorneys

"*This manual provides the answers to the many perplexing questions for potential caregivers. Wexler's book is not a do-it-yourself volume...It is a guide for people who must provide for an elderly loved one. Wexler is a pioneer in the field of private geriatric care management. She presents a convincing case for the need for qualified personnel in this new field...It is an important manual for professionals and for families with elders...*"

Sol H. Marshall
"B'NAI B'RITH MESSENGER"

"*I ordered <u>Mama Can't Remember Anymore</u>—I am so impressed with the content. It is excellent for professionals as well as lay caregivers! The style and flow make it easy to read and understand. Everything about it is unique, different from other books about dementia. Congratulations on a difficult job being done very well.*"

Lois M. Brandriet, Ph.D.,
Nurse Gerontologist, Highland, Utah

See further testimonials from clients and professionals on page 371

Mama Can't Remember Anymore

Care Management of Aging Parents and Loved Ones

Newly Revised & Updated 2nd Edition:
Resources/Bibliography/Glossary

NANCY WEXLER, MA, MFCC

with Wesley J. Smith and Ron Norman
Foreword by Dan Osterweil, MD

In order to keep this edition of the book as current as possible, the author will periodically provide updates to readers, as important new information becomes available. Please send your name, address, and telephone/fax to Nancy Wexler at the address below.

Note:
"MAMA CAN'T REMEMBER ANYMORE: CARE MANAGEMENT OF AGING PARENTS AND LOVED ONES" is not intended as medical, legal, or financial advice. The book's intent is solely informational and educational, to be used in an ongoing partnership between caregivers, professional geriatric care manager, and other medical, legal, or financial professionals. All readers are urged to consult with these professionals.

Since all governmental services and benefits are currently being intensively debated in Congress, check with the proper agencies, organizations, and professionals to verify the status, benefits, and availability of any given assistance program.

For permission to reproduce any part of this book, please contact:

Nancy Wexler, Director
Gerontology Associates
P. O. Box 572499
Tarzana, California 91357, USA
(818) 342-3136

Cover and book design by Sharlene Wein.
Cover photography by Ed Wein.
Partners Publishers Group,
Austin and Nelson
Typesetting by Victoria Graphics, Orange, CA
Printing by KNI, Inc., Gail Foor, Anaheim, CA

First edition: June 1991
Reprinted: March 1992
Second edition: March 1996
Reprinted: August 1997

Library of Congress Catalog Card Number: 92-60279
ISBN: 0-9629358-2-4
Printed in the U.S.A.

Table of Contents

Acknowledgments

I am indebted to all my clients and their families. Their poignant stories over the past fifteen years have laid the foundation for this book and helped make it into a living human document.

I am particularly grateful to:
My husband, Charles Wexler, MD, who has devoted unlimited time, love and patience as a sounding board for my ideas and teammate in my work.

My daughter, Karen Wexler Scheffler, JD, a successful lawyer, who has lovingly supported me along my often difficult and bumpy journey, and helped edit the first edition of this book.

My son, Michael Wexler, MD, who graduated Tufts Medical School with an honors award in geriatric medicine, and has a special interest in geriatric psychiatry.

My father, the late Honorable Raymond Reisler, Supreme Court Judge in New York, who was always extremely supportive and inspired me in my work.

My mother, Harriet Spitzer Reisler, who is in good health and celebrated her 86th birthday, December 16, 1996.

My father-in-law, David Wexler, MD, a nonagenarian who has been there for me over 30 years, as a role model for successful aging.

My gratitude goes to Dan Osterweil, MD, a pioneer in the field of geriatric medicine, for his superb leadership in the profession. He has been a friend and mentor for over a decade.

It is impossible to sum up my warm feelings towards Harold Paulus, MD, Stanley Marcus, MD, Burt Liebross, MD, Daga Peterson, RN, Terry Voges, RPT, Francine Snyder, Ph.D., and Jeanne Levy, who literally saved my life and helped me through my greatest battle.

Heartfelt thanks go to Paula Richwine, Leslie Feibelman, Emma Parica, RN, Maria Mariscal, Steve Pearson, and Ilene Fletcher, for their many years of loyal friendship and encouragement.

I want to acknowledge Laury Adsit of the National Association of Geriatric Care Managers, for her extraordinary management skills, warmth, and invaluable support.

Thank you to Betty Field, MFCC, my Supervisor of many, many years, whose loyalty and passion in her life and work have served as an example in my own career.

I was fortunate to have trained at OPICA, under the guidance of its inspiring founder, Yung Huo Liu, PhD.

I want to particularly thank Priscilla Ebersole, co-author with Patricia Hess, for their landmark book, *Toward Healthy Aging: Human Needs and Nursing Response.* It was an inspiration and helped me take off in this chosen field.

I remain indebted to Sharlene Wein for her assistance in editing the first edition. The book seemed to fill an unmet need and touched so many readers, assisting in the acceptance and growth of the new field of geriatric care management.

Deep appreciation to Karen White, MSW, for her original ideas, commitment to my work, and friendship. Also, to Susan Latta, MFCC, for her ongoing professionalism, loyalty and friendship.

For those who have admired my professional assessments, my gratitude goes to Susan Latta, MFCC, Karen White, MSW, Niamh Doyle, RN, Kathy Sawyer, MSW, Kathy Martinez, RN, Ellen Thaler, MSW, Cheryl Hubert, OTR, Susan Widen, MA, Pat Jackson, MA, Darlene Weiner, Ph.D., and Kathy Black, MSW, MSG, MPH, LVN.

My appreciation to Jennifer Feuerstein, who brought her youthful energy and great sense of humor to my office, to Carla Schlesinger, who has organized my office in such a positive manner, and to Sheryl Katzovitz for wearing so many hats and helping out with every conceivable task.

Special acknowledgment, thanks, and friendship to my Editor, Ron Norman, who has taken time off from his filmmaking to persevere long editorial nights alongside my roses and cats, sharing interminable tuna sandwiches, and somehow managing to keep his (Groucho) Marxian humor, while maintaining a sense of the literate and humane.

There are so many other friends and colleagues I would like to acknowledge, some of whom I have known over a twenty year period. Further professional and personal acknowledgments continue in Appendix F. My only real regret is that a deluxe leather-bound book can't be published to thank them all.

See Appendix F, pages 299-301, for additional acknowledgments.

<u>Dedicated to Nomie</u>

*Naomi ("Nomie") Wilkin, age 93,
my dear friend and role model
for self-actualization in old age.*

<u>**Cover:**</u>

Yes, the cover is my four-generation family photograph...The center of attention, of course, through no fault of my own, is Baby Nancy.

Prologue

A DIFFERENT PERSPECTIVE ON AGING AND CARING

by Paul E. Ruskin, M.D.

I was invited to present a lecture to a class of graduate nurses who were studying the "Psychological Aspects of Aging." I started my lecture with the following case presentation:

"The patient is a white female who appears her reported age. She neither speaks nor comprehends the spoken word. Sometimes she babbles incoherently for hours on end. She is disoriented about person, place and time. She does, however, seem to recognize her own name. I have worked with her for the past six months, but she still doesn't recognize me.

"She shows complete disregard for her physical appearance and makes no effort whatsoever to assist in her own care. She must be fed, bathed and clothed by others. Because she is toothless, her food must be pureed; because she is incontinent of both urine and stool, she must be changed and bathed often. Her shirt is generally soiled from almost constant drooling. She does not walk. Her sleep pattern is erratic. Often, she awakens in the middle of the night, and her screaming awakens others.

"Most of the time she is very friendly and happy. However, several times a day she gets quite agitated without apparent cause. Then she screams loudly until someone comes to comfort her."

After the case presentation, I asked the nurses how they would feel about taking care of a patient as the one described. They used words such as, "frustrated," "hopeless," "depressed," and "annoyed" to describe how they would feel.

When I stated that I enjoyed taking care of her and that I

thought they would too, the class looked at me in disbelief. I then passed around a picture of the patient: my six-month-old daughter. After the laughter had subsided, I asked why it was so much more difficult to care for a ninety-year-old patient, than a six-month-old with identical symptoms.

We all agreed that it's physically easier to take care of a helpless baby weighing 15 pounds than a helpless adult weighing 100 pounds, but the answer seemed to go deeper than this.

The infant, we all decided, represents new life, hope, and almost infinite potential. The demented senior citizen, on the other hand, represents the end of life with little potential for growth.

We need to change our perspective. The aged patient is just as lovable as the child. Those who are ending their lives in the vulnerability of old age deserve the same care and attention as those who are beginning their lives in the vulnerability of infancy.

-Reprinted with permission from:
Journal of the American Medical Association
(11/11/83, vol. 250, p. 2440).

Foreword

by Dan Osterweil, M.D.

As a Geriatrician, I have known and worked with Nancy Wexler for over a decade. We recommend her book to our patients and their families at the S⁺AGE Clinic at the Encino-Tarzana Regional Medical Center, where I am the Medical Director. In fact, it's on the coffee table in the waiting room, and judging from the pages, it is the most thumbed-through piece of reading material we provide.

Nancy Wexler was in the business before there was a business. This is not to say that Nancy is old. In fact, she's young and beautiful (and more importantly, joyful and full of a zest for life). But the entire *profession* of private geriatric care manager is as "young as the hills"... only about 15 years old.

It may be strange, calling "helping people" a business, but like everything else involving humankind (other than martyrdom, which we all praise but don't aspire to), it is. It's one of the blessed businesses.

Imagine! Earning one's living, doing something you truly love, and giving elderly people the curtain call they deserve, if for no other reason than having survived (no mean feat in today's world of pure chaos)...and...giving the caregivers of these wonderful, difficult elderly people the possibility of a guilt-free, honorable, intimate farewell with their loved or unloved aging family members.

Say what you want about politicians, bankers, and lawyers (to be politically correct, *some*): They may be community-minded and charitable, but few of them, with all their power, can have such an immediate, precise, no-nonsense effect for the good.

Geriatric care managers, along with priests, ministers, rabbis, mullahs, good shrinks, and perhaps a few physicians, can actually affect the lives of needy human beings. And once we get old, real old, we are all needy.

This book, a second revised, updated, and reformulated edition, is part of Nancy's legacy. The first edition was explosive in its quiet ability to fill unmet needs of a society which more or less ignored its elderly and lacked knowledge on how to deal with them. The second edition continues and expands the work of the first. Additionally, it adds a well thought-out series of Appendixes, Resources, Bibliography, and Glossary.

May Nancy Wexler continue to write new editions, ad infinitum. I, myself, can't wait to read the twentieth edition.

DAN OSTERWEIL, MD, MScED, AMDA, is the Medical Director of the S⁺AGE Clinic (Specialized Ambulatory Geriatric Evaluation) at Encino-Tarzana Regional Medical Center. In addition, he serves as Associate Professor of Medicine and Geriatrics at University of California, Los Angeles, Director for Academic Programs at the Jewish Home for the Aging of Greater Los Angeles, Grancell Village Campus, and Director of the Mini-Fellowship Program at both the California Geriatric Education Center and UCLA.

Dr. Osterweil's areas of expertise are cognitive and functional assessment, particularly fall assessment, management of dementia, and pressure sores. He has lectured and consulted throughout the world on the needs and problems of the elderly.

Preface

In recent years, as aging children and their aging parents have pioneered new caregiving experiences, **private geriatric care management** has become a compass for families charting unknown territories.

As a founder and five-year member on the Board of Directors of the National Association of Professional Care Managers (GCM), I am proud to have been an integral part of this profession's growth.

In meeting the challenges of aging, when dependence and depression strike an older loved one, a family needs much more than a doctor's prescription. The family must learn as much as possible about the conditions, and what options are available.

Concerned family members are usually overwhelmed when they face an immediate crisis with a beloved **elderly family member (EFM)**. Suddenly, they must confront a maze of possible interventions, critical medical and financial decisions, and complex long-term planning strategies.

Family caregivers need to know what choices and resources are available, to be certain that nothing "falls through the cracks." They want to do the right thing. Whether they love, like, dislike, or even occasionally hate their EFM, they don't want to feel guilty or have regrets later on.

Family members desperately need a caregiver's map and a dedicated professional guide, to achieve the optimum benefits for their EFM, as well as for themselves. This is where a good geriatric care manager comes in.

First and foremost, a professional care manager tries to improve the EFM's quality of life. Quality of life, not length, is the key word. At the same time, the GCM attempts to protect the family's hard-earned savings by suggesting cost-efficient options.

This book is not a do-it-yourself manual. It doesn't offer easy solutions or New Age miracles. Nor does it suggest how to treat specific cases, which are as individual as human beings are unique.

Most importantly, a book does not substitute for a competent professional assessment and care management.

This book does supply facts, dispels myths, and corrects misinformation. It alerts caregivers to the crucial need for **early intervention**, so they can prepare a plan of action for the immediate and long-term care of elderly loved ones.

The book can also serve as a caregiver's bible during times of crisis, when families really need it. Because some people may not read the entire book, but only selected chapters of interest, many important topics are referred to and detailed in more than one place.

Throughout this book, I use true stories and syntheses of true stories about some of my clients and patients as examples. This allows the reader to relate to real-life situations similar to their own, gaining what they can from others' mistakes, successes, and courage. Of course, names and details have been changed to protect their privacy.

It is not possible to completely cover the ever-expanding field of care management for the elderly in a single volume. Instead, this book deals with the subjects of interest to most caregivers, and asks forgiveness from those whose questions and particular situations have been omitted.

The goal of this book is to empower caregivers to become knowledgeable, competent care managers for the elderly loved ones they are entrusted with.

Preface to Second Edition

When the first edition of this book was being written, I had no idea how deeply the new concept of private geriatric care management would resonate and take hold in our society,

Over the past five years, the response to "Mama Can't Remember Anymore: How To Manage the Care of Aging Parents" has been so widespread and gratifying that I felt inspired to do a revised, updated edition, so the book could continue to empower families.

My commitment to providing down-to-earth, useful education and realistic help to families is even stronger now. With the growing numbers of people needing professional geriatric help for their elderly family members, and with governmental support systems and medical care for seniors presently in such flux, I believe this book is needed more than ever.

- Nancy Wexler
Tarzana, California
February, 1996

CHAPTER 1

My Story: Denial
or
"I've Walked a Mile in Their Shoes"

One of the most demanding dilemmas facing families involves the care of older members who can no longer competently care for themselves. At such times, family relationships can short-circuit. Terrible strains can be placed on emotions and finances, escalating into family crises.

Believe me, I know of what I speak. While I have not yet reached the winter of my life, I've been severely disabled. In fact, disabled seems too polite a word for the hell I endured when I fell severely ill with a muscular disease that left me paralyzed from the neck down.

It all began innocently enough. I started to feel fatigued after a normal day of work and play. Soon, it was arduous getting to the top of the stairs without resting half-way up.

So what did I, a trained and licensed family counselor, do? What did my husband, a licensed medical doctor, do? Just what most people do when faced with an impending crisis: we went into denial.

Let me tell you about denial... When it takes hold, you refuse to admit your avoidance of a very real problem. After I found it all but impossible to climb stairs, did we go to a doctor to find out what was wrong? No. We waited until I could no longer even walk before going to the doctor. Now, that's denial!

The bad thing about denial is that it doesn't make the problem go away. All, it does is prevent any chance of finding an early cure or solution. And it increases the likelihood that the problem will continue to grow into a crisis...a crisis that could involve the ultimate issue of life and death.

But that may not be the worst of it. More painful to handle than a physical breakdown are the emotional issues that go along with it.

How do I describe what it feels like to watch in horror as one's own body refuses to do the normal, everyday things that we take so much for granted? How do I let you see into the dark room of humiliation and despair that I entered, when I could no longer control my own bodily functions?

1984: I was flat on my back in bed. Three months later we celebrated our 20th anniversary, and I was still lying flat on my back in bed...I didn't get out of bed again for a year.

How can anyone who hasn't lived through the feeling of helplessness and impotence, understand the raw panic that arose as I was forced to rely on others for every human want and need? It's not easy. And how can I stress enough the absolute necessity of having a loving and understanding family just "be there" for the disabled person - to sit through the hours of agony and depression - to share the little victories that lead toward renewed independence - to simply hold their hand or stroke their brow, as the dependent person escapes into sleep?

It is during a crisis when family and friends mean so much. These times of hardship test the mettle of family, either renewing it stronger than ever, or rending it down the middle, leaving a legacy of bitterness and hurt that can last for generations.

When I became totally physically dependent, my family reacted in different ways. Again the key word was "denial."

My husband, Charles, did his best to make sure I had all the comforts of home. Fortunately, he is a physician, which facilitated making the decision that I should stay at home, with around-the-clock nursing care.

This, of course, cost a small fortune. Soon, we found ourselves deeply in debt, as we tried to "ride the tiger" until I recovered.

It deeply hurt Charles to see me bedridden, unable to move my head. As many of us do when facing fear and despair, he turned elsewhere for solace. Happily in our case, the "other" wasn't a woman... it was a computer. Charlie became a computer addict. Now, his expertise with the microchip has made both our professional lives far easier to organize and manage.

My daughter, Karen, had a different way of coping with my illness: She pretended nothing was wrong. There was always a smile on her face and a forced lilt of happiness in her voice. She popped into my room to give me a quick kiss, then off she'd go to spend as much time as possible with friends and at school activities...anything but face the powerlessness and disability that her mother was enduring.

Karen told me it took an entire year to work through her tremendous fears about my illness, to be able to face it - and me - squarely. I am glad to tell you that we have a wonderful honest and open relationship, which is one of the great joys of my life.

My son, Michael, then a teenager, angrily withdrew because he suddenly was burdened with a no-longer-functioning mother. At the same time, he felt guilty about his anger. This caused us both a lot of pain and adversely affected our relationship for some time.

I am delighted to report that all's well that ends well. Michael and I have reconciled. In the end, perhaps my illness had a positive impact on him... I'm now the proud mother of a doctor who intends to devote his career to being a psychiatrist for the elderly.

So my family, perhaps like yours, plunged full-speed into escapism. We denied the seriousness of my predicament. Once that was impossible, we finally started to confront the problems, the *surface* problems. But at least we handled them effectively.

The inner crisis...that was another story. Our failure to deal with my near-death intimately, as a family, led to feelings of estrangement and bitterness that took real work to cure.

Fortunately, I slowly recovered from my visit to disabilityland. I learned to walk again, to manage my medications, and to cope with my devastating illness.

The things I experienced, while in such a totally dependent

state, gave me invaluable insights into what it is like to be disabled, needy, and old. I know what someone in that unfortunate condition wants and requires from caregivers. Happily, I learned how to continue working and live a productive, rewarding life with a chronic disease.

Incorporating these insights into my work enables me to provide vital assistance, advice and direction, otherwise unavailable, not only to those as acutely ill as I was, but to all seniors who become unable to function independently.

The awesome power and danger of denial never ceases to amaze me.

As in the case of Bill...

Bill

One of my clients is a health care professional of national repute who suffers from early Alzheimer's. This disease causes loss of memory and other symptoms of dementia (*see Chapter 3*).

Bill had been successfully covering up his affliction for a long time. I realized that something must be afoot when he retired at the very early age of 62, even though he was brilliant and loved his work.

Bill still refuses to acknowledge the truth of what is happening to him, or what it means for his family's future.*

Bill's wife Mary, a take-charge CEO who always confronts business realities head-on, has all her corporate problems under control. But she cannot bear to face the more personal reality of her husband's condition. Mary actively encourages Bill to continue driving. This is extremely dangerous denial.

Their son, Chuck, finally told me what was going on. Grief stricken over his father's prognosis, Chuck was greatly concerned about the refusal of his mother to confront Bill's true

---

*If a person with early-Alzheimer's patient does acknowledge the disease, there are now very useful supportive seminar groups for dementia patients and their caregivers. Such discussions may help relieve anxiety, clear up misinformation, improve family communication, increase trust, and alleviate the sense of isolation.

condition. He asked me to make an informal assessment.

Bill may have early Alzheimer's, but that doesn't mean he has lost his ability to judge other people's agendas.

Bill knew I came to check on him and he was furious: "My son betrayed me!"

Yet, his symptoms of dementia were easily observed by the trained eye. Shortly after insisting that he was fine, the telephone rang. My heart sank as I watched Bill vainly crying, "Hello! Hello! Hello!"...unable to communicate with the caller because he forgot how to push the flashing button to activate the line.

My colleague checked on him again later and found Bill wandering in the street, totally confused, without his house keys. We told Chuck that someone must accompany Bill to make sure he is safe. They spoke to Mary, who responded, "No! Bill doesn't need help!"

Bill is often left at home alone, where he could easily hurt himself. He is endangered because Mary refuses to deal constructively with the bad hand dealt to the family.

Sadly, Bill and Mary continue in denial as these words are written, insisting, "we can handle it," every time their children express concern. But they can't handle it. Their situation is a time-bomb waiting to explode.

Despite all the loving intentions, Bill is being ill-served. At this stage of the disease, good professional assistance would make a major positive difference in the quality of life for Bill and his family.

Bill is slowly descending into severe memory loss, which will impair his ability to continue the life he used to lead. Dementia will prevent him from safely getting through the day. Now, before an emergency occurs, is the time when a plan of action must be created to assist him.

Denial prevents Bill from receiving the nurturing support he deserves. Denial stops the family from making vital legal and financial arrangements. None of the things that should be done now, to ensure proper care later, are being done.

Not confronting the real issues hurts Bill, hurts Mary, and

will most likely hurt the family. Avoidance simply forestalls and worsens the painful decisions that are surely to come.

Bill's case, as well as my own family embracing the false comfort of denial, illustrate a vital truth: When physical or cognitive symptoms indicate a gathering storm, don't ignore the dark clouds on the horizon...confront them openly with each other and with the family doctor.

If the worst comes to pass, don't run from the pain. Face your fears, share the agony, problem-solve together as a family, and work with professionals who specialize in problems of the elderly.

CHAPTER 2

A Growing Profession

Let us take note...
It is the old apple trees that are decked with the loveliest blossoms.
It is the ancient redwoods that rise to majestic heights.
It is the old violins that produce the richest tones.
It is the old wine that tastes the sweetest.
It is for ancient coins, old stamps, and antique furniture
*   that many eagerly seek.*
It is when the day is old and far spent
*   that it displays the beauteous colors of the sunset.*
It is when the year is old and has run its course
*   that Old Mother Nature transforms the world into a fairyland*
*   of snow.*
It is the old friends that are the dearest, and it is the old people
*   that have been loved by God for a long, long time.*
Thank God for the blessings of old age:
Its faith, its love, its hope,
*   its patience, its wisdom, its experience, its maturity.*

- Adapted from a publication of the
Older Women's League (OWL)

In the original edition, the title of this chapter was *"The Newest Profession."* Since that time, the field of private geriatric care management has blossomed in influence and importance. The **National Association of Professional Geriatric Care Managers (GCM)**, has over 1000 members throughout the United States who operate under the highest standards.

Serving on the Board of Directors for five years, and writing this book, have been my ways of contributing to this fine organization's growth and excellent work.

For more than a decade, GCM has helped families and patients who are overwhelmed with the stressful challenges of aging. The organization has established a nationwide network of respected professionals in 47 states, and has created a "Constitution" and "Bill of Rights" that sets strict ethical standards, establishing client rights.

The Baby Boomers and our population as a whole are aging. In 25 years, 50 million of us will be over the age of 65. There is a more critical need for professional geriatric care managers than ever before.

WHO WE ARE

We are here for you...when Mama doesn't remember anymore, when Dad suffers a stroke, when your favorite Uncle or Aunt no longer can live alone safely...when you are trying your best to take care of an elderly loved one, and all your efforts just don't seem to be enough.

Whenever a family is in crisis because a relative's golden years have begun to tarnish...it is the right time to seek out a professional.

I am a Private Geriatric Care Manager. Simply stated, I'm hired to make sure that the wants and needs of older people requiring assistance are provided for. In essence, I am the "hub" of their senior-care wheel, making sure all aspects of their lives are attended to properly.

This dedicated outside aid gives senior citizens and their loving families the freedom and opportunity to live fuller quality lives. A thousand of my colleagues perform such services for many thousands of families throughout America.

It must be understood that we are not public health workers, employed by the government. We work for you. Our commitment is to our clients.

Unlike public health workers, we are free to accept the clients who will most benefit from our skills and individual personalities.

Nor should we be confused with the "gatekeeper" type of case managers, whose goal is cost-containment in whatever domain they work. For instance, one of the major roles of such medical case managers is to look over the shoulders of doctors and hospitals, to limit treatment whenever possible. Their responsibility is to the companies who hire them.

On the other hand, private geriatric care managers are hired by individuals and families. Our responsibility and commitment are solely to you.*

While "case manager" is often used as a buzzword for "cost effective," the emphasis of *care* managers is on *quality* of life. Care managers attempt to be cost-effective, working within what the family can afford, but always using the elderly family member's needs and the quality of life as the guideline.

Geriatric care managers charge varying fees for their services. Some of these may be partially covered by insurance, others are not. Like lawyers, accountants and most other professionals, we bill you for our time spent in crisis intervention, consultations, care management, traveling, and telephone calls. Discuss financial arrangements during your initial consultation.

It's to your advantage to consult with a geriatric care manager *before* making crucial decisions about your elderly parent. It's as much of a priority as getting a good road map, and checking out your car's safety before a major trip. Most clients wish they came to us sooner, before they "took the wrong road," or made mistakes resulting in "accidents."

We are highly trained to do what we do. We provide our time, training, and experience. A degree is required to be a member of the National Association of Professional Geriatric Care Managers. Many of us have Masters or Ph.D. degrees and/or licenses in gerontology, psychology, family therapy, social work, or nursing.

---

*During my years in the profession, I estimate that I've received and responded to approximately 150,000 telephone calls, not to mention consultations in the office. There obviously is a tremendous need for the services of geriatric care managers and other professionals who are specifically trained in helping the aged. As the number of elderly people escalate, personal finances dwindle, government benefits vanish, health care remains in flux, and life gets ever more difficult, the need is rapidly growing.

Geriatric care managers do not personally perform many of the hands-on services provided to the people we assist...for instance, companion care. That is why we are called "managers." Instead, we evaluate what services our clients require, and then select, supervise, and/or direct their implementation. The essential part of our job is to assess the condition and the needs of an elderly person. Then, we go through our files, collected from years of personal contact and experience with other professionals. *We pull together a multi-disciplinary team.* We assist in selecting and supervising those who work directly with your loved one.

In other words, we find the right people for the job, and make sure it is done right.

The intervention of a geriatric care manager will save you hundreds of hours of research time. The stressful search for the right answers to aid your elderly loved-one is like a TV game show: Make the right decision and you get the prize. Make the wrong decision and you can lose everything.

Such professional guidance alleviates the frustration of coming smack up against bureaucratic brick walls in your community or with your HMO, as you try to find the correct "care doors" to enter. It saves you from mistakes which can cost you and your loved-one too much money and pain.

OUR RAISON D'ÊTRE

We all get old. This is not an extraordinary observation, yet it's a powerful fact which, at least sometime in our lives, we all deny. And sooner or later, we will all need some help with daily living.

The difficulties confronting a family that takes care of an elderly relative are daunting and can be frightening. For instance...

You realize that your parents need assistance with the chores of daily living. Should you hire a part-time or full-time companion or home health aide? Can you afford it? And how do you find one who is trustworthy?

What if your parents absolutely refuse to accept a stranger

in their home, and insist on receiving help only from you? Can you afford to quit your job? How will your own family accept this major disruption in their lives?

What if your parents live hundreds or thousands of miles away? You might try to fly home once a month, to look in on them. You'd certainly earn a lot of frequent flyer miles, but what would these visits really accomplish, except leaving you with terminal jet lag and an empty bank account? Short visits aren't useful enough for parents who need daily care.

You can try to convince your parents to move near you, but where? Should they move into your home...assuming you have the space, your family agrees, and you can live with them on a daily basis? These are large assumptions.

What if your spouse and children start to resent all the time you spend helping your parents? Will you argue with them?...Probably. Cry?...In all likelihood. Pray?...If you are a believer, that's certainly a rational act.

Should your parents move into senior citizen housing, where they'll be on their own, just as they are now? Or a retirement hotel? A board and care facility? A nursing home?

Are they depressed? Do they have Alzheimer's or a related disorder? Exactly what kind of assistance do they need and how much of it? What is best for them...and for you?

So many questions. And you probably have so many doubts. You may feel you have no choices. You have to make major decisions, perhaps even make major compromises which will satisfy no one. Ultimately, you must find a way to accommodate all the feelings and responsibilities for your aging parents, your family, and yourself...

Maybe you *can* find a solution which will satisfy everybody. When you are overwhelmed by questions without answers, and choices you don't even know you have, it is the best time for a professional geriatric care manager to step in to clearly outline your choices, making order out of chaos and panic.

It may seem strange to hire a stranger, called a "geriatric care manager," to make sure that Mom or Pop is adequately cared for. You may wonder why you should have to pay for services which were traditionally performed by the family and community.

The answer to such doubts and questions can be found in the dramatic changes that have taken place in our society during the last thirty years.

The ties that bind are not as strong as they once were. For most of us, life in the USA no longer resembles a Norman Rockwell painting (if, indeed, it ever really was).

Nowadays, people simply do not have the time, training, or understanding to fulfill the needs of dependent older family members. They may deeply desire to give their loved-ones rich and fulfilling, or at least comfortable Golden Years, but they don't have the ability to do so.

The reasons for this major societal change are several fold:

People are living longer

In my practice, it is not unusual to meet adult children in their 60s or 70s, who have to disrupt their own retirements in order to care for parents in their 90s or even early 100s! No longer will TV's Willard Scott have enough time to wish "happy birthday" to all his centenarian viewers.

We truly live in miraculous times. In this century alone, the medical, pharmaceutical, technological, safety, and nutritional breakthroughs have almost doubled our expected life spans. People over the age of 85 are the fastest growing segment of the population.

Many diseases that once killed us quickly, at relatively young ages, no longer have their deadly bite. In 1918, over a half-million people in the United States died of influenza. Imagine! That tragic toll is unthinkable today in this country. Not even the devastating AIDS epidemic approaches such numbers in one year.

Tuberculosis, polio, measles, diphtheria, and many other acute infectious diseases, have been largely controlled (although TB and polio are threatening to make a comeback). Smallpox, the once-feared mighty killer, has been wiped off the face of the earth.

Oh, what people throughout the ages would have given for the second, third and fourth chances that many of us receive to live long, healthy lives.

And yet, this increase in longevity extracts a price, some-times a heavy price. Old age usually won't be denied its pound of flesh. Our bodies grow weaker. Bones become brittle and memories less acute.

Other slower diseases have taken over from the old stand-by quick killers... We may suffer chronic medical conditions, such as diabetes and heart disease, These slowly debilitate and restrict our bodies, energy, and perhaps worst of all, our spir-its.

Diseases such as cancer strike seniors much more frequently than younger people, and treatment may cause significant im-pairments. (Thus, the old proverb, "The treatment is worse than the disease.")

Alzheimer's disease is the fourth leading cause of death in the United States. It affects more and more older people, some-times taking 8-20 years to kill its victims.

For these, and a host of other reasons, the older population is in greater need of care than ever before.

We no longer have large extended families

"Family" used to play a much bigger role in our lives. Par-ents had a half-dozen or more children, instead of today's 1.5 children. And "the kids" tended to stay closer to where they grew up.

So, when older family members began to show signs of wear-and-tear, the extended family took over. There were al-ways plenty of sons, daughters, nieces, nephews, assorted spouses and children, to assist them in times of need.

In contrast, today's traditional and non-traditional families are more likely to be isolated. When children leave the nest these days, they really leave the nest. Sometimes they move 3000 miles away from where they were raised, from where their parents live.

Modern seniors are also mobile. They, too, may move a thousand or more miles from their original snow-bound home-steads, to retire in the sun. *Many adult children cannot physically be there for their parents*, even when they really want to.

For example, one of my cases involved a daughter who lived in Los Angeles. She was forced to grapple with caring for parents who lived in New Jersey.

Such long-distance care giving would be traumatic even under the best of circumstances. But this case was particularly formidable: one of her parents suffered from Alzheimer's disease and the other from Parkinson's disease. Geriatric care managers see such double-whammy hardship cases everyday. More and more, they are not the exception.

Add up the one-two punches of smaller family size and greater distance from parents, and you have a knock-out. There is no longer the strong network of family care that once existed.

More women are working than ever before

The old saying, "a woman's work is never done," was and is still true. Previously, a woman worked an endless shift as housewife and mother to a large family. Now, after "being liberated," she works an endless shift as housewife, mother (or single-mother) to a smaller family, and also works at the office.

For better or worse, women no longer can afford to restrict their work to the home. They are alongside men in all areas of work and public life in America.

Of course, women's wages are still not commensurate with men's. But more often than not, it is the women who have the responsibility to care for aging husbands, their own elderly parents, their husband's elderly parents, and often other elderly relatives, such as aunts and uncles, who have no one else.

Far more daughters and daughter-in-laws consult geriatric care managers than do men, because women generally live longer and have to take care of all their aging loved-ones.

Adding working careers to their traditional roles has created a profound change in family interaction. Women were always designated by the culture to nourish and care for both the youngest and the oldest in the family. Now, they may not have time or energy to even manage their households the way they would choose, much less attend to the expanding needs of their seniors.

For example, one of my clients valiantly tried to juggle her roles as careerwoman, wife, mother, and caregiver...

Kay

Kay worked for a large corporation as an executive on the fast-track to the top. She enjoyed the challenges and intensity of corporate life, and was able to effectively balance those demands with the joyful work of raising a family.

All seemed well, then, up popped the devil. Her mother, who was only age 67, developed a serious psychotic condition and Kay's life soon became obsessed with mom's crisis-of-the-week. Kay felt guilty, because no matter how much she did, it was never enough.

This additional burden on "Super-Kay" proved more than even she could handle. By the time she finally admitted to herself that she needed assistance and consulted me, Kay was a mere shell of her former robust, assertive self.

I arranged for her mother's psychiatric treatment and for help in the home. Also, I counseled Kay about her unproductive and totally misplaced guilt.

Fortunately, this acted as a safety valve, before the family boiler (or Kay) exploded. Now Mom is doing quite well, and so is Kay's career, marriage, and family.

It's not easy to care for a parent for so many years

Helping a parent through their final years is fulfilling, honorable repayment for the love of a lifetime. But even at best, the task is stressful and emotionally draining. Many people who take on the challenge ultimately find it's much more than they bargained for.

"Second childhood," is commonly used to describe the needs of a frail or impaired older person. It implies that caring for that individual is similar to rearing a child. Nothing can be further from the truth.

In reality, _it is usually much easier to raise a child, than to care for an aging loved-one._ Most of the time, parenting a child is a joyful experience. Caring for an failing parent often is not.

Children are used to being dependent and like the benefits, no matter how stubborn and defiant they may act. Parents, in contrast, often chaff at the bit, and intra-family friction of the worst kind can easily develop when their independence must be restricted. They spent their entire adulthood functioning independently, and they darn well don't want to be "ordered around" by their own children!

However, the exact opposite can also occur...Some parents, instead of protesting that they don't want to "be a burden," *do* expect their children to take care of them. Such older folk were once dependent upon their husbands or wives. Now, they rely on their "kids," who find this an impossible situation. It's a very stressful and sometimes impossible situation for adult children.

Eventually, something has to give. More often than not, that "something" is the stressed caregiver.

Caregivers often desperately wish for a helping hand, feeling angry and trapped in their roles, yet guilty when they don't attend to their loved-ones. That's when they need a geriatric care manager.

Government services can be confusing

Up until now, our government has tried to keep up with the changes in society, much to its credit. Taxpayer-funds from all levels of government exist to assist older people.

Unfortunately, the bureaucratic path to the "promised land" is very confusing. Many citizens, and even government workers in other social services departments, don't know what services are available.

Many people know that their loved-ones qualify for services, but they don't know where or how to get them. At such times, many an intelligent, able, calm caregiver has been known to yell for help.

The uninitiated, faced with escalating geriatric challenges, try to solve the problems without professional assistance. They will often find themselves playing "ring around the telephone."

Here's how the game is played: You call a local senior service center to ask a simple, but necessary question. Trying to be helpful, the operator gives you a clue: another phone number. You dial the new number, wait, and wait. Finally, a harried switchboard operator refers you to yet another phone number, which you hurriedly scribble down before the line goes dead. You take a deep breath, pray, and call the next number. Of course, you're referred to still a fourth phone number, only to have a harried civil servant answer and refer you back to the first number you called.

Then, there's voice-mail hell, too gruesome to fully describe in these "G-rated" pages. This nightmare begins when a synthetic voice rattles off an encyclopedia of menu and sub-menu options. Too confusing for even a Rhodes scholar to comprehend, you must backtrack and listen a second or third time. At this point, you either hang up in rage, or wind up leaving a message in the wrong box and no one calls you back.

If, through the persistence of Job and the luck of a lottery winner, you manage to get living, concerned human beings on the phone, they frequently do not know the answers to your questions.

You've heard the slogan: "Reach out and touch someone?" Well, after going through such a phone odyssey, all you feel is: "Reach out and strangle someone!"

Government services are becoming scarce

Now, for an apparent contradiction. It's true that over the years more services have been extended to include the elderly than ever before. However, the complete truth is that government services, especially in this era of budget crises and major budget cuts, frequently don't go far enough.

Long-term nursing home care, for instance, isn't covered by Medicare. In order to receive financial assistance from a companion program, known generically as Medicaid, needy seniors have to be virtually driven into poverty.

As of early 1996, the Medicaid program was still functioning, but it may be severely diluted and ultimately abandoned.

In-home services, which make daily living activities easier, can keep an old person from going through the nursing home door, but they're often not compensated by any government benefit.

In northern Europe, governments sponsor progressive, creative programs to help the elderly. _Aging is considered part of the human condition_, whereas in the United States, we often see aging as a medical condition...a disease.

Even dementia is not treated as an embarrassment, sin, or crime. Caregivers are respected as professionals, and given proper training. Housing, in conjunction with community services, is considered as vital as personal care needs. To preserve independence and choice, seniors are encouraged to live in the least restrictive environments they can handle. Flexibility, change, and user-friendly environments are encouraged, not resisted. (For instance, elderly citizens are allowed to have cats, dogs, and even a glass of wine with dinner! How personal and humane...a true definition of "compassion.")

These are not pie-in-the-sky fantasies, but social ideals, and as ideals, of course they do not always function perfectly in reality. However, America might look at the health care system in Sweden, for example, and work to integrate much of its humanity into our own medical system. We can learn a lot.

In America, families must look to the private sector for service providers. But what services exist? Who is qualified to render care? Where can help be found?

The era of managed health care is here

If your elderly family member is enrolled in an HMO or other managed health care plan, you may need an advocate on your side. For one thing, it may be difficult to get an appointment quickly, and in many cases, time is of the essence. Someone is needed who knows how to put a little pressure on an over-loaded, slow system.

Even when the patient gets an appointment with their managed care doctor (or a fee-for-service private doctor), without the supervision of an adult child or geriatric care manager, don't count on the fact that an older person will actually go on their own. Your loved one might not want to burden you with transportation, and will no way spend money to take a cab* (especially after living through the Great Depression). So the hard sought-after, much needed doctor's appointment is missed.

People are living so much longer. An elderly person may be afraid of not having sufficient savings to get through old age, and doesn't want to "waste" money on their health and well-being. Also, your EFM often secretively saves the money for your "inheritance," although such false economizing can lead to further physical problems.**

If you are over-burdened by all the pressures, multitude of needs, and scheduling conflicts in your own life, you may need a caring professional "to keep on top of things" and get through the maze.

WE'RE HERE TO HELP

All right, already. Enough about how much geriatric care managers are needed. Let's cut to the chase: what exactly is it that we do?

Assessments

Families frequently wait until a crisis has fallen upon their heads before they reach-out for aid. The status quo may be only barely working, but working nonetheless. When it finally collapses, a desperate need for new ideas and solutions becomes the priority.

Perhaps Grandpa refuses to eat since Grandma died. Maybe Mom breaks her hip or has a disabling stroke. Quite possibly, Uncle Charlie has undiagnosed Alzheimer's, wanders away from his retirement hotel and gets lost, setting in motion a frantic search. Or, caring neighbors call to report that Aunt Edith can't take care of herself any longer, and the closest family member is hundreds of miles away.

---

*Some caring cities provide low-cost/no-cost "taxi coupons" to the elderly or infirmed.

**It should be mentioned that, with costs of care escalating, and government benefits in the process of going down or even being partially eliminated, there might not be much in the way of an inheritance to leave your children.

Usually, a concerned adult child contacts me about an aging parent. Occasionally, the older person or their spouse calls. Whatever the case, the first job of a care manager is to figure out exactly what is going on, then decide what should be done about it. This is known as an **assessment**, the cornerstone of geriatric care management.

Geriatric care managers include in their comprehensive assessment, a *functional* assessment, evaluating how an elderly patient gets through the day, and their quality of life. Many physicians who are not specifically trained in geriatric medicine, do not assess whether older people can cook, feed, toilet, or dress themselves.

While the focus of physicians is on medical problems and prescribing proper medications, GCMs assess the elderly family member's strengths and needs, psychological and social functioning, physical limitations, financial resources, and ability to take care of the Activities of Daily Living (ADLs).

We also speak with physicians and other involved professionals, as well as family, friends and neighbors who help form an accurate picture of what has led up to the current state-of-affairs.

After gathering all the information, issues are identified, recommendations are made, and a care plan with short-term and long-term goals, including ways to implement them, is developed.

Together, the family and the geriatric care manager decide on the best care plan, which is updated as needed. A family may wish to carry out recommendations by themselves, or choose to have the GCM coordinate and implement necessary on-going services.

The GCM is often seen as an extension of the family. This special, caring relationship between a geriatric care manager and a family is invaluable.

A geriatric care manager's in-depth knowledge of local senior services, government benefits, and other sources of assistance to elders and their families, is of tremendous benefit to the client. Simply stated, a good care manager knows where the keys to the kingdom can be found...where to go, whom to see, what to say, and the costs involved.

Professional geriatric care managers may have different procedures, but the objective always is to come up with a meaningful, realistic plan of action that gets the "most bang" for the "fewest bucks." Hopefully, this will result in increased comfort and dignity for the older person, creating harmony in the family.

In-home assistance

Over 9.4 million Americans over age 65 live alone...41% of all older women and 16% of older men.

When a crisis rears its ugly head, the first fear of most people is, "Uh-oh, we need to find a nursing home." Perhaps a family doctor may have told them this.

The fear of most older people is that their family is going to "put them away," into a nursing home. Well, as Ira Gershwin once wrote, "It ain't necessarily so."

On a scale of 1-to-10 (with "10" as the most drastic solution) placement in a nursing home is about an "8." Luckily, most geriatric problems have solutions that fall into the 1-5 range. Try these first.

Usually, the first **intervention** to help a frail older person is **in-home help**. This can include meal preparation, housekeeping, laundry, assistance with hygiene, bathing, grooming, toileting, medications, and companionship.

Often, with in-home assistance and a little TLC from family and friends, an older person can continue to live independently, or can be temporarily assimilated into a family member's household with a minimum of friction.

If the client wishes, a geriatric care manager will screen, interview, select, arrange, and monitor in-home services. Their knowledge of quality, cost and availability of in-home help is extremely useful in choosing the right service providers. Continuing hands-on involvement can guarantee that a senior gets all the quantity and quality of services that are paid for.

Sadly, the family home is probably not where an aging parent with dementia or multiple medical problems will live out the rest of their life. While a geriatric care manager cannot promise that the elderly family member will never need to be placed in a nursing home, they can provide compassion and assistance through this difficult chapter in the lives of the patient and family.

Information and referrals

A geriatric care manager has the objectivity and resources to support clients, with a "world-class Roladex and rugged network of professional relationships. It would take months or years to gather the same information."[6]

Knowing that professional assistance is needed is one thing... Knowing which professionals to select is quite another.

Let's take psychiatry, for example... If an older person appears to be suffering from deep depression and needs the services of a psychiatrist, which one should you choose?

Do you just open the Yellow Pages, close your eyes, and point at a name? Do you go to the psychiatrist who once saw Cousin Jerry for his obesity problem, or the one who worked with Aunt Beth on her alcoholism, or the one who patched-up things between your married friends when he had an affair?

There is no doubt that you can find a psychiatrist without the right referral, but will he or she be the *right* one? Unfortunately, probably not. At one time, child psychiatry was the only sub-specialty in the field. Now there's a recognized sub-specialty known as **geriatric psychiatry**. Geriatric psychiatrists have undergone special training, taken exams in order to get board certification, and have the necessary experience. Unfortunately, geriatric psychiatrists are still few in number and are often difficult to locate without assistance.

One of the most valuable services geriatric care managers provide to clients, are excellent referrals to other professionals who are equally expert in alleviating the concerns of the elderly. Just as important, they *like* to work with aging people. Older people have *unique* needs which are best served by those

---

6 From: "The Lawyer, the Geriatric Care Manager, the Forest and the Trees," by **Lenise Dolen, PhD**, *Elder Law Attorney* (vol. 4, no. 1), New York State Bar Association.

professionals who specialize in geriatric concerns.

I cannot overstate this point... There is often a major difference in commitment, ability, and that vital elusive quality, called "bedside manner," between professionals who are generalists and those who focus on working with the elderly.

If the senior needs an internist, a geriatric care manager knows committed internists with special training and certification in geriatric medicine.

If a lawyer is called for, a geriatric care manager knows the ones with expertise in the new specialty of elder law, who emphasize estate planning, asset conservation, and financial preparation for long-term care.

A geriatric care manager will know which registered dietitians to consult about possible food and drug reactions, if your parent needs a special diet, such as a low-sodium or diabetic diet.

In short, when it comes to finding professional services, a geriatric care manager serves as both the Yellow Pages, and the "fingers that do the walking."

Placement services

There comes a time in many senior citizens' lives when they can no longer live on their own.

Sometimes this means that a nursing home is required. More often, placement in a retirement hotel, assisted living facility, or a small board and care home may be the best decision. It all depends on the needs of the individual and their unique situation, as determined by an assessment.

Families turn to geriatric care managers for needed assistance. These professionals know what level of care is needed, which facilities should be considered, and *when* to place the senior. It is their responsibility to know the quality of facilities at each level of care, and the specific services offered.

Many people do not believe they need professional advice. They think it's easy to randomly select an alternative living arrangement for the elderly family member, choosing blindly from an alphabetical list in the phone book. When such a placement doesn't work out, the well-meaning caregiver often frantically calls a geriatric care manager during a crisis.

Remember, selecting a senior residential facility is one of the most important, far-reaching decisions in your life, for both the EFM and the family.

Help in finding the *right* assisted living facility, nursing home, or other placement option, can mean the difference between a life of quality, comfort and dignity for the person being placed, or something far less.

Matching needs to services

One of the keys to good placement is finding a facility whose level of hands-on services most closely meets the requirements of the person being placed.

Matching needs to services is *essential*. Choosing a facility that offers too much assistance can be a disservice to the elderly person.

First, it will doubtlessly be more expensive, wasting money on services which are not required.

Second, "over-placement" can prove to be socially unproductive, if the other residents function at a lower level. They may not be able to provide the social stimulation which everyone needs in order to enjoy a satisfying life.

Being around people with lower-functioning abilities can lead to a self-fulfilling prophecy. The newly placed person may begin to feel more dependent than he/she really is, instilling a faulty belief that even more assistance is needed.

This, in turn, often leads to an actual loss of functioning, which gradually reduces their quality of life to the lowest common denominator. Let me give you an example of what I mean...

Akira

Relatives placed 87-year-old Akira in a nursing home when the family determined that he could no longer live alone. In "the old country," Japan, families always took care of their elderly, who usually lived in the same home.* But this was America, and "things worked differently here."

Despite their well-meaning attempt to make Akira's life better, his family made a miscalculation. Akira didn't need the intensity of care that the nursing home offered, and he didn't appreciate the lack of freedom. No longer could he grow his prize-winning bonsai trees. The environment made Akira feel old, which, quite frankly, made him miserable. And his misery made his family equally unhappy.

When they called me into the case, I recommended that Akira move to a really good retirement hotel, where he made friends with seniors who were as vibrant as he was. His best "buddy" was an extroverted Irishman, and they got along fabulously.

Perhaps most important to his spirit, Akira could continue growing the beautiful bonsai. He even gave classes to the other seniors.

The added independence and companionship did wonders for the old fellow. When his depression lifted, the women at the hotel were suddenly attracted to him like kittens to catnip! As this is written, Akira is one happy and popular octogenarian.

Just as over-placement can be detrimental, so too can "under-placement." Caregivers also go wrong by placing an elderly relative in a facility that doesn't offer enough care. This only leads to frustration, unexpected hurdles, and a new crisis a little way down the line. When the facility is unable to provide needed care, it will regrettably tell the family the patient must be moved.

A less-supervised environment could be unhealthy for the patient if they don't eat properly, take prescribed medicines, or care for personal needs. In addition, under-placement can be a waste of money, since the level of required assistance is not being given, The senior may wind up as needy as ever, or more

---

*This tradition is true in all Asian countries. Refugees and immigrants who came to America from Taiwan, China, Korea, Vietnam, and Japan face severe problems between generations, largely due to the differences in cultural attitudes towards age and the elderly.

so, if their condition worsens because of too little care.

One of the key jobs of a geriatric care manager is to match the client to the right facility, making sure that they fit like comfortable shoes. GCMs evaluate both the elderly family member and the family, to determine which level of care will provide the best physical support, while maintaining as much independence as is possible under the circumstances. Professional instinct comes into play, because some placements are like new shoes: they take a little time to be properly "broken-in."

Matching facilities and budgets

Each family must decide how much can be spent to provide a place to live for their loved-one. Sometimes the money will come from the senior's own estate, sometimes from children or siblings, or from a combination of them. Other times, the only money available is from Social Security, SSI, and/or Medicaid.

The more money there is to spend, the better the facility that may be available to you, although _expense does not guarantee quality._

If a Rockefeller or Bill Gates should come knocking at my door, believe me, I could place them in a super-elegant retirement home for the elderly. Unfortunately, few of us are Rockefellers, but that doesn't mean we want any less for our loved-ones. We want the best we can afford.

A creative, knowledgeable geriatric care manager works with the client and family to figure out what money is available, then makes sure it is well spent. I always shop around to find my clients the best value for their money, in terms of quality of care, comfort, and location.

Helping clients avoid the "black holes"

We've all heard horror stories of residents being neglected or abused in senior care facilities. The use of experienced geriatric care managers goes a long way toward avoiding the pitfalls, alleviating the guilt, and debunking the myths that make elderly placement seem so scary.

Care managers know the true reputations of facilities in their areas. Their professional guidance is especially useful because, as the old saying goes, "you can't tell a book by its cover."

Many residential facilities may look good or make wonderful claims of service, but they don't come through. Geriatric care managers steer clients to homes or hotels that *really* treat people under their care with dignity, respect, and accountability.

They monitor nursing homes, residential, and other non-medical facilities. GCMs follow through as advocates for elderly patients, in hospitals, HMOs, and managed care plans...wherever the person may need support and advocacy. This helps assure their quality of life.

Surrogate family services

Because of modern economic strains and the desire to live independently, family members frequently don't live near each other anymore,

Despite these massive cultural changes, it goes without saying...but I'll say it anyway...families love each other just as much as they did when they all lived as an extended family, in one house or in the same community. I know. I work with loving families every day of my professional life.

When a parent's or relative's situation deteriorates, and no one lives close enough to give on-going assistance, many families turn to a care manager. We give the needy elderly person our compassionate commitment and knowledge, making sure their needs are fulfilled. Of equal importance, we care and can be a friend. For instance, a care manager might stop by and chat with a patient, to see how things are going.

A care manager, acting as a surrogate daughter or son, is not the same as being there yourself, of course. But when distance, health, or conflicting priorities prevent your personal hands-on assistance, a dedicated care manager is the next best thing. Remember, we all need to experience the demonstration of real interest and affection.

Helping businesses hold on to valued employees

If you are an employer and one of your key employees is having problems dealing with his caregiving responsibilities at home, or with the company's managed care plan, the stress of constant crises will definitely show up in his/her work. This, in turn, may cause a crisis for your company. What do you do?*

One useful tool is to work with the employee and a geriatric care manager, to find ways to take some of the burden off, free up more time, and allow for much-needed R&R. An employer often hires a geriatric care manager to do a one-time assessment of the employee's elderly family member. This helps both the employer and employee understand what they're up against, and helps in the development of a practical caregiving plan to alleviate the problems.

For instance, the GCM may suggest hiring appropriate in-home help, which could make all the difference in the world if the elderly family member is living in the employee's house, or if the employee must make constant emergency trips to visit the EFM.

Another reason an employer may hire a geriatric care manager is to actually implement the recommendations. The GCM can work with the caregiver employee to find good in-home help, adult day-care, or the right placement for the needy family member, if needed.

An employer might even consider the value of paying for professional help for the EFM, and/or counseling for the caregiver employee. After all, if an employee is indispensable

---

*"Employers don't need to turn themselves into aging-service providers...nor do they have to spend a lot of money," says Donna Wagner of the National Council on Aging. "They need to alter the culture within the company so it supports family caregiving."— Quoted in **Sue Shellenbarger's** excellent article, "In Caring for Elders, Sometimes Less Can Accomplish More," from *The Wall Street Journal: Work and the Family* (8/2/95).

Shellenbarger's article also points out that employers deal with the issue of elder care by offering flexible scheduling, resource and referral services, elder care seminars, long-term care insurance, and one-time case assessments by professionals.

to a company, whatever works may be worth it.*

An employer's humane, financially-sound gestures of support for a severely stressed employee can reap a harvest of gratitude, excellent work, and loyalty in the future.

Crisis intervention

As much as 50% of a geriatric care manager's practice is crisis-oriented. Events in a senior's family tend to move in sudden fits and starts. In other words, things will be going along fine when - *BAM!* - the flood gates suddenly open and a crisis bursts out.

A medical emergency might require immediate changes in the senior's lifestyle. The death of their spouse will turn a loved-one's life upside-down. Or suffering the personal indignity of losing the ability to drive may be "the straw that breaks the camel's back."

When it comes to gerontological matters, it's not unusual for families who only yesterday were sailing on balmy seas, to unexpectedly find themselves in the eye of a hurricane.

When such a crisis happens to an elderly person, the entire family is pulled into the crisis. Things seem to occur all at once, which makes even the strongest feel like "a poor little lamb who has lost its way."

(Isn't it startling how accurate the old cliches, nursery rhymes, and pop tune lyrics can be? Ultimately, they reflect the truth about life.)

Frequently, families simply don't know where to turn during an emergency, how to solve the crisis, or whom to see to

---

*According to Kathleen J. Roberts, an executive at Carrington Enterprises: "The inventive idea to consult a professional geriatric care manager, and hire him on behalf of our valued employee, was one of our best investments. Not only did the company weather the projected loss of one of its key executives due to the pressures of family caregiving, we also helped a terrific man through a devastating crisis when his father's dementia deteriorated. This is the kind of personal crisis which, I fear, we may all have to face, sooner or later. No matter how much we paid the geriatric care manager, it wasn't enough for his highly effective work."

make things better.

That's where geriatric care managers come in...to quickly analyze the problem and its causes, find the right resources, and immediately coordinate all the elements and people into a cohesive plan of action.

A case in point occurred just before these words were written...

Sarah

Sarah had invited her older sister from the East Coast, Ginny, to visit her in Los Angeles. Ginny, age 84, had never married and always remained a loner. The sisters hadn't seen each other for a year.

To Sarah's horror, during the entire visit, her sister was obsessed with the plane tickets and talked only about going home. But it was obvious that Ginny was too confused to return to the East Coast and live alone, where she had no family, no close friends, no one to care for her.

So Sarah and her husband took care of Ginny for three months, far longer than the scheduled visit. Soon the couple was arguing every day about their long-term guest. They panicked and simply didn't know what to do to solve the problem. The full realization sunk in that they couldn't care for Ginny in their home forever, because it would break up their marriage.

In desperation, Sarah called me. We did a complete assessment and found an excellent living facility where she could get proper care. In short order, we had the crisis under control.

This is not an unusual type of case. Variations on it happen every day throughout America. A declining elderly person alone is sad. If they cannot find the right support, it is tragic.

That's the job of a geriatric care manager. They know how to respond to a crisis, the same way that a doctor responds to a patient who suffers a medical emergency.

Geriatric care managers are specifically trained for crises and are able to spring right into action, seeing to it that what must be done is promptly accomplished. These emergency care situations provide some of the most critical and personally satisfying opportunities to serve our clients.

Personal counseling

Counseling is a profound and valuable part of my work. And not just for the older person who is experiencing the many trials of aging. Families also need assistance to emotionally prepare for the pending death of a loved one, to deal with the fear this brings up about their own aging, or to vent the anger and frustration that often occurs when caring for an elderly person.

Caregiver clients who come into my office don't always have great relationships with their elderly family member, but they come in anyway. Even though they may have ambivalent or negative feelings toward the EFM, they may still feel a sense of responsibility, guilt, confused emotions of love and hate, or personal pride and self-respect. They consult with me seeking help and solutions to the problems of caregiving, which weigh so heavily on their minds, hearts, and wallets.

As a licensed family therapist, one of the services I'm trained to provide is family counseling, if needed. However, even if geriatric care managers are not licensed in the field of counseling, they can make appropriate referrals.

Before seeking such assistance, it's not unusual for an adult child or other relative caring for an elderly family member to be more needy than the patient. If both spouses, or if an EFM and the caregiver have problems, stress and strain multiply tenfold. For example...

• Mr. Mannheim is now legally blind, and his wife, who must take him everywhere, has congestive heart failure.

• Mr. and Mrs. White both have the beginnings of dementia: she has Parkinson's, he has Alzheimer's.

• Mr. Andersen has diabetes and just had a stroke, while the caregiver, his 49-year-old daughter, has been in a wheelchair for years with multiple sclerosis.

Who can help whom? These are truly overwhelming situations, where professional help can make all the difference.

When a new client first comes into my office for a consultation, it is not unusual for the overwhelmed caregiver to cry out: "I don't have a life of my own! I had a handle on life, but it fell off."

For instance, one courageous client was taking care of her beloved terminally-ill husband, knowing he could die any day. She was also caring for the spouse's aging parents, as well as raising four deaf children! Can you imagine her time and energy commitment, and the emotional stress?

Caregivers feel totally alone and believe they have to handle the ever-escalating problems all by themselves. Although they may not even know what a geriatric care manager does, by the end of the initial session, concerned family members have learned that a geriatric care manager can pull together a multi-disciplinary team of professionals to help. Caregivers leave with a new sense of hope. *They are not alone.*

A previously stressed-out caregiver sighs with relief, "I *can* have a life. I *can* manage the care of my loved-one!"

It is important for caregivers to realize that *their* lives are just as important as that of needy elderly family members.

When caregivers burn-out and reach "the end of their ropes," they feel overwhelming guilt. They may fantasize escaping or vanishing...a natural, healthy response to impossible problems, which makes them feel even more guilty.

Sandy, a school teacher and client, told me that every day when the school bell rang, she imagined reading a headline in the *Los Angeles Times*: "Northridge School Teacher Vanishes Without a trace!" She said it was the only way she could get through another day of caregiving.

The roll of life's dice is often extremely unjust. Overwhelmed caregivers are usually doing the best they can in terrible situations. Yet, despite doing such stressful, exhausting, selfless work, caregivers may feel a sense of undeserved guilt for "not doing enough." A geriatric care manager honestly and correctly is able to offer caregivers "permission" to give up such guilt. This allows caregivers the freedom to seek outside help, so they can finally get some well-earned respite and relief.

Appropriate home help can be arranged to assist the adult child, spouse, or other primary caregiver. Or the time may finally come to place their elderly family member in the right residential, small board and care, or nursing home, which will be able to take better care of the seriously ill or demented EFM.

A caregiver needs guidance for the emotionally difficult process of placement, and often feels a tremendous sense of relief when a geriatric care manager helps them... Sometimes, sharing the weighty responsibility with a sensitive GCM can save the caregiver from being pulled-under and drowning.

The immediate principals aren't the only ones who may be affected by problems with an aged family member. There can be unexpected ripple effects in the family... as in the case of Edith, a very caring woman who brought her parents from Illinois to live with her. Both parents needed an enormous amount of attention and Edith provided it.

Meanwhile, her sensitive young son, Kenny, felt abandoned and intensely jealous. For the first time, he began to have severe behavioral trouble in school, which intensified the crisis atmosphere already in the home.

Because of my training, I was able to spot the trouble and incorporated the boy into his mother's counseling sessions with me. This increased attention did the trick. Kenny eventually became his well-behaved self again.

Teenagers, in particular, are very vulnerable and can even become suicidal when a needy elderly family member suddenly disrupts their home life. They have the second-highest suicide rate, after males over the age of 65.

When an elderly family member moves in, a teen may fear bringing friends home, because the behavior of their demented grandparent embarrasses them.

Teenage years are when children are under the most stress: learning how to function independently from their parents, how to stand up to peer pressure, how to handle their raging sexuality, how to get into college or get a job.

Teens don't handle stress well, even in the most loving families. The added pressure of their parents taking care of an EFM may be too much for them.

In conclusion, there are many different, equally valid reasons why a caregiver may need personal counseling. Every family has its own unique circumstances and story.

It's certainly okay to consult with a geriatric care manager, even if you don't have a positive relationship with your EFM, even if your relationship has always been distant, even if you don't have fond memories of your childhood. We fully understand that every person brings a lot of emotional baggage to their role as caregiver. None of us are saints, none of us has had perfect parents, and none of us has had flawlessly joyous childhoods.

You may still decide to be a caregiver, despite your understandable reservations due to mixed emotions and all the practical hardships, because of your strong sense of responsibility. If so, be secure in the knowledge that you are helping out an older person during a time of their greatest need. This generosity of spirit will leave you with a sense of fulfillment.

Caregiver Effectiveness Training (CET)

Caregiving is one of the most complex, vital, and blessed roles in life, yet one we initially know so little about.

Like so many other things in life - how to repair a car, how to fix a leaky toilet, how to balance a checkbook, how to get information and cooperation from the government, how to be a good parent - the most useful things aren't taught in school. We are expected to somehow learn complex necessary facts and procedures through osmosis.

Who teaches us how to be good caregivers when our parents get sick and we have to take care of them for more years that we took care of our own children?

Caregiver education is one of the major functions of a geriatric care manager, because families need to learn caregiving skills. GCMs teach caregiving effectiveness, modeling appropriate behavior that will help adult children deal with their loved-ones. They offer books, tapes, and information to be used as road maps, and provide the compass.

Knowledge can be power. Knowledge sustains caregivers day-by-day, and gives them the ability to be effective. CET skills help caregivers make advance plans and difficult decisions before the chaos of a crisis hits, putting them into a panic. Foresight prevents future emotional upheavals from becoming devastating emotional killers.

Please don't be an ostrich and stick your head in the sand. The problems of aging do not go away.

Forming a team - advocacy and ombudsman services

Part of what geriatric care managers do is to make referrals to, and work as a team with other professionals in the aging network. GCMs have developed special relationships with doctors, lawyers, financial advisors, carefully selected nursing and home-care services, residential facilities, adult day-care centers, and other community resources which serve older people and their families. A geriatric care manager often pulls together this array of professionals and specialists into a cohesive team, whose goal is to work for the best interests of the elderly family member.

Because of such personal relationships, care managers are frequently able to get special attention for clients. And we do have clout. Clients often ask me to communicate with other professionals on their behalf. This works well for many reasons:

• I usually work with the same multi-disciplinary team on more than one case, which makes for clear, easy, open communication.

• Since I am a substantial source of referrals for the best professionals, they want to keep my clients happy. And when my clients are happy, I'm happy.

• As a professional, I'm treated as a colleague by other professionals and can intervene on behalf of my clients.

The involvement of professional geriatric care managers does not stop with recommendations. They follow-up to ensure that clients receive the quality of services they need, which they are paying for and have a right to receive. If not, they speak up! There is no excuse for slip-shod care.

So, I guess you might say that care managers are the hub of the gerontological wheel for clients. When clients first walk in for a consultation, they are frequently muddling along in partial denial, stuck. unable to confront the many painful hurdles they must overcome.

When they walk out, they no longer feel alone, without support. They now have a professional problem-solver on their side...someone who truly enjoys working with the elderly. I often get hugs from grateful families and their elderly loved ones.

Clients who consult with geriatric care managers are assured of immediate access to a pre-screened dedicated support team, specializied in working with the elderly. Families take comfort in the fact that their geriatric care manager is both a concerned spokesperson who can pull the right strings, and a friend...someone who will be there in time of need.

Come to think of it, maybe we can live in a Norman Rockwell world, after all.

CHAPTER 3

The Scourge: Alzheimer's

There is a plague in our midst.

It is not contageous, nor is it caused by virus, bacteria or any other "germs." In fact, no one really knows what causes the affliction.

Its principal victims are an estimated 4-million older people over age 60. And the yearly cost of their care is about $47,000 per person, $188-billion a year.

It is invariably fatal. In fact, it is the fourth greatest killer in the country.

Its name: **Alzheimer's disease (AD).**

Of all of the tribulations faced by seniors and their families, this is the most devastating...and I do mean devastating.

Most people have heard about Alzheimer's. Some confuse it with the normal mild memory loss that many older people experience as a natural part of the aging process. The two are nothing alike.

AD is a neurological disease which causes a degeneration of brain cells, leading to symptoms of profound memory loss and confusion.

Alzheimer's disease is the leading cause of **dementia**, (although there are more than 50 diseases that can cause dementia, or that have symptoms similar to Alzheimer's).

Dementia is the loss of cognitive ability and judgment that enables us to function, i.e., "the loss of mind." There are many forms of dementia (*see Glossary*). This chapter will deal only with progressive, irreversible dementia caused by Alzheimer's disease.*

---

*To learn about reversible dementia, read "Reversible Dementia," by Jeffrey L. Cummings, D. Frank Benson, and S. LoVerne Jr., in the *Journal of the American Medical Association* (JAMA, 1980, 243:2434-9).

In its early stages, the symptoms of Alzheimer's usually progress slowly, beginning with *short-term memory loss and/or mild confusion.*

In the middle and late stages, the symptoms escalate, gradually becoming a nightmare of profound memory collapse, inability to control bodily functions, and complete destruction of the patient's intellectual capacity...finally leading to death.

Alzheimer's first robs the mind, then much later, kills the body. (The opposite is true with Parkinson's disease, where first the motor system deteriorates for many years, then dementia may set in.)

We don't know what causes Alzheimer's, and as of now, there is no cure. For reasons that are not understood, neurons (the basic cells of our nervous system) in the cortex (outer layer of the brain) begin to deteriorate. Messages are sent from neuron to neuron, between the brain and the body, across synapses between neurons. When these are affected, messages cannot be completed or properly understood.

To put it another way, a train (the message) runs out of track, or the direction of the track suddenly changes. Messages get lost or connected to the wrong responses.

Changes in the brain tissues of Alzheimer's victims can be seen under a microscope with a brain biopsy, but this procedure is almost never done prior to the death of a patient. These changes determine the degree of gradual brain function loss.

The longer we live, the more vulnerable we become to Alzheimer's. After age 65, the chances of getting this disease double every ten years on an average. If we lived to age 150, we'd probably all have AD.

THE UNRELENTING PROGRESS
OF ALZHEIMER'S

We suffered through the year-long "Trial of the Century." But the real trial of the century is Alzheimer's disease, and it lasts much longer than one year.

Alzheimer's disease has an insidious onset and progresses slowly over a long period of time. Frequently, a family takes

4-6 years to recognize and admit the symptoms of deterioration in a loved one. Only then, the dementia becomes so pronounced that they come in to see me.

It often takes even longer for the family to overcome their understandable emotional reaction of denial, admit the truth, and seek real solutions. Unfortunately, this may not come until a crisis, such as a car accident.

Denial is, in a way, hope...hope that the AD victim will recover and everything will be the way it was before. The fact that this hope is not based upon reality, makes it both sad and dangerous.

Blaming a family member who has AD is another defense against accepting the inevitable. Rather than yelling in anger at the horrible disease, a caregiver may yell at the victim. Don't be judgmental if your EFM cannot do something which seems simple to you, and which always came easy before they got the disease. Always remember: _Alzheimer's is not the patient's fault, nor is it yours._

The course of Alzheimer's disease, from initial symptoms to inevitable death, can take anywhere from 8-20 years. The time in-between is filled with heartaches...emotional pain, guilt, and financial devastation.

The stages of an Alzheimer's victim regression are, ironically, almost a reverse mirror of the stages of a child's growth. What a child learns last, leaves the AD sufferer first.

With Alzheimer's disease, mental abilities go first. In the beginning, denial is so strong that the person's loved one frequently takes over the roles of the patient who has Alzheimer's, doing the checkbooks, driving, cooking, reading, etc. A healthy spouse or "significant other" quietly becomes the primary caregiver, covering up to keep the reality of AD from the adult children, family, and friends...for as long as they can.

Sometimes concerned neighbors will call when they see garbage piling up, or perhaps the elderly person wanders around in the middle of the night, repeatedly knocking on their door and disturbing them. Then the sad charade is exposed.

In the early stages of AD, many patients feel very frustrated and say some variation of: " I don't know what's wrong with me... My memory isn't what it once was... I'm losing my mind... There's something wrong and I don't know what it is... Am I going crazy?"

Alzheimer's causes a gradual and complete loss of self...short-term memory... communication skills...orientation to time, place and person...the ability to care for personal hygiene and the daily tasks of life.

Visual and spatial loss can lead to wandering. The part of the brain that keeps a person knowing where they are is damaged. Some AD patients just need to be on the move and have no awareness about where they are going, while others are frightened about becoming lost and do not wander.

Depth perception shrinks and rapid movement cannot be processed. Don't call to your elderly family member from a distance. It's best to slowly walk directly up to them, making eye-to-eye contact. This simple, but effective habit will help decrease combativeness about 50%. And use clear gestures while speaking.

It's not always easy to do, but being cheerful and friendly helps put the elderly person at ease, facilitating communication, easing possible resistance, and helping to get them to do what you want. Flexibility, not entrenchment, is the key.

With Alzheimer's, the ability to initiate things, ask pertinent questions, and participate in activities deteriorates. Sadly, the AD victim can no longer prepare even a simple meal, balance a checkbook, or play a familiar card game without supervision.

AD causes severe communication and comprehension problems for the patient and family. Words like "pill" and "purse" are regularly confused. Frustrated family members learn that they have to play guessing games, just to find out what the patient really wants to communicate. Eventually, at the end of the disease's progress, many Alzheimer's patient speak what their families refer to as "gibberish."

An AD sufferer can get confused and attempt to unlock the door with a lipstick tube instead of a key, or use a trash can instead of a toilet. (The objects "look the same" to the demented patient.)

Often, with Alzheimer's, there is a change in personality, perhaps radically. A kind, contented elderly patient may become combative and suspicious...literally a stranger.

Stunned family members often exclaim: "My mother/father is another person!" or "That's not my husband/wife!" The realization that they are losing the very essence of their elderly loved ones can be emotionally devastating.

Alzheimer's victims often develop psychiatric symptoms and conditions, such as paranoia, hallucinations, delusions, and depression. They may accuse their loving spouse of 50 years of philandering, stealing, or trying to harm them. Judgment and insight are eventually lost. The patient may even denounce their caregiver: "It's all your fault!"

A family member may start fearing that they, too, are getting Alzheimer's, as if it's contagious. It's not. A personality trait that was lightly dismissed as "scatter-brained" when they were young, and "on overload" when they were middle-aged, might be mistakenly attributed to Alzheimer's when they hit age 65.

Another worry that arises for family members when confronting the devastating effects of Alzheimer's is, "What will happen to me? Who will take care of me?" Many caregivers find such questions frightening.

When family members first start caring for their elderly loved ones, they usually are able to leave them alone while they go to work or shopping. But as the disease progresses into its middle stages, this is no longer safely possible.

After the early stages, handling an Alzheimer's patient at home is as fraught with problems as leaving a toddler alone. Caregivers think they are taking care of a 75-year-old, but windup with a 2-year-old whom they can't take their eyes off for more than a moment. If you make the mistake of leaving them alone, you may find things very different when you return.

For example: While "cleaning-up the house," one elderly AD patient put the milk in the bedroom closet and carefully put all the dirty dishes in the trash bin outside. Unfortunately, the garbage truck came and emptied the bin.

Another example: After a stressful day of caregiving, one wife stayed up late, doing all her bills and writing long-overdue letters. She piled them neatly on her desk, stamped and ready to be mailed in the morning. Imagine her reaction when she awoke to find all the mail opened, letters torn up in the garbage disposal, and checks disappeared.

Most AD victims are fortunately unaware of the extent of their troubles. They truly lead an existential existence. But for families, Alzheimer's is the perfect recipe for hell on earth, because of the extreme stress on caregivers. Their frustration doesn't go away. It's like seeing the same bad movie over and over. Caregivers, unlike patients, are fully aware of what is happening and cannot forget about it.

Even if an AD victim does know what's happening to them, memory loss softens their on-going stress and their frustration dissipates. They truly lead an existential existence.

Many times the spirit of the Alzheimer's victim transcends the terrible regression and disintegration of the person. Other times, Alzheimer's strains, to the extreme, close family ties built over a lifetime. By the time the AD patient dies, in most cases their family has long ago lost the person they once knew.

After years of chronic grieving, the long slow funeral, the piece-by-piece disintegration of a loved one, death is frequently seen as a relief for both patient and family. The affected loved one is finally at peace, and the family can begin to go on with the rest of their lives.

Statistics

In 25 years, 50-million Americans will be over age 65.
Ages 65-75...3% have Alzheimer's.
Ages 75-85...18% have Alzheimer's.
Ages 85+...47% have Alzheimer's.

The Alzheimer's Road Map

I know of no circumstance faced by the elderly and their families where there is a greater need for the assistance of a knowledgeable professional geriatric care manager, than when Alzheimer's rears its exceedingly ugly head.

There is so much to do, both to accommodate the needs of the patient and to prepare the family for the ordeal that is to come. The overwhelming stress of Alzheimer's disease can be destructive to family relationships, careers, marriages, and in worse-case scenarios, even lead to abuse or suicide.

One way to avoid such tragedies is to consult a geriatric care manager, and to follow the **Alzheimer Disease Road Map...**

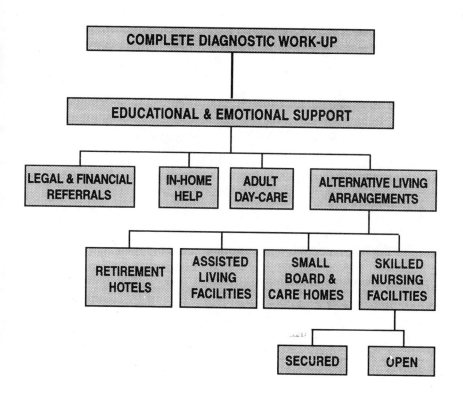

Step #1: Complete Diagnostic Work-Up

The first step on the Alzheimer's map is diagnosis. Why is this necessary? Because many patients who are diagnosed with the dreaded disease, really don't have it. AD is frequently diagnosed incorrectly. Disturbingly, there are estimates that the frequency of mis-diagnosis exceeds 25%!

The earliest symptoms of AD may be hard to detect. Alzheimer's always has a *gradual* onset. The first indication usually involves memory loss. Thus, if the person has a sudden onset of forgetfulness or sudden personality change, the cause is unlikely to be AD.

With beginning Alzheimer's you probably will not notice drastic changes, but slowly come to a realization, "Gee, Pop isn't as sharp as he used to be."

Such an observation may not sound any alarms, since it is easy and more comfortable to assume that the loved one may be "simply growing old." This **age-associated memory impairment**, also known as **benign senescence**, is not Alzheimer's disease.

After a period of time, what was at first easily dismissed as a little forgetfulness, becomes recognized as something more serious. An elderly person may become easily confused, or no longer be able to perform their usual tasks well.

If Alzheimer's disease is suspected, it is important to do a complete diagnostic work-up as quickly as possible. First, the elderly patient should be examined by an internist, a neurologist, and a geropsychiatrist, to rule out other causes of the dementia symptoms. Then, an assessment should be made to determine the person's level of functioning and social behavior.

If the disease is Alzheimer's, medical and financial decisions will have to be carefully made, to plan for the care of the patient during their progressive decline.

Denial is such a strong force that families often delay getting a diagnosis until long after their EFM is capable of making competent decisions.

The possibility of misdiagnosis mentioned above cannot be over-emphasized: the patient's symptoms may not be caused by Alzheimer's at all. Many *treatable* afflictions share symptoms with AD. For example, are infections or metabolic problems in a dementia patient due to the disease or simply due to a lack of water or good nutrition? Does anyone monitor the patient's water intake and diet?

The quicker a diagnosis, the quicker a possible cure or treatment if it is not Alzheimer's.

A case that turned out not to be Alzheimer's was that of a 90-year-old man, Peter, who was found lying in his own feces. He hadn't been out of bed for two weeks and obviously had no interest in his hygiene. Completely disoriented, the poor man was malnourished, dehydrated, and confused. Confusion is one of the most common symptoms of AD. The diagnosis seemed easy.

"It's Alzheimer's," a doctor confidently declared. Fortunately, the family didn't leave it at that. They sought a second opinion from a geriatric psychiatrist, who found the real affliction.

Peter was diagnosed with **major depression (clinical depression)**. His wife recently died and he was suffering such intense grief that it induced psychosis. Today, after treatment with medications and talk therapy, he lives cheerfully in a board-and-care home, in full possession of his faculties.

Without the extra effort by his family, and the prescribed medications, chances are this man would have been improperly left in his treatable condition. Peter might have been consigned to a nursing home, waiting to die, with the erroneous terminal diagnosis of Alzheimer's on his chart.

In all fairness to the doctor in the case above, Alzheimer's can be a tricky disease to diagnose. There are no sure-fire objective tests that can determine the condition, although a few tests show great promise. Check with your doctor, and get all the up-to-date research from the Alzheimer's Disease Education and Referral Center (*see Appendix G*).

AD cannot be diagnosed by X-ray, MRI, CAT scan, PET scan, SPEC scan, or any other imaging procedures available today.

None of these tests can prove a person has Alzheimer's, however, they can be very helpful in the clinical diagnosis of the disease. In addition, such tests are extremely useful in revealing other serious conditions, such as brain tumors.

The only way to positively know that a person has Alzheimer's is with a brain biopsy, which is too dangerous to consider. Only when the victim has died, can an autopsy definitely prove AD. A family may request a brain biopsy, by filling out a form ahead of time, *before* the death of their loved one. This may ease the family's plaguing question about whether the patient actually had AD. (The biopsy is also invaluable to researchers, who urgently need information for their studies of Alzheimer's, as they seek to find a cure for this dreaded disease.)

However, Alzheimer's disease can be **clinically diagnosed** with 90% accuracy by first ruling out other possibilities, then carefully examining the patient's behavior. This is a better percentage of certainty than for many other diseases.

Unlike other diseases, one of the best indicators of AD is to *observe* the social behavior of the person. Behavior is essential in making an accurate diagnosis of Alzheimer's. I urge all families who suspect AD, to keep a journal noting changes in their elderly family member.

Changes in personality are so insidious that it's necessary to evaluate it over a period of time, to determine the progress of the disease. For instance, inappropriate behavior may be caused by a stroke, not Alzheimer's.

When a family member has been told that a parent has Alzheimer's, the first thing I do is suggest a second or even third opinion. To get a correct diagnosis, your loved one deserves to be given a complete *physical and psychological work-up for dementia*, not just a prescription to reduce symptoms.

If your EFM is enrolled in an HMO or other managed health care plan, you may have to go outside the plan to see private specialists or to do certain procedures.

Geriatric care managers are becoming advocates in the HMO system, helping families get the work-ups needed, as well as finding the best resources outside an HMO to fill the gaps.

Step #2: Educational and emotional support

Concurrent with obtaining an accurate diagnosis, is the necessity of educating and giving emotional support to the family. The Alzheimer's victim is in for a long, slow slide down a slippery slope. But in many ways, they don't have it as bad as their family, who must endure years of watching a beloved parent or spouse slowly fade away. Families show amazing valor through years of 36-hour days and chronic grieving, as they lose a loved one, piece-by-piece. They know their loved one would never want to live out life this way.

Ongoing stress and pain can set the stage for elder abuse by a family member, at wit's end, who simply "loses it." To alleviate a trying situation before it escalates to this point, to prevent guilt, to preserve sanity, and to hold the caregiving unit together, families need *a lot* of comfort, support, and education.

There are many excellent organizations that offer such help, such as: Alzheimer's Association, Alzheimer's Disease Education and Referral Center (ADEAR), and Family Caregivers Alliance (*see Appendix G*).

Taking care of an AD patient is one of life's more Herculean and emotionally-draining tasks. I've led Alzheimer's support groups and held educational seminars for many years, featuring many top professionals in the geriatric field. Families of patients receive information and solid mutual emotional support. Many geriatric care managers throughout the country offer such on-going support groups and seminars. The love, commitment, and mutual assistance offered by those who are in a similar situation can be invaluable.

There are also excellent **early-Alzheimer's support groups** with useful cutting-edge programs for both AD victims and their families. Caregivers have the opportunity to meet other families in like circumstances, exchanging information and emotional support. Such resources are often under-utilized because of denial.

At this mild stage, AD victims still have many of their faculties, and can greatly benefit from interaction with others who are going through the same frightening experience. However, early-Alzheimer's groups may not be right for all patients. Some elderly people may want to know they have a diagnosis of AD. For others, diagnosing a terminal illness may devastate the patients and families. Even though early-Alzheimer's patients may know something is wrong with them, some may not benefit from knowing the full truth about their condition.

For years, AD sufferers were satisfied with the explanation that they had "hardening of the arteries." Now they are told they have "a memory problem," like so many other people of their age. They should be informed that there are special doctors for such problems, called geriatricians. This explanation may be beneficial to relieve their anxiety about an incurable condition they cannot control.

If and when to tell a patient that they have AD is a very complex, emotionally and ethically-loaded matter. It should be thoroughly and carefully discussed with professionals, before making a decision.

A geriatric care manager can analyze the individual's needs and their particular set of circumstances, then suggest a practical, caring approach. The early-Alzheimer's stage is the best time to formulate plans for the long-term care of the patient.

Step #3: Financial and legal referrals

It is essential to work with a **financial planner**, who specializes in the needs of the elderly.

One of the burdensome aspects of an Alzheimer's case is the incredible cost. Remember, we are talking about providing for the residential and medical care of a terminally ill patient who will in all probability take many years to die. That costs a lot of money!

Don't expect Medicare to save you. The long-term care that all AD patients require is not paid for by Medicare or most insurance policies. And in order to qualify for Medicaid, which will pay for such bills, the patient must be virtually impoverished.

Some **long-term care insurance** will pay benefits for Alzheimer's, but the policy must have been procured prior to diagnosis. Although most modern policies no longer have "Alzheimer's exclusion" clauses, there may be other subtle exclusions. Read the policy carefully. Investigate the history and strength of the insurance company, to guard against it going out of business before the policy is needed.

Long-term care insurance pays for nursing homes, and more often now, for in-home care and **respite care*** (including adult day-care) to give the family relief. The financial planner may work with a good insurance agent to obtain the best policy available.

You are also going to need to work in conjunction with an **elder law attorney**. For referrals, contact the National Academy of Elder Law Attorneys (*see Appendix G*).

The reasons for this are decidedly practical: preservation of assets, preparation for long-term care, and an answer to your loved one's unspoken stressful question, "Who will decide if I cannot?"

Elder law attorneys deal with estate-planning matters, and are especially knowledgeable about changes in laws that protect the aged. They will try to preserve as much of the estate as possible from the high costs of Alzheimer's disease. This is especially vital if there is a spouse involved.

The 1988 Medicare Catastrophic Coverage Act made changes in the amount that the spouse at home may keep. The law seeks to prevent spousal impoverishment, guaranteeing a minimum amount of income and resources.

---

*California has a landmark **respite program**, called the Caregiver Resource Center (CRC) system. It was legislated to replicate the excellent model support program developed by Family Caregiver Alliance, where **Kathleen Kelly, MPH**, is the Executive Director (*see Appendix F*). Other states have adopted their own respite care programs for caregivers, subsidized with different amounts of funding...usually too little. If you are a stressed-out caregiver (and who isn't), check to see if your state has such a program, find out how to qualify, and use it.

Elder law attorneys can also provide the legal tools to enable adult children to take over when necessary, such as...

• **Durable Power of Attorney for Health Care** and **Durable Power of Attorney for Finances.** These give a family member or caregiver the legal tools needed to care for the physical and financial well-being of a patient who no longer can care for himself/herself. It is greatly preferable to get Powers of Attorney while an Alzheimer's patient is competent enough to give decision-making power to whomever they choose. Having such foresight relieves the caregivers of the emotionally-wrought, sometimes intricate and costly necessity of later going through the court system.

• **Conservatorship (Guardianship).** This alternative may be necessary if the patient is no longer competent to handle their own affairs. Conservatorship must be established through the courts. When the estate is small, a *Conservatorship of the Person* may be sufficient. However, when the estate is large, a *Conservatorship of Assets* will probably be necessary, which is expensive.

In rare cases, a patient may still be able to participate in the decision-making. Usually, however, the family understandably rationalizes and denies their loved one's insidiously deteriorating behavior until it is too late. Then the dementia victim is no longer legally competent to make decisions.

Step #4: In-home help

When families are confronted with the bleak future of AD, many are determined to "handle the burden" completely on their own. They may let the Alzheimer's patient live at home for as long as possible, then move them into the caregiver's home. As many as 70% of AD patients are cared for at home.

The in-home solution may be viable - for awhile - if, and usually only if, the spouse or adult child is willing to accept (and pay for) in-home help. They need assistance with the job of caring for the patient who will become progressively unable to care for her/himself.

Among my professional responsibilities is to assess families' needs and the affordability of in-home help. Geriatric care managers help families determine the amount of in-home help required as the disease progresses, and assist in hiring, training, and monitoring the in-home workers.

Some families want to work with a home care agency. Others want to interview and hire on their own. Be aware that there are over 15,000 Medicare-certified and non-Medicare home health agencies, Medicare-certified and non-Medicare hospices, and home care aide organizations. These multitude of providers are definitely not all equal in quality. Choose very carefully.

The person hired may be a **homemaker-companion** or a **certified home health aide**. The latter is trained to do hands-on care, CPR, and other health-related procedures.

In the earlier stages, around-the-clock assistance is not required, but may begin with only a few hours two or three times a week. Later, a live-in caregiver will be required to supervise the patient 24-hours a day.

In-home help is an *essential service*. People need to work and play, and everyone needs to sleep. If the family is to have any kind of personal life apart from caring for the Alzheimer's patient, hiring a caregiver is not a luxury, it is a necessity.

What many caregivers don't realize or accept, is that you cannot successfully take care of an Alzheimer's patient by yourself. At some point, you need a team.

Safely is a big issue. Think of what can happen in the bathroom alone... The bathtub railings may pull out from the wall. An elderly family member may slip and be unable to get up. Can you imagine trying to lift a patient (who is dead-weight) from the bathtub by yourself, throwing your back out, and waiting for someone to come to rescue you both?

It's interesting (and sad) that parents don't feel guilty about hiring a baby-sitter for their young children so they can go to a movie, but when they think of hiring a caregiver for a demented elderly family member, there's often a lot of guilt.

If and when the decision is finally made to employ in-home help, the reality of health care costs really sinks you.

Currently, there are totally about 3- million people over age 65 receiving home care services in the United States, many of whom are Alzheimer's patients. Nearly 75% of those relied solely on family members and unpaid help. Annual expenditures for all home care exceeds $23-billion.

Custodial care at home costs about $15/hour, usually with a 4-hour minimum. If the patient requires live-in custodial care around the clock, the cost is about $160/day...$1120/week...$4800/month...... $58,760/year. How many of us can afford such expenses for more than a year or two? Remember, a loved one with Alzheimer's can live many more years than that.

And if the services of a **Registered Nurse (RN)** or **Licensed Vocational Nurse (LVN)** are medically required, the rates are much higher.

Unless you are former President Ronald Reagan, or rich like the CEO of an HMO, such continuous professional in-home care is simply not affordable.

Though your heart may be in the right place, bankrupting your entire family is not the right way to go. Placement should be utilized sooner, rather than later, in many cases. However, almost all families try the in-home route until they can't manage it anymore, financially or emotionally. Sooner or later, the realities of AD make it virtually impossible. There's a lot of truth to the saying that one parent can care for ten children, but ten children can't take care of one parent with Alzheimer's. AD patients exhibit behavioral difficulties, the tendency to wander and get lost, and the need for constant supervision as the disease progresses.

Inappropriate or disruptive behavior can be embarrassing, irritating, or even dangerous. One patient thought the logical place to put toilet paper was in the drawers, so every drawer was stuffed with it. Another brushed the walls with shoe polish, instead of brushing their teeth with toothpaste. Still another patient lit the cat's tail, instead of the stove.

Because of the intensity of the task and the emotional trauma that results, keeping an Alzheimer's patient at home without getting help can be a mistake. Family caregivers frequently suffer stress-related disease, loss of job, and psychological or emotional dysfunction.

In fact, 85% of spouses who are caring for a husband or wife with AD, will die *before* the Alzheimer's patient. This shocking statistic is undoubtedly due to the constant stress of caregiving.

Ironically, most AD patients don't experiencing stress-related illness, due to their profound memory loss. Physically, their health may even improve, because they are continuously under the supervision of caregivers. (For example, diabetic patients almost always improve because they don't cook their own meals.)

Patients forget the bad times. Caregivers have to go through intense emotional pain and/or guilt daily, and often hold in feelings until they become unbearable.

I remember Joanne, one very quiet, elegant lady, in the truest sense of the word. She deeply loved her husband, who had Alzheimer's, and was taking excellent care of him at home. Yet one day, she unexpectedly slugged him when her pent-up emotions exploded.

Even the most loving caregivers "lose it" sometimes, and feel terrible about losing control for months afterward.

If you choose to keep your elderly family member at home, a geriatric care manager can offer experienced guidance and supervision, making sure the family gets excellent service by well-trained employees. Hiring in-home help is a serious responsibility for all caregivers, especially those caring for a loved one with Alzheimer's.

Ask Family Caregiver Alliance to send you their excellent fact sheet, "Hiring In-Home Help" (*see Appendix G*).

Step #5: Adult day-care

Often the best prescription for an AD patient is referral to a quality **adult day-care center** in the community, which can be found in hospitals, senior centers, and as privately-run businesses. At the right stage of Alzheimer's, such day-care can be extremely beneficial for the patient.

Developed in the 1970's, adult day-care centers provide quality of life programs for the frail elderly, offering failure-free activities which give AD patients a sense of dignity. (Note: Adult day-care centers are different than senior citizens centers, which primarily cater to the elderly who do not have severe mental problems or physical problems that interfere with daily functioning.)

Adult day-care also provides respite for the family, allowing them free time with the confidence that their loved one is in a safe, loving, professionally supervised environment. Many centers run support groups for family caregivers.

The centers serve nutritious meals, and staff members see to it that the elderly really eat the food. This is particularly important, because one symptom of AD is that patients who aren't closely watched frequently forget to eat, leading to malnourishment and dehydration.

Attending an adult day-care center makes life more joyful. Like all of us, people who suffer with AD need human contact to get the most out of life.

A day-care center is often the only place where Alzheimer's patients can be with their peer group. Some creative centers also bring-in children and pets, which always seem to delight the seniors.

Older people enjoy telling stories to peers and professionals who really do want to listen, instead of only to their family members who are exhausted after hearing the same stories a hundred times. It gives AD patients a sense of meaning.

Many adult day-care centers have **reminiscence groups** for AD victims to share their long-term memories which frequently remain intact.* Patients enjoy leisurely reminiscing and the sense of camaraderie, even when their short-term recall is poor to non-existent.

Leaders frequently use music as a magnet for bringing out old memories and common experiences. Music can be used to soothe or stimulate, and is the one thing almost all Alzheimer's patients have in common, which they all respond to. They enjoy listening to Lawrence Welk or Glenn Miller, and love to dance. Even elderly with severe memory problems somehow remember the words to their favorite old songs and join in sing-alongs. Amazing!

The frustrating thing for caregivers is that, unlike children who like to brag about everything that happens each day, AD patients who have wonderful experiences at adult day-care centers often can't remember that they did anything or even attended. Even so, the next morning these patients are enthusiastic about going again. And their peers at the centers welcome them like old friends they haven't seen for a long time. The elderly feel young and useful, as if they're going off to school.

Adult day-care programs create a positive, creative atmosphere for confused patients so they are able to feel more independent. Patients get back their self-esteem. Their experiences at centers can be a real "upper," providing socialization and stimulation for the patient, and respite for the caregiver, often preventing premature and inappropriate institutionalization.

In advising my clients on the selection of an adult day-care center, I work hard to find programs which are sensitive to the special needs and predicaments of Alzheimer's victims. These centers cost about $40-50 per day, according to the region. Unfortunately, Medicare doesn't pay, unless the adult day-care center has a "rehabilitation license." But if you can afford it, an adult day-care center is well worth the cost, because of the love and understanding given to the patient.

An innovative new concept in day-care is the growing num-

---

*One elderly man vividly remembered: "When I was about eight years old, I decided to raffle my rabbit off. I sold tickets at 10 cents each. The night before the raffle, a storm dropped a tree branch on my rabbit box, and in the morning, I found I had a dead rabbit on my hands...I didn't know what to do, so I put the dead rabbit in a big cigar box and went ahead with the raffle. The winner looked into the box and said, "What am I going to do with a dead rabbit?" I gave him his dime back... The other kids just walked away. I figured nobody lost anything. But when my dad found out, he gave me a good lesson in ethics and made me return the remaining dimes."

ber of **intergenerational day-care centers,** where children and the elderly interact together in a single program. Still relatively few in number, the idea is taking root and expanding. The young and the old have an extraordinary bonding experience, with deep intangible benefits that cannot be measured. This concept may go a long way toward reviving a much-needed respect for the elderly in our culture.

Step #6: Alternative living arrangements

Sooner or later, almost every caregiver is put in the position of seeking an alternative living facility for their loved one with Alzheimer's. The family is no longer able to handle the AD patient, who must be cared for in a non-home environment.

Placement becomes a necessity.

If there is no family or support system, an alternative living arrangement may be necessary early-on. For most, the subject of alternative living arrangements usually comes up about 5 years after the family notices symptoms of AD. For the hearty few who are able to hang on until the bitter end, the decision may be put off until the disease reaches its final stages.

But whatever the case, this must ultimately be done to preserve the patient's health, and the family's sanity when they reach the end of their rope. Action is finally taken when caregivers are ready to admit they need help, because they've exhausted all other ways to handle the stressful, deteriorating situation.

Placement options include:

Retirement hotels

"Independent living" retirement hotels, for seniors who needed minimum care, were once the rage.

However, today's **retirement hotels** are usually licensed and function, in a sense, like large board and care facilities. They've expanded the depth of services available, offering **assisted living** at several different levels, with the cost increasing as more personal care is needed (e.g., *incontinence care*).

Retirement hotels which accept patients with Alzheimer's or related disorders, must be licensed for "non-ambulatory" status. Even if AD patients may be physically ambulatory, they are not considered *mentally ambulatory*.

The facility should have installed a "Wander Guard," or other type of electronic system to monitor wandering. Whenever a patient wearing the special bracelet tries to leave the building, the system buzzes and alerts the staff. These systems provide an alternative to medicating patients who wander, thus providing a better quality of life. AD facilities should also have secure, protected, nicely landscaped areas for wanderers.

If the facility does not have such an electronic system, patients require constant one-to-one supervision to prevent them from endangering themselves or others... We expect parents to constantly watch over their toddlers (or put them on leashes). Alzheimer's patients need the same intensity of supervison.

The facility must be specifically set-up for the safety of such patients. For instance, hot water temperature has to be set low enough so an elderly person with memory loss, slowed reactions, or physical disability, cannot be scalded.

Retirement hotels with assisted living are able to offer a variety of services, both for patients who are more alert and for confused patients with memory loss. They should offer different activities for higher-functioning and lower-functioning patients.

These alternative living facilities provide meals, religious services, laundry, maid service, security, and sometimes medication supervision. There are usually parties, exercise classes, and crafts. When appropriate for the patient's condition, there is transportation to adult day-care centers, shopping, banks, doctors, and sightseeing trips. A hair stylist, podiatrist, psychologist or social worker, and medical doctor may visit regularly.

The criteria for assisted living facilities are being developed and defined as I write. Standards are changing daily.

In order to qualify to live in a licensed retirement hotel, patients must meet minimum physical standards, which vary from facility to facility. But all retirement hotels require that patients be able to get around (not be bedridden), even if movement is with the assistance of a standard or 4-pronged cane, a walker,* or in some cases, a wheelchair.

However, retirement hotels are not licensed for extensive skilled nursing care. For that, a nursing home is needed. Investigate a facility carefully to determine what services are offered and what level of care it is licensed to provide. The patient's future must also be considered. Remember, Alzheimer's disease is on a one-way trip to complete mental incompetence and total dependence.

Even if the patient is well enough to meet the retirement hotel's standards today, tomorrow will be a different story. So, if the patient is close to the physical or mental point of no-return, as far as the hotel's minimum standards are concerned, it is probably better to look elsewhere.

For further information, contact the Assisted Living Facilities Association of America (*see Appendix G*).

Small board and care homes

At some point, a retirement hotel or licensed large board and care facility will cease to be a viable living alternative for the AD victim, unless it is an assisted living facility that offers sufficient security, supervision, and care.

---

*The AARP will send a free copy of their product report on canes and walkers. A physical therapist should always be the one to prescribe the correct walking aid for your EFM. Elderly people often trade canes and walkers, which is a mistake. Just as a patient shouldn't take someone else's medication, using a walking device which is the wrong height, for example, can be harmful.

If needed, a walker is one of your EFM's most important, most used personal possessions. Don't settle for the standard, least-expensive type. Some better walkers are equipped with wheels, hand brakes, baskets for packages, fold-down seats, and can be collapsed in order to fit in a car. Be creative: You could even add a bicycle horn, a safe side-view mirror (like on the EFM's former car), and paint the typical cold-looking aluminum with cheerful colors. You and your EFM can work together to make this unpleasant necessity more fun and individualistic!

Ultimately, Alzheimer's will render the sufferer disabled, incontinent, unable to find the dining room, and otherwise mentally incapacitated. At such time, a retirement hotel, in fairness to its other guests and in order to keep its state license, will be forced to ask the Alzheimer's patient to leave. The next stop is frequently the **small board and care home (residential care facility)**. Sometimes, a small board and care may even be the first place selected when a loved one can no longer be adequately cared for at home.

Good small board and care homes are marvelous for patient and family alike. These facilities are usually single-family dwellings which may house six elderly people who need constant care and supervision. Some cater to seniors in relatively good health who desire a higher-level of care in a home environment, but most residents are very frail. As with the larger retirement hotels, small board and care homes have different atmospheres and offer varying levels of care.

Some licensed homes are run by owners who live there, and are devoted to the care of the elderly residents. Patients are considered to be "family members." This has negative and positive aspects. The live-in owners can become stressed out from the round-the-clock contact with residents, turning the board and care home into one large dysfunctional family. On the other hand, some of the most warm, caring, beneficial environments for Alzheimer's patients are such board and care homes.

However, in most cases of family-run board and cares, the owners and/or administrators do not actually live there. They come by daily and are very involved, carefully training and monitoring their 24-hour staffs.

Families should seek homes that specialize in assisting dementia patients. The board and care home has to cater to all the patient's physical needs: hygiene (bathing and toilet), nutrition, medications, dressing and undressing appropriately. Seek homes where there are two staff members who live on the premises and are willing to give 24-hour care. If the staff of the board and care are not able to help residents in the middle of the night, then this is not the home for your EFM. Look elsewhere.

Small board and care homes bridge the gap between in-home or retirement hotel care, and nursing home care. They often act in conjunction with home-health agencies to provide skilled nursing care. Patients' medical needs may include: incontinence, healing wounds in the early stage, oxygen use, colostomy care, special diets, diabetic care, and/or other special care.

A nursing home doesn't always have to be the final destination anymore for an Alzheimer's patient who has medical problems, although it must be considered when it is really needed.

The best thing about a small board and care facility is that it feels like home. The patient isn't in a hospital or a large nursing facility with hundreds of people, which are institutional and can feel impersonal. There are no uniformed nurses, nor that awful "hospital smell." The care is virtually one-on-one.

Most patients enjoy the company of their peers. They find the relaxed, informal atmosphere of a small board and care ideal. High quality homes also provide daily activities, making life more interesting and pleasurable.

Families also respond positively to the small board and care choice. The feel far less remorse or guilt over the loved one's plight, when visiting them in a clean, quiet, home-like setting.

Remember, though, that "fancy" does not necessarily mean "better." Exterior luxury may make the family feel good, but less beautiful board and care homes often give the patient better care. Look beyond the surface for quality of care.

Financially, a small board and care home is a easier to handle than a nursing home, costing many hundreds of dollars less per month.

Many states require such facilities to be licensed. If your state does, make sure the board and care home you select has a license. This isn't an absolute guarantee of quality, but at least it ensures that there will be inspection and a higher supervising authority to turn to, if you are dissatisfied with the care.

Nursing homes

In many cases, the last stop for the AD sufferer is a **nursing home** (also known as a **convalescent hospital** or **skilled nursing facility**). But you don't want just *any* nursing home, if it is financially and logistically possible to avoid it.

When it comes to Alzheimer's disease, all nursing homes are definitely not created equal. About 40% of the nursing homes certified by the U.S. Health Care Financing Administration have repeatedly violated Federal standards during recent inspections. One wonders about the uncertified nursing homes.

Patients are often placed in nursing homes for financial reasons when a family cannot afford a small board and care, or when nursing care is truly needed...e.g.: tube feeding, turning the patient in bed, decubitus ulcers (major bed sores), or the patient was just released from the hospital. If the family is impoverished and their only means of payment is Medicaid (when they qualify), they will have to choose a nursing home rather than another alternative living facility. Nursing homes are appropriate for patients with advanced and final stages of dementia, and serious physical illnesses.

A nursing home that caters, at least in part, to sufferers of Alzheimer's and other forms of dementia is a must for families who want the best possible care for their loved one. Finding such a facility should not be too hard, since many nursing homes are now developing special Alzheimer's wings or units. Currently, 1 in 10 nursing homes have such units.

AD patients have special needs. Most Alzheimer's sufferers are mobile and, for reasons not fully understood, have a need to "wander." At any time, day or night, they will decide to take a stroll for hours on end, often saying they want to "go home." This is why so many AD patients get lost. They simply wander away and forget how to get back.

Nursing homes with Alzheimer's units have locked areas reserved for dementia patients, to prevent them from leaving and getting lost. As with retirement hotels which are prepared for dementia needs, some nursing homes have secured perimeters, such as fenced outdoor areas, so that the patients' urge to wander can be satisfied without endangering them.

Nursing homes which are *not* set up for Alzheimer's may use some type of physical restraints for the convenience of staff or patients' safety, but such a drastic remedy is now in disfavor, for ethical reasons and because patients may injure themselves trying to get free.

Nursing homes may also use chemical restraints, another practice under fire. When agitated or combative Alzheimer's patients are drugged, they may forget how to do such primary skills as walking, getting into a car, and feeding themselves.

On the other hand, medications can be helpful to dementia patients, if properly prescribed and *monitored,* and used for reasons other than restraining them. A geriatric psychiatrist, trained in Psychopharmacology, will be able to prescribe the right drug in the right dosage.

Check out the video tapes and books describing environments for dementia patients which maximize their quality of life.

Select a nursing home where the staff is familiar with Alzheimer's patients, and *chooses* to work with them. In some nursing homes, staff yearly turnover rate can reach nearly 100%. In such facilities, it's difficult to find anyone who has more than a passing familiarity with your EFM, and consistent caring is virtually non-existent.

Many skilled nursing homes emphasize physical rehabilitation, not dementia. There is a huge difference between a broken hip and a broken mind.

If an AD patient breaks a hip, often they can temporarily go into a nursing home that specializes in *physical rehabilitation.* After the patient hopefully heals, she/he can return to the previous nursing home that specializes in Alzheimer's (a broken mind)... That's the ideal goal.

Alzheimer's units employ mental health professionals who specialize in communicating and providing activities for AD patients, making the use of drugs far less necessary. Unfortunately, like most other skilled nursing facilities, nursing homes which have areas reserved for Alzheimer's patients are expensive, costing in excess of $3000-$6000 per month, according to regional differences.

As Alzheimer's worsens, concerns over a patient wandering will lessen in most cases. The sad fact is that the disease continues to attack the brain for so many years that, in the final stage, the demented patient usually is totally bedridden, unable to eat, unable to even remember their family or their past.

At this point, the distinction between a secure nursing home which caters to dementia patients, and other nursing homes which do not, begins to lose its meaning. Oh, having a staff that understands the special circumstances of Alzheimer's certainly is the ideal. But, care and consideration are certainly not restricted to Alzheimer's nursing home facilities.

As death approaches, loving care, soothing touch, music, kindness and consideration are about all that can be given to the patient. It is still quite a lot to offer, and makes all the difference in the world to the family.

MEMORY LOSS AND CONFUSION

Noted author E.B. White observed that, "The aging mind has a bagful of nasty tricks, one of which is to tuck names and words away in crannies where they are not immediately available."

There is a crucial difference, however, between mild forgetfulness and Alzheimer's dementia. We all forget things, but they come back to us. With AD, information doesn't come back.*

Older people may search for a word on the tip of their tongue which cannot quite be grasped at the moment, but eventually will be retrieved. Benign senescence is like the old person making a call to China. The connection is made. It takes longer, but they get connected.

Unfortunately, in the case of Alzheimer's, the connection is usually never made...or if made, disappears so quickly it's as if

---

*Lisa E. Dolan invoked this useful image of Alzheimer's dementia: "Picture the human brain as a library, and all the books are brain cells, filled with knowledge and memory. Now, imagine the books are slowly being checked out, but none are returned. The library slowly loses its knowledge and memories."

the connection never existed at all.

Alzheimer's disease also leads to a state of confusion. All AD caregivers can cite countless sad examples of this...

Ma is found walking the streets, carrying bags of groceries from the supermarket a block away, because she cannot remember how to get home. Always an overly careful driver, she has her first car accident because she literally forgets that a red light means "stop."

Grandma has always knitted beautiful sweaters for the family, but now she forgets the stitches she's done a million times before. Everybody lauded her delicious cooking, but lately she mixes up ingredients in the rugala, burns her prize-winning stuffed cabbage, and her light-as-air angel cakes fall flat.

Dad has always fixed the family car, but these days he can't even remember how to change the oil. Always accurate to the penny, he forgets how to balance his checkbook.

Granddad cannot find the way to his favorite armchair, or he doesn't know how to fill his pipe. In fact, he may leave the burning pipe unattended on the couch.

Most early-Alzheimer's victims know when they are "losing it." Often unable to finish a thought and unable to initiate activities, they suffer tremendously because they're losing their memory and control of their lives. Self-esteem sinks to the bottom of a dark pit.

Extremely frustrated that they no longer can accomplish what they used to do so well, AD victims desperately try to cover-up their mistakes.

When asked why she doesn't sew anymore, Grandma quickly offers the excuse, "Well, I've just lost interest." At a restaurant, Dad may ask you to order for him, or order the same thing you do, because he no longer can comprehend the menu.

Once vital and outgoing loved ones may start to withdraw, unless someone encourages them.

How do you talk with a elderly family member who asks a question, then immediately forgets the answer and asks again?... Who starts a story, then completely loses the thought?... Who endlessly hunts for the right words, but winds up using the wrong ones?

The AD sufferer can be compared to a tape recorder, with no record button. New tapes can't be made. Long conversations and explanations don't work, so don't drive yourself crazy.

The best way to handle this frustrating and sad reality is to bring up your EFM's fond old memories, or when the person is still partially able to carry on a conversation, learn to do "The Alzheimer's Dance." The steps are emotionally complex, but the theory behind them is simple: move wherever the patient moves, following their lead, from fox-trot to waltz to rumba to square-dance...from subject to subject. Don't demand logic, succinctness, rapid comprehension, or remembering. Above all, a lot of good-natured patience and humor are required.

It's very painful for family members to understand or accept why their formerly sharp, competent, aging parent is now confused and "scared to death" about so many seemingly simple things in life.

The healthy spouse tries to disguise the deterioration to "protect" their children. Or the children may try to protect the "reputation" of the AD victim. In fact, family members may be hiding their loved one's condition from each other. Everyone wants to protect everyone else. They may not even be aware of covering-up the truth.

Memory loss and confusion frustrate the AD victim, but it's also devastating to the family, particularly in the later stages of Alzheimer's. I can't think of any pain more acute than visiting your own parent and not being recognized.

Equally traumatic is when a loved one accuses you of stealing from them or betraying them...verbally abuses you with the vilest curses... or even physically attacks you. The most difficult thing to accept is that this behavior comes from a beloved spouse or parent who, in healthier times, would have laid down their life for you!

Fortunately, there is a smorgasbord of Alzheimer care interventions and options available to educate and guide caregivers, unfortunately none of them make the disease any easier to accept.

DOCTORS

Before making any decision about the proper care of their elderly family member, and before a crisis hits, a family should become more educated about dementia and Alzheimer's. If you plan a long family vacation in the car, you get a complete check-up at the garage. Why would you do any less for your loved one?

Too many people simply accept a single doctor's diagnosis at face value and base their decisions on partial or flawed information. Just as we take a baby to a pediatrician, we should take an elderly person to a specialist experienced in correctly diagnosing the symptoms of Alzheimer's, as well as possible causes which are not Alzheimer's. There are several medical specialists that should be consulted...

The first person to see is a **geriatrician, internist**, or another doctor who has had additional training and experience in geriatric medicine - Board Certified, if possible. Unfortunately, there aren't enough geriatric specialists, but it is well worth the effort if you can find one.

A good geriatrician will do a lot of ruling-out (and hopefully, some ruling-in) before diagnosing the possibility of Alzheimer's. If the diagnosis is not AD, say "thank God!" and toss away this Alzheimer's Road Map.

After ruling out any medical cause that an internist can diagnose, see a **neurologist**, who will investigate possible brain damage, whether from a tumor, stroke, or other neurological cause of your EFM's symptoms.

Then, both a **geriatric psychiatrist** and a **neuropsychologist** should be consulted, in the continuing hope of eliminating the probability of Alzheimer's disease. Many older people suffer from depression (pseudo-dementia) or other treatable temporary mental illness which mimics the symptoms of AD.

If the patient is acting inappropriately, the geriatric psychiatrist can prescribe the proper medications.

Neuropsychological testing is an excellent way to find out vital facts which can confirm the diagnosis of a geriatric psychiatrist.

Such testing also gives important information to the family about an EFM's capacity to function. If tests show that the AD patient still has the capacity to accomplish a specific task, encourage them to do it. If a well-meaning caregiver mistakenly does everything for an elderly family member with Alzheimer's, the patient may permanently forget how to do things.

On the other hand, a caregiver might blame their EFM for purposely acting obstinately or mean, when in fact, testing could reveal that the AD patient really can't do a specific task. Hard as it is for us to imagine or emotionally accept, our parent with dementia may actually forget how to make a cup of coffee or get into a car. It is painful to see a once-vital parent so dependent, but yelling at them will do no good, and will cause you great stress.

Ideally, it is only after a thorough review by a geriatrician, neurologist, geropsychiatrist, and neuropsychologist that the tragic diagnosis of AD must be accepted and acted upon with great courage.

MEDICATIONS

There are no known drugs that cure Alzheimer's. However, after many years of clinical trials, there is an Alzheimer's drug known as **Cognex®** (generic name, tacrine), which *may* improve reasoning, memory, language skills, and the ability to perform simple tasks, such as bathing and getting dressed.

Cognex® *does not cure Alzheimer's disease*. Unfortunately, any positive effects it may have cease over time as the disease progresses.

It is tempting to jump right into using Cognex®, but the drug is not without side-effects. Liver damage is a primary concern. The medication may also cause nausea, loss of appetite, loss of muscle coordination, and muscular pain. The patient must be frequently monitored with blood testing.

It should be noted that not all AD patients benefit from Cognex®. The earlier the diagnosis, the more likely it is that your doctor may determine it can be of some value.

Recently, Aricept™ (generic name, donepezil) has become available. Its potential positive effects are similar to Cognex®, but the drug has a different set of side effects. Be sure your physician is knowledgeable in the proper use of either of these medications.

Early diagnosis of Alzheimer's gives you the opportunity to decide whether your elderly family member qualifies and should participate in any other clinical trials of new medications.

Participating in a drug trial may or may not help the patient. However, it may help millions of other AD victims, by either proving that a new medication works in the treatment of Alzheimer's, or demonstrating that it does not. Remember, even Cognex® took over 10 years of clinical trials before it received government approval.

For information on eligibility requirements for participation in an experimental drug trial, contact your doctor, local hospital, or Alzheimer's organization.

AN ALZHEIMER'S FAMILY

Discussing this terrible disease in the abstract is one thing. But to see how Alzheimer's affects real, living people, is quite another.

And to see the heroic love offered by the families of these tragically ill people is one of the most heartening and fulfilling aspects of being a care manager. Every black cloud can, indeed, have a silver lining.

One of the most compelling stories of what I call an Alzheimer's family is that of the Steiners...

Mel

The extended Steiner family:
> MEL - the family patriarch with Alzheimer's disease
> SHIRLEY - Mel's wife
> DANIEL - Mel's and Shirley's oldest son
> BETTY - Daniel's wife
> FRED - Mel's and Shirley's younger son
> LI-ANG - Fred's wife

Mel was born in New York in 1906, and moved to California when he was ten. At age 15, he quit high school and went to work for a major corporation in the Los Angeles area.

During his long career, he worked his way up from office boy to office manager. Mel was employed by that corporation for 50 years, and only retired because of company policy.

As the son of Hungarian immigrants, Mel was fiercely patriotic. When World War II broke out, he was too old to join the service, so instead, he became a civil defense block warden for his neighborhood in the West Side of Los Angeles. In addition, he worked a second job at nights at McDonnell Douglas to assist in building "liberty's arsenal."

In 1926, Mel's brother introduced him to Shirley, a vivacious young woman, whose sister would eventually marry Mel's brother. Shirley was two years older and two inches taller than Mel, but that didn't matter. They fell in love and married that same year.

The two of them got right to work: Daniel was born ten months after the wedding and his brother, Fred, followed soon after. And they weren't alone. Mel's brother and his wife were also following the Biblical injunction to be fruitful and multiply.

Soon Mel, Shirley, his brother's family, and all the kids were one of those good old-fashioned extended families that loved and supported each other through good times and bad.

Daniel's favorite childhood memory of his father was when the family decided to buy their first new car. Rather than accept delivery in California, Mel decided to treat his oldest son to a little adventure. He and his son took a train to Detroit and picked up the Plymouth right at the factory gate. Then, they spent a week driving the car home to see the countryside.

Mel and Shirley had a love affair that lasted over 50 years. Daniel speaks movingly of the beautiful memories he has of his parents going out for walks, holding hands like two love-smitten teenagers.

Throughout their years together, Mel and Shirley traveled widely to Asia, Alaska, Europe. On their 25th wedding anniversary, they took off for six weeks , touring the United States, just to see what they could see.

Mel was a good family man, always making time for the

kids, and later, the grandkids. He took them to wrestling matches, baseball games, and the circus, whenever it was in town.

Both elder Steiners were notably active socially, committed to volunteerism and community service. In fact, Mel rose through the ranks and became a Shriner.

When he finally was forced to retire, Mel went to work for his sons, joining them to build the grocery business they had started together. He took care of the books and pitched-in at the store.

So, as the 1980's came around, 68-year-old Mel and his 70-year-old wife of almost half-a-century, were very happy. Seemingly healthy, they looked forward to many more years of fruitful retirement living, until one day...

Fred came to Daniel with a disturbing observation: "Something's wrong with Dad. He doesn't seem to be doing the books as well as he used to."

Daniel had to admit that his father seemed to be "slipping," but none of the family could or would really believe it. The early symptoms of AD that Mel exhibited are typical: loss of short-term memory and mental acuity, the inability to initiate activities, loss of words and communication.

As Mel's bookkeeping skills increasingly faltered, the boys were forced to make other arrangements. But since they wanted their dad to continue to feel part of the business, they arranged for him to make some of the store's deliveries. Unfortunately, that didn't work out either. Mel began to get lost in the city he lived in for decades.

Things soon came to a head. Mel had to make a delivery at the local airport, and somehow, wound up driving onto the runway. Shortly afterwards, he had an auto accident.

One of the principal reasons that it took so long for the family to realize the depth of Mel's disorder, was Shirley. Like any good wife, she was fiercely protective of her husband. Their sons later realized that she spent years covering up for Mel in every way that she could.

Little clues which they ignored suddenly became clear: Mel

asking Shirley what he should order when the family went out to dinner... Shirley reviewing the check before Mel paid it. (Mel used to be the one who gave a tab the old eagle-eye.) Mel had a few minor accidents before, but his wife never reported them. After all, Shirley couldn't drive and depended on Mel to drive her. If he lost his license, she would have to change her lifestyle.

The latest accident finally cracked open the shell of denial that the family had mutually built up for several years, since the first signs of Mel's mental slippage.

I first became professionally involved with the Steiners in early 1984, when I was brought in to assist the family. Ironically, it was not to care for Mel, but for Shirley, who had been diagnosed with abdominal cancer.

At the time, Mel had not been diagnosed with AD and his family was unaware that he, too, suffered from a terminal disease.

Daniel still believes that his mother's cancer was at least indirectly caused by the pressures of living and coping with Mel, as he declined over an eight-year period.

"Mom was always such an optimist, such a fighter," he once sadly told me, "but I think she finally gave up. She covered for Dad and dealt with his illness for so long, that she just gave up."

This is not as improbable as it may sound. One of the disturbing things I've noticed in my years of working with Alzheimer's families, is the frequency in which the primary caregiver of a demented patient (in this case, Shirley) dies long before the victim does.

Sometimes it's cancer, sometimes a heart attack, but I have seen Shirley's fate repeated over and over again. The stress just seems to get to them, which underscores the need to reach out for professional assistance.

I arranged hospice care for Shirley, and she benefited from it as she lay dying at home. (*For more about hospice care, see Chapter 9.*) Members of her extended family would stop in to visit...people that Mel had known and loved for a lifetime. But instead of being comforted, Mel grew angry: "Who are these people coming into my home and eating my food?!"

Mel had forgotten his own relatives. And, while he had not forgotten his sons or daughters-in-law, he often resented their presence.

"It was like his whole personality changed," Daniel's wife, Betty, reported. "He was always so generous, and now he's become stingy and distrusting."

Then, the other shoe finally dropped. Mel was diagnosed with "dementia." His doctor didn't explain the term, and the family had no knowledge about the affliction, so they chalked it up to senility. Little did they know what was in store for them.

The first time I met Mel, he was brought in by Daniel and Fred. The ostensible purpose of the visit was to discuss Shirley's illness, but I also wanted to have a first-hand view of how far Mel's AD had progressed.

I'll never forget that scene. Just months before, Mel almost fainted with grief when his older brother died. But Mel suddenly slipped so badly that he wasn't even aware his wife was dying.

This illustrates how AD patients can be stabilized for relatively long periods of time, only to suddenly and dramatically worsen.

We were talking about what to do about finding hospice care for Shirley. The boys had such a deep, loving respect for their father that they kept turning to him and asking, "Dad, what do you think?"

Mel would start to speak, and after the third word, forgot what he wanted to say. The frustration on his face was so vivid and disturbing, I couldn't stop thinking, "What must it be like to know you are sinking beneath the waves and there is nothing you can do about it?"

May you and I, dear reader, never learn the answer!

A few months later, Shirley passed away. To illustrate just how horrible AD can be...when Mel was told his wife of over 50 years had died, he grieved a little, but soon forgot. Every week or so, he'd ask where Shirley was. Mel would be gently told that she died, and he would again grieve for a brief period of time, only to forget again. After a while, the decision was made to stop this torture, by saying that Shirley "was away." Soon, Mel stopped asking about Shirley altogether.

A decision had to be made about what to do with Mel. While Shirley was dying, in-home help had not only assisted her, but her husband as well.

Now, the prospect of Mel living there alone, where Shirley suffered her final illness, was more than the family could emotionally handle. They deeply hoped that Mel could still get some enjoyment out of life, which he couldn't get by living at home.

The family decided to try a retirement hotel, where Shirley had once expressed a desire to move. I counseled against this, because I believed Mel needed much more hands-on care than a retirement hotel could give. The family disagreed, and since Mel met the physical requirements for the facility, he was moved in.

As I feared, the retirement hotel simply didn't work out. Mel wasn't able to handle life, even in the protected environment of this upscale, service-oriented facility.

His disability wasn't physical, it was mental. For example, Mel would forget to show up for meals, and even when he did come, he refused to eat.

The staff tried to make it work, but in the end, the hotel couldn't sacrifice service to the other residents in order to give extra attention to Mel.

The decision was then made that Mel would live with one of his sons. I warned them that they were asking for a tough row to hoe, but Mel was their father! They wanted everything that could be done for Mel, should be done. This is a unusually common and noble reaction of many Alzheimer's families.

Often families want to go through such a learning process, ignoring the professional's advice. Each son had an emotional need to have Mel live in their home.

Knowing this, I advised the family: "Do what you can do, and only what you can do." I hoped they would base their caregiver decisions on realistic expectations, not raw emotionalism.

So Mel moved in with Daniel and Betty, and for several months things held together pretty well. Then, the inherent problems of caring for an Alzheimer's victim began to take its toll. Mel's personality (as with most AD victims) continued to change and deteriorate. He became moody and tough to deal with. Daniel was out all day working. Even though Betty had in-home help, the strain of the little things got to be too much. There was the "battle of the 39¢ head of lettuce." I'll let Betty explain:

"Dad was living with us and we knew he couldn't be left alone, so we hired Latasha to be his companion. Latasha was a real delight and soon became one of the family.

"One day, I needed a head of lettuce, so Latasha and Mel walked to the store to buy it. I forgot to give Latasha the money, and she didn't have change on her, so Mel paid.

"As soon as they got home, Mel started to scream and carry on about how the store owed him 39¢, and he wanted it "right now!" Latasha tried to calm him down, but he wouldn't stop yelling. So I got angry and yelled back at him, and gave him his damn 39¢.

"Of course, I didn't care about the money. It wasn't even my father-in-law's rudeness that got to me. It was the grief of watching one of the most wonderful people I had ever met turn into a stranger...a difficult, cantankerous stranger."

Betty also reported a more disturbing episode:

"On another occasion, Mel suddenly appeared at the door with his packed suitcase in hand. He yelled that he was going to move out because his papers and bank books were missing, and he accused us of stealing them.

"Well, I wasn't about to let him out, so I locked the door and called my husband and his brother. They came right away, but I got quite a scare, because Mel became so enraged and physically aggressive that I feared for my safety!"

Betty's first confrontation with Mel may seem small, and when viewed in a vacuum, it is. But such episodes cannot be viewed in a vacuum. Each day, the Alzheimer's victim annoys and vexes the caregiver in every possible way.

Add in the normal ups and downs of life - illnesses, marital strife, financial woes - and it is easy to sense why family caregivers begin to desperately need their own R&R.

Betty's second disturbing story is all too common. As the disease destroys normal brain functions, many victims become so paranoid and moody that they actually become violent. They are unable to care for their own safety. Living with such unpredictable responses is too much for most people to take.

So Mel moved in with Fred and Li-Ang for a short time. Almost immediately, Mel dripped chocolate syrup over their white carpet, because he thought the carpet was vanilla ice cream and wanted to make a hot fudge sundae.

This incident almost destroyed Fred and Li-Ang's marriage... after all, it was *her* home and Mel wasn't even her father. Li-Ang was normally a warm, loving person, but she was under too much stress trying to take care of her own mother *and* grandmother.

When they discovered Mel putting toothpaste on a razor blade, intending to brush his teeth with it, the frightened family finally accepted defeat. They got Mel accepted into a small board and care home. Mel was agitated, verbally abusive and uncooperative.

The owner of the facility called me and said, "We'll keep him if you can make him behave." Sadly, I told him, "I can't make him behave."

So I recommended to the family that Mel be placed in a highly regarded nursing home which specializes in Alzheimer's care. In this secured facility, he adjusted well, and it is where Mel's long life finally ended.

He lived at the nursing home for several years, as contentedly as could be expected. The facility had a loving, committed staff who treated him, as they do all of their patients, with the respect, kindness and dignity they deserve.

Mel's family visited him twice a week for the rest of his life, offering as much love as they could, even though it was not always returned. They reported that when they were with Mel, he would smile. Perhaps that is return enough.

During Mel's final years, his family also participated regularly in my Alzheimer's Support Group, where they interacted with similar families, giving each other support and sharing their experiences. None of the family felt guilt, because they knew they did all they could to make Mel safe, secure and happy.

If you are interested in the latest research findings on AD, call the Alzheimer's Disease Education and Referral Center (*see Appendix G)* and ask for, "PROGRESS REPORT ON ALZHEIMER'S DISEASE: Research is the Key to Unlocking the Mysteries of Alzheimer's Disease."

———

"When I paint
I can go anywhere.
It doesn't matter
if I remember or forget.
It's still there."

Pearl
Alzheimer's patient

CHAPTER 4

Absence Makes the Heart Grow Fonder... Long-Distance Care Giving

The United States is a remarkably mobile society, especially for the young. For many, career objectives have them packing-up and moving-out. Others want to escape the unfortunate circumstances of their childhoods.

For the upwardly mobile, "moving up" frequently means "moving away." Some people nest wherever they meet their mates. Some have a sense of wanderlust. Whatever the reason - business, pleasure, or necessity - adult children of aging parents often live far away from "home."

Take, for example, the case of Maria, a stressful situation which certainly isn't unique, and often doesn't end as pleasantly...

Maria

If a concerned neighbor had not called her, Maria, a long-distance caregiver in Houston, would never have known about the condition of her mother, age 77. The neighbor revealed a terribly distressing picture of Mrs. Sandoval's life in California: a refrigerator full of spoiled food, stacks of paper covering the floor, filthy bathrooms, a broken stove, dust everywhere.

Maria was heart-broken, for she truly loved and respected her mother, who throughout childhood had always kept their home immaculately clean and orderly.

Feeling helpless, Maria confessed: "It's a terrible feeling to be working full-time, 1500 miles away. My job and family situation don't allow me any time to fly out to help my own mother!"

Fortunately, Maria called the National Association of Professional Geriatric Care Managers* and was referred to me. She flew to California and was present when I assessed her mother's condition.

With the information gathered from the assessment and a complete diagnostic work-up, I was able to create a care plan and quickly brought matters under control. Maria decided to place her mother in a fine board and care home, where she receives truly wonderful assistance. They talk daily on the phone. It's not as good as being there, but they are happy.

Younger people are not the only ones who have dancing feet. Older citizens also choose to relocate far from former hearth and homes.

Retirement may mean moving to a warmer climate and leaving the children, as well as the snow, far behind. The illness of a sibling or spouse may require relocation. As neighborhoods change, older residents may "flee" to safer, if less familiar, surroundings.

Of course, families may feel almost as close to each other as in years gone by. The telephone can keep loved-ones in continual contact, and the miracle of modern transportation means that even the most far-flung relative is usually only hours away.

Then there's the fun of sending and receiving mail. Maybe I'm old fashioned, but I think a good, long letter from someone I love is one of the great pleasures of life.

For those who no longer write letters by hand, we have fax machines and e-mail. Soon, there will be video phones, which may reveal more than you want to know! So today, out-of-sight need never be out-of-mind, or out-of-heart.

Families can get along swimmingly for years in this fashion. They often see each other ritualistically during celebrations and the major holidays in their cultures: Christmas/Passover/Ramadan/Asian New Year; births/weddings/funerals;

---

*The telephone number for GCM is 520/881-8008, or you may fax the organization at 520/325-7925.

50th Anniversaries; and occasional summer vacations. This may be enough family contact, when times are good.

The rest of the years and decades, they keep in touch any way they can...until...up pops the devil, wearing the guise of a gerontological crisis: stroke, Alzheimer's, a broken hip, or significant psychiatric impairment.

When this comes about, the whole family is affected. Love may know no boundaries, but the ability to spend the time and effort it takes to really aid Mom or Dad sure does. Soon, the family may wind up in a frenzy of discord and guilt.

Sister Sue yells at Brother Bob: "You're the closest. You should be the one to go take care of Ma."

Brother Bob yells back: "I can't take the time off work and keep my job. You go and I'll pay half the airfare."

Sister Sue screams: "I just had a baby and she needs me. Use your vacation time."

Bob retorts, "No can do. I only have a week and I promised the kids I'd take them skiing."

And so it goes. Meanwhile, the old folks may be in desperate need of support.

Luckily for many families who are separated, there is a solution: the friendly, thoroughly capable professional geriatric care manager who lives and works in your community.

Even families who are not separated by distance can benefit, since it may be impossible finding enough time to truly care for one's elderly parents, considering the demands of job and family that modern life places on us all.

Not only do we understand what the elderly experience, we also have the time, ability and know-how to make sure they receive TLC...the TLC that their children really want to give them, if only they could. A sensitive geriatric care manager becomes, in a sense, a "surrogate child" for the needy patient.

When I receive a call from a client who needs help with an elderly loved one living in my service area, time is of the essence. Fortunately, I am almost always able to jump right into action...

First, within a day (and sometimes within hours), I personally visit, or send a trusted associate to visit the patient and make an assessment of the situation. After talking with neighbors, friends, doctors and clergy, in order to get a clear picture of what is going on, I report back to my client.

Assessments are the corner-stone of geriatric care management. This service can be vital, not only to the elderly person in need, but also for the family, which is also in crisis. Readily available on-the-scene professionals reduce intra-family tensions, healing painful breaches that otherwise might last a lifetime.

I know of one case where a dispute over the care of an elderly father became so embittered that the family was torn apart. When the father finally died, half the family didn't attend his funeral. Later, when one of the brothers died, the siblings only sent the briefest condolences to his wife. Such tragedies are all too common.

Second, I make sure the immediate crisis is stabilized.

For example, I was retained by Robert, a highly successful lawyer who lives in St. Louis. His 92-year-old father, Sam, a California resident, suffered a medical emergency. Robert was in the middle of an important trial and couldn't get away to be with him, although he dearly loved his dad. Sam's HMO had been changed, and they were confused about the procedures and benefits of the new HMO.

As my client's advocate with the HMO, I was able to have Sam seen by the right doctor in a reasonable amount of time, so he didn't fall through the cracks. Accompanying Sam to the doctor, I suggested that if his depression didn't improve, he could consult a geriatric psychiatrist in the HMO, or see one privately.

With HMOs and some other managed health care plans, patients are usually not free to choose any doctor they want, so this approach isn't as easy as it once was.

Third, after a crisis is stabilized, I recommend options for the elderly family member's best long-term care. It may be to arrange for in-home care at the patient's residence. Or it may be to find an alternative living arrangement, such as a retirement hotel, small board and care home, or skilled nursing facility.

We also discuss many factors that must go into the family's decision-making process, such as cost, service, availability, and expectations for the patient's future prognosis.

In the example above, it was determined that the lawyer's father would do best living at home, with in-home custodial care, intermittent visits from a nurse and a physical therapist, and housekeeping services, So I arranged these things. As a result, my client did not have to drop his busy practice to fly to California.

Fourth, I continue to monitor the patient's progress, reporting back to my client on a regular basis. In essence, I'm an extra pair of eyes, ears, legs and hands, doing what the adult children would do themselves if they were available and had the expertise. They may ask to me to provide such services for years. Strong friendships often develop with both the patient and family.

A typical example of how useful and consequential long-distance care managing can be to families and patients, is the case of Otis...

<u>Otis</u>

At the time of my involvement, Otis was in his mid-80's, living by himself in Los Angeles. He recently lost his wife, and the tragedy hit him hard. The family worried so much about his welfare, that they called me for a consultation.

The initial telephone call came from his daughter and only child, Joyce, a writer for a prominent national women's magazine. A few years prior to the death of Otis' wife, Joyce was also widowed. She had recently remarried and was happily beginning a new life when her father ran into trouble.

Even though Joyce lived in Georgia, 3000 miles from her

father, she never failed to keep close tabs on him. She called Otis almost every day, and arranged for his neighbors to let her know if they ever felt that something was wrong. A cousin in the area promised to keep a sharp eye out for trouble.

One day, Joyce received a call from the cousin, who had been talking to the neighbors. Apparently, Otis had stopped socializing with them and rarely left his apartment. They reported that when they did see him, he looked terrible. When the cousin visited Otis, he could only agree. Joyce's father seemed to be sinking, and sinking fast.

This confirmed the fear that had been gnawing at Joyce for several months. Ever since her mother died, it seemed her father was slowly drifting away. Otis didn't sound sharp on the phone. He spoke about an imaginary friend in the mirror, who helped him brush his teeth. Clearly, something had to be done.

But what? Joyce was writing under a deadline. If she turned in her articles late, she'd violate her contract with the magazine... and it wasn't as if her father was dying. Otis was still living independently, and there were no special orders from his doctor.

Joyce decided to bring her father back East to live. His answer was simple and to the point: "Over my dead body!" No matter how hard she argued, Otis was adamant. He would not move. And Joyce couldn't force him, since her father wasn't sufficiently incompetent for her to legally seek conservatorship.

A retirement hotel was out, too, because Otis wouldn't leave his apartment. Considering her job and new husband, Joyce couldn't move to California. So, what to do? She asked her father's doctor, who referred Joyce to me.

The first thing I did was visit Otis. He was a feisty old fellow, determined to prove to me and his daughter that he was fine and could live alone. To prove this, Otis climbed on a rocking chair and changed a light bulb!

We got along fine, but he made it absolutely clear to me that my assistance was not needed. He also stated that any in-home help hired by his daughter would be immediately fired. Talk about a dilemma...how to deal with an octogenarian, severely depressed because of his wife's death, who had mild hallucinations and needed in-home help, but wouldn't accept it. (In a free country a person has the right to be miserable and unstable, just as long as they don't endanger themselves or others.) "Think, Nancy," I said to myself. "It's time to come up with a plan."

It was obvious, after talking with Joyce and others who knew him, that Otis liked women. He enjoyed looking at them, talking with them, flirting with them (and wasn't above making a little proposition to them from time-to-time). He was in desperate need of companionship, as well as someone to watch over him.

"Yes, " I decided, "the time is right. Time to call in my secret weapon...my one and only Martha."

Many private geriatric care managers have one or more persons on staff who are employed to assist patients with daily living needs. They provide transportation, shopping assistance, and other light services for the patient, as well as companionship.

Martha is a senior citizen herself, so she develops rapport easily with patients. Such closeness makes it easier to fulfill Martha's two most important functions: friend, and quiet observer for the care manager.

Martha could always be relied on when the chips were down. She was in her early 70's, going on 35. Bright and articulate, Martha was fearless. She was trained to watch for warning signs that an old person was headed for trouble. I knew that Otis would receive as much as he gave, if he tried to give her a hard time... But how to get Otis to accept Martha's friendship, when he had thrown out all his previous in-home helpers?

The answer came in a flash: corned beef. Otis loved corned beef sandwiches. So, I arranged a lunch for the three of us at a local deli. Martha and Otis hit it off like gangbusters! A true friendship was born.*

Initially, Martha took Otis out for lunch once a week. Soon, it was up to twice a week, with phone calls in-between. Martha managed to get Otis to go shopping, and made sure his refrigerator was filled with healthy food. Yet, their connection always centered around corned beef sandwiches at the deli.

Martha's task was far from easy. While acting nice to her, Otis had not changed his stripes to the rest of the world. He'd often create a scene at the deli or supermarket, arguing with anyone and everyone whom he imagined had gotten in his way.

However, Martha did make my job easier. As long as she was there, Otis seemed to enjoy my visits. Plus, she gave me weekly updates on his welfare.

Otis' doctor agreed to refer him to an excellent geriatric psychiatrist, whom I often worked with on such cases. We wanted to know if he was in an early stage of dementia, or whether his hallucinations were caused by loneliness and/or depression.

After a thorough evaluation, it was determined that the basis of Otis' distress was grief over the loss of his wife. His hallucination of a friend in the mirror was not harmful, because it provided him with comfort. The psychiatrist scheduled visits every two months to monitor Otis' emotional state.

For over a year, things worked out well for everyone: Otis was being seen by the physician to make sure he was doing well; he had a good friend in Martha; Joyce was able to live her life with the peace of mind that her father was being tended to by a "surrogate daughter" (me); and I had the satisfaction of a job well-done.

Then, matters took a turn for the worse. Otis' invisible friend started to become hostile. Rather than helping Otis with brushing his teeth, the "friend in the mirror" began to upset the old man quite a bit. He threw water at the mirror to make the friend go away. I feared the next step might be for Otis to throw a punch at the mirror and cut himself badly.

---

*In my years as a family counselor and geriatric care manager, I've found that it is often the most practical, down-to-earth idea that solves a problem, rather than some deep psychological insight which would make Freud proud... Whatever works!

This new symptom was accompanied by a change in Otis' personality. He began to act more like a dementia patient, suffering short-term memory loss and some confusion. He wouldn't even let me in the house unless Martha was with me. Moreover, she reported that he wasn't as sharp as he had been. He was having trouble sleeping. Even his beloved corned beef sandwiches seemed to have lost their appeal.

I discussed the matter with Joyce and Otis' doctor, and we again decided it was time to call in the geriatric psychiatrist. This time, it was determined that the neurosis of the secret friend had grown into a full-blown psychosis, which had begun to get a real grip on the old man.

The psychiatrist decided to "bring him in" for a 72-hour hold, which was extended to a 14-day hold.*

While Otis was in the hospital, the psychiatrist tried to stabilize him by prescribing anti-psychotic medication. Other doctors evaluated him, to rule-out a tumor or any other organic causes.

I visited Otis regularly to follow his progress, and to make sure the hospital staff treated him well. Martha usually came with me, since I knew that he felt deeply lonely without her.

Happily, with a little fine-tuning of treatment here and medications there, Otis became stabilized, his hallucinations were gone, and he began interacting with people again.

However, because he was functioning on a lower level than before hospitalization, I strongly recommended to Joyce that the time had definitely come for Otis to move near her. So I referred Joyce to Suzanne, a colleague who works in Atlanta. Such a referral, to a professional geriatric care manager in the family's community, is one of the essential elements that guarantees continuity of care.

Joyce, Suzanne, and I discussed the case in a conference

---

*In California, for instance, people who are reasonably suspected of being a danger to themselves or others can be brought into a psychiatric hospital for observation. The initial time period is 3 days, which can be extended to a 14-day hold. Thereafter, the State must prove beyond a reasonable doubt that grounds exist for the patient to be held against his/her will. The laws of your state may differ.

call. We all agreed that the best thing for Otis would be to move to a small board and care home close to Joyce.

Joyce still had to talk Otis into flying home, or face the prospect of filing for conservatorship and forcing him. We were finally able to convince Otis to move by agreeing that it would only be a trial visit, and he could come back to California if things didn't work out.

When Otis moved back South to be near his daughter, I knew in all likelihood I'd never see him again. There was sadness in parting, but it was satisfying, because I was able to make a difficult time in his life more bearable.

Postscript: When I last heard from Joyce, Otis was contentedly living in the board and care home. He was doing as well as could be expected, considering his age and precarious health. Otis was enjoying his daughter's proximity, and he established a new friendship with his granddaughter. Interestingly, Joyce maintained a friendship with Martha through the years, providing intangible benefits to them both.

Not all long-distance cases involve a child in another locale and a parent who lives in my service area. Sometimes, it's the reverse, as in the case with Frances...

Frances

74-year-old Frances lived in Phoenix, Arizona. Her daughter and son-in-law, Marge and Gary, live in Ventura County, about 60 miles north of downtown Los Angeles. Their young family keeps them extraordinarily busy.

Frances and Marge have had a notably poor relationship over the years and, while there was still love between them, no attempt had been made to work out a close living arrangement.

The only medical contact Frances had in California was with an internist, who treated her for a minor ailment during one of her occasional visits. Marge knew none of Frances' doctors in Phoenix.

As is often the case, word that trouble was brewing came from Frances' neighbors. They called Marge to report that a personality change was occurring: Frances was becoming the neighborhood recluse. She rarely appeared outdoors, and when she did, seemed to go out of her way to alienate one and all.

To make matters worse, Frances was seen wandering aimlessly around the neighborhood from time-to-time. This was quite upsetting to Marge, since her mother had no prior history of psychological disturbances.

Marge had no idea what to do. It was impossible for her to take an extended-leave from her family and job in order to take care of her mother in Phoenix.

Since Marge didn't know anyone in the Phoenix medical community, she didn't feel secure trusting her mother to strangers, even if they were professionals. So she called the California internist who treated Frances, and he referred Marge to me.

The first thing I did was to call Paula, a professional geriatric care manager in Phoenix, and asked her to do an assessment of Frances' situation and state of mind.

This wasn't going to be easy. Frances had decided there was nothing wrong with her, and made it quite clear that she would not cooperate with any of Marge's ideas about seeking medical assistance.

My colleague had to tell a little white lie in order to see her patient...* Paula learned that Frances had become obsessed with the fantasy of selling her house for an exorbitant price, and would constantly call real estate agents to come to her home. They were her only social contact. Creatively using this information, Paula identified herself as an real estate agent, to see if the elderly lady would let her in.

Frances opened the door immediately, without even ask-

---

*When obtaining an initial assessment of a mentally or physically frail older person, it is sometimes best not to tell them that they are being assessed by a gerontological professional. Some elderly will act on their best behavior, putting on an Oscar®-winning performance which makes an objective evaluation impossible. Others will be hesitant to cooperate, even though the professional opinion is that it's in their best interest to evaluate them. As a result, caregivers may introduce us to their loved EFM as "family friends," in order to allow us to see the patient as he/she really is.

ing for identification... This set off Paula's professional alarm bells. Remember, the point of the assessment had to do with whether Frances was truly able to care for and protect herself. Despite her paranoia, the defenseless old lady let in a total stranger with no questions asked. This significant clue to Frances' mental state became a crucial part of the evaluation.

After spending about an hour with Frances, Paula came to some unfortunate initial conclusions:

"It is too easy for anyone to gain access to Frances' home, despite her paranoia. She is not only paranoid, but appears to have some senile dementia or Alzheimer's-related condition. Her logical thought processes are pretty much gone, as are judgment and critical cognition.

"Frances recently visited her unmarried adult son in Boston, but said the only reason she wanted to go was so she could 'be his baby-sitter.' The son's home was immaculate, yet Frances admitted she still cleaned it obsessively.

"Frances' only activity seems to be a weekly walk to the grocery store, although there is little edible food evident in her refrigerator. She isn't eating well and is obviously deteriorating mentally. There is a paranoid twist to everything she says. My impression is that Frances lives an almost totally isolated existence.

"While matters have not reached a crisis point yet, they may, unless intervention occurs within a relatively short time."

It is at this point when our roles as geriatric care managers typically begin with most families. It is a little late, but better late than never.

Clearly, something had to be done immediately. Frances had no family in Phoenix. Marge decided that since Frances trusted my ability and my contacts, she would bring her mother to Los Angeles.

Marge also preferred to work personally with a local care manager, rather than by phone or mail with one in Phoenix. The real question became, "How do we get her here?"

Interestingly, Marge's husband Gary rode to the rescue. A

compassionate, successful attorney, Gary had no objections to spending whatever it would take to make his mother-in-law's life better. More significantly, he and Frances got along remarkably well, which was the opposite of Frances' and Marge's relationship.

Gary flew to Phoenix to pick up Frances. A mild subterfuge was used, only as a last resort. (Subterfuge is only used in times of crisis.) Frances wasn't told that she was going to a hospital for evaluation. She thought she was coming to visit her family (a half-truth).

Upon arriving back in Los Angeles with Frances, Gary drove directly to a hospital which has an excellent gero-psychiatric unit.*

One major advantage of utilizing the services of a private geriatric care manager is that we are often able to get an extra measure of service from the professionals treating our clients and patients.

Although it was Sunday, his day off, the geriatric psychiatrist I referred Marge to, met them at the hospital and admitted Frances. (He swore never to work on his "rest day," but that's what he always says!) This was of great value to Frances, since Sunday was the only day the family could be there with her, easing her adjustment to the psychiatric unit.

During the next 2-1/2 weeks, Frances had a complete diagnostic work-up, and was carefully assessed as to what medications, if any, were needed.

The consensus of the medical and mental health professionals was that she could no longer safely live independently.

---

*A geriatric psychiatric unit is a locked hospital area, ideal for evaluating an elderly patient. Such security actually allows the patient more freedom, since on a regular hospital floor, they might have to be restrained physically or chemically, for safety reasons.

It's getting more and more difficult these days to find such an excellent geropsychiatric unit, one which allows enough time to work with depressed and demented patients. I've seen depressed people totally turn-around as a result of treatment, and I've seen many unmanageable dementia patients become stabilized, their medications fine-tuned, so they can return home or to their board and care.

I agreed. Frances would do best at a board and care home in the Los Angeles area.

Before making the placement, I arranged a lunch for Frances, her family, and the owner of the board and care home. All seemed to go well, and Frances moved in.

All's well that ends well, right? Well, not quite yet. Frances lasted exactly one hour at the first home she was placed in. It came as quite a surprise to the family, because they had carefully selected this particular home after evaluating several others.

But Frances immediately decided that she didn't like the way things were run, and she wasn't about to keep quiet about it... Oh well, back to the drawing board. This isn't so unusual. After all, we're not dealing with machines, but people. It sometimes takes a little while to find the "square hole" into which the "square peg" fits smoothly.

So, the family decided to have Frances live at home with them. Wrong move. Frances and Marge still didn't get along. Soon, the entire family was in the middle of a crisis.

One more try at a board and care home also proved a failure, when Frances got upset one evening and decided to leave.

By this time, many families would have given-up and gone the nursing home route, even if it meant putting their loved-one into a locked facility. But not Marge and Gary. No quitters, they.

First, Gary filed a request, granted by the court, to become the conservator of both Frances and her estate. In other words, he had the legal right to make decisions about her life, under court supervision.

They tried keeping Frances in their home again, this time with a live-in helper. The situation worked...barely. Everyone's sanity seemed held together by spit and bubble gum.

The stress became so great that two of their children began acting out in school and needed the assistance of a child psychiatrist. Such ripple effects are not uncommon.

Finally, there was an opening at a unique, larger board and care home, the size of a small retirement hotel. This wonderful facility specializes in demented and psychologically disturbed older people. It seemed perfect for Frances, who was suffering symptoms of early Alzheimer's, so she moved in. Lo and behold - it worked! Frances loves the place and they love her. The home is close to Marge's, so the family visits Frances often. An ideal solution to her ordeal has been found at last. Correct placement is not an easy process.

Not every case of long-term caregiving is so complex. As in the case of Emil, sometimes less is more...

Emil

Emil's beloved wife, Goldie, died a year ago, after 52 years of marriage. Emil was staggered by her death. Always a passive fellow who prided himself on fulfilling his traditional roles of husband, bread-winner, and father, he had been content having Goldie run the household and the family's social calendar.

But now she was gone, leaving 86-year-old Emil bereft and bereaved. Overnight, his home became just a house, and it felt empty.

So Michael, who lived in California, flew to visit his Dad in Florida and gave him a beautiful long-haired Angora cat for company. Emil and the cat, now named "Mimi" for unknown reasons, eyed each other warily...just whose home was it?

Even though he always had a good-natured joke when he exchanged pleasantries, and everyone who met him seemed to like him, Emil was a shy introvert at heart. He lacked self-confidence socially and had almost no social contacts, since they all had been initiated by his wife. So he stayed at home with Mimi Cat.

A major added burden was all the household responsibilities, which now fell completely into Emil's lap... How to do laundry? What to buy at the supermarket? How to cook for himself? What to eat? When to change clothes? What outfit to wear? How to clean the house??? Goldie had collaborated on, or made decisions about all these "housewifely" responsibilities.

To top off the year of terrible troubles, when his whole world of half-a-century suddenly collapsed around him, Emil was experiencing severe short-term memory loss. Perhaps worst of all, he was fully aware of his mental deterioration. Profoundly lonely and depressed, he panicked under the emotional stress.

Always trying to do the "right thing," Emil voluntarily gave up his driving license and car, despite never having an accident in over 65 years of driving. He had an older sister 30 miles away, but when you could no longer drive or take a bus alone, 30 miles was the same as 3000 miles.

Michael was a busy independent filmmaker who sometimes had to work seven days-a-week. He didn't have the financial resources or free time to spend long "vacations" in Florida, calming and caring for his father.

Yet Michael was devoted to the old man and wanted to move him to California. Recently, he heard from Emil's friendly neighbor that his father was sinking. Concerned about the rapid decline, Michael came to my office for a consultation. He didn't know what to do.

But I did... I immediately called Miriam, another professional geriatric care manager who fortunately lived in Emil's community. (I trust Miriam so much, that ten years ago my husband and I retained her to manage the care of my mother-in-law.) Michael described the situation to her on the phone. Miriam promised to visit his father the next day, to conduct an initial assessment.

True to her word, Miriam did just that. The situation was not as bad as was feared. Emil needed assistance, but thank goodness, it was not an emergency case. Miriam arranged for some in-home help, took him to the doctor for a check-up, and visited Emil once a week to make sure that he was okay, always remembering to bring Mimi Cat a little snack.

That gave Michael a sense of security. It wasn't necessary for him to drop everything and immediately fly to Florida. He could go about his business without guilt or the fear that he was not taking care of his father properly.

This also gave me the luxury of time to search for the right placement option. As these words are written, Michael and I are working closely to find Emil's future home, a placement that will maximize his quality of life and allow him to live close to his son.

By the way, Emil now insists on bringing Mimi. I'm sure we'll find an excellent small board and care home that would love to accept a nice man and another cat in residence.

Having a network of colleagues throughout the United States who can be contacted, allows a member of the National Association of Professional Geriatric Care Managers to quickly respond or intervene, averting many a geriatric crisis. And it can all be started with a phone call, as in Emil's case, from one coast to the other.

CHAPTER 5

I've Got Those "Placement Blues"

There comes a time in many oldsters' lives when they simply can't make it on their own anymore. Maybe it's a stroke that keeps Grandma from walking like she used to... Perhaps chronic diabetes has led to blindness in Uncle Phil... Or Aunt Sue's Parkinson's disease has become so severe that she can no longer be left alone, and her husband who used to care for her has died.

When crises such as these jump-in with both feet, families often feel like they have been picked-up by a tornado and dumped into a twisted version of the Land of Oz. Only this land doesn't have friendly Munchkins to point-out the yellow brick road. No, this land seems more like a nightmare, a nightmare of uncertainty and guilt, where no sign posts point the way toward a better tomorrow.

If it's tough on families when loved ones can't live alone anymore, imagine what it feels like to the old person who realizes that their time of independence has come to an end, perhaps a permanent one. Imagine the feelings of depression, helplessness and fear that would strike you if you found yourself in such a dependent circumstance.

I know how painful this time can be. My own illness was so debilitating, my family and I had to wrestle with the issue of whether or not I would have to be placed in a nursing home.

We chose not to do that, and instead, opted to hire around-the-clock nursing. But many families can't afford that luxury. We almost couldn't, either. It nearly broke our pocketbooks and family spirit. Yet, eventually we thrived... You and yours can, too.

DETERMINING WHEN THE TIME HAS COME

It's all well and good to counsel people to face tomorrow honestly, with dignity and courage, come what may. But how do we really know when the time has come that Mama can't live alone anymore?

Sometimes, it's easy, such as when a stroke paralyzes or Alzheimer's robs a loved one of their ability to dress or recognize the caregiver. Sometimes, the approaching disability is subtle, walking on cat's paws.

At these times, it is best to be safe, rather than sorry. Hopefully, the following test will make an on-coming crisis clearer, so you can act on it before it acts on you.

QUESTIONS TO ASK WHEN AN EFM LIVES ALONE

These questions should give you a pretty good idea if the time has come for an elderly family member (EFM), currently living alone, to find a suitable alternative living arrangement:

Safety needs
1. Has your EFM had accidents because of weakness, dizziness, or the inability to get around?*
2. Has use of the stove, oven or appliances become a safety hazard because of forgetfulness?
3. Are there conditions in the EFM's home that are safety hazards, such as steep stairs or a lack of adequate heating?
4. Does your EFM refuse to use a cane, walker, wheelchair, or other assisting apparatus necessary for safety?
5. Has your EFM lost interest in living or expressed a desire to die?

---

*Researchers have just developed a light thin pad worn on the hip, which reduces impact from falling by 65%. It may soon be approved by the FDA, so physicians can prescribe it. Watch for it.

Nutritional needs

1. Is your EFM unable/unwilling to use the kitchen for food preparation?
2. Is there a demonstrated nutritional concern, such as weight-loss, illness, anemia?
3. Does your EFM eat only inappropriate foods which do not supply nutritional needs?
4. Does your EFM "forget" to eat?

Personal hygiene

1. Is your EFM unwilling/unable to go to the toilet without assistance?
2. Is your EFM unable to change their own clothing or bedding to remain clean and dry?

Medical needs

1. Does your EFM forget to take necessary medications?
2. Is it likely that your EFM would take the wrong dose of medicine by mistake, or purposely?*
3. Is your EFM physically unable to handle medications, spilling them, or unable to administer needed injections?
4. Is your EFM unwilling/unable to obtain help in case of need?

---

*The U.S. General Accounting Office estimates that more than 5 million elderly who are on Medicare take prescription medications which are wrong for them, increasing the possibility of negative reactions, including falls, car accidents, drowsiness, and confusion. And FDA Commissioner Frank Young estimates that 800 million prescriptions are taken incorrectly each year.

Non-compliance with doctor or medication instructions accounts for almost 30% of all hospital admissions over age 65. It is the primary reason patients are initially admitted to long-term care. Shockingly, approximately 125,000 people die each year from non-compliance.

The effects of a drug may be entirely different if prescribed for a patient at age 15, age 40, or age 80, even if the directions on the vial are the same. This is another reason why it's so important to use a physician experienced in treating the elderly, who knows their unique problems, and who will carefully monitor the effects of a medication.

Social needs
1. Is your EFM unable to handle money?
2. Does your EFM get lost in familiar surroundings?
3. Has your EFM left home without a destination?*
4. Has your EFM behaved inappropriately in public, such as exposing himself/herself or threatening others?
5. Does your EFM have mental or emotional problems which might be a threat to self or others?

If you honestly answered all these questions "no," then rejoice, count your blessings, and challenge your EFM to a hard-fought game of tennis.

However, if you found that many of the answers you gave were "yes," then you must begin to face the fact that a crisis may be fast approaching. In such case, you can either act now and hopefully head danger off at the pass, or go into denial and wait for your family to feel like General Custer did at the Little Big Horn.

PLACEMENT ALTERNATIVES

When an EFM can't live alone anymore, and in-home help is ruled-out as an option, suitable accommodations must be found as soon as possible. This process is called **placement**.

For most people, the emotionally wrought subject of placement brings forth dark visions of dank, dark nursing homes from hell. In truth, placement need not be bleak and, if handled correctly, can be a positive blessing to both the beloved elderly person and their family .

When people think of placement, they may envision putting their beloved EFM into a nursing home with all the horror stories that option brings to mind. Luckily, those stories are more myth than reality. And, in fact, most elderly people who

---

*You can register your EFM in Safe Return, a program operated by the Alzheimer's Association for the protection of "wanderers" (*see* *Appendix F*).

need placement can find alternative living arrangements other than a nursing home.

Placement in an adult child's or relative's home, retirement hotels and assisted living facilities, small board and care homes, and life-care homes, are all alternatives to nursing homes that are not only viable, but as we shall discuss in the next chapter, can actually enhance the older person's enjoyment of life, serving to extend life itself.

Living with an adult child or relative

We hear so much about how seniors of today are not cared for by their families, like they were in "the good old days." Well, I don't buy it. Every day I see committed and loving families doing all they can to make sure their loved ones needing assistance are properly cared for.

The first option for most families is to explore the ways in which an EFM can be cared for in the home of a child or relative. Sometimes this proves to be impossible, but more often than you may think, it works out unexpectedly well.

Having your parent live in your home or in a **granny-house** on your property is becoming a trend. Currently, some zoning laws prohibit this, but when all the baby boomers and the next generation reach old age, there won't be enough facilities to house them. In the future, the granny-house option may very well become a necessity, especially since the government is pulling out of financing elderly care.

The benefits for the elderly person are, of course, enormous. There is nothing that can replace the sense of belonging that comes with living in a familial environment. The love and care a family can give cannot be matched by "strangers" who are paid to do the job, no matter how much they truly empathize with the oldsters in their care.

On the other hand, the burden and responsibility of caring for an EFM in one's own home can be truly overwhelming. This is especially true for those in the "sandwiched generation," who also must take care of their spouses, children, and grandchildren, while holding on to their jobs. The addition of another dependent loved one can put a whole family on tilt.

I have even handled cases where grandchildren in their 30's wind up taking care of their grandparents, because their parents have either divorced, died, or are unavailable.

Nowadays, with most women working, it's even more complex, and the aging parents may also be divorced, with more than one set of children and grandchildren.

Who has the time and energy to take care of an EFM with Alzheimer's,* especially one who is in constant motion? Such a patient needs supervision for safety reasons...to protect them and to protect your home.

The following test should give you a good idea whether or not to place an EFM in your home:

Health and safety

1. Is your home an adequate, safe environment for an elderly person, i.e., warm, adequate plumbing, laundry facilities, etc.?

2. Would it be necessary to modify your home to increase safety and assist with mobility, such as adding railings, a lift, etc.?

3. Does your EFM require nursing services that are too demanding for you to physically perform, such as assisting them to a toilet or turning them in bed?

4. Does your EFM regularly disturb the sleep of others by calling-out, needing care, or walking around at night?

5. Is your EFM likely to wander away if left unguarded or alone?

6. Does your EFM create safety hazards due to forgetfulness or carelessness, such as falling asleep while smoking, leaving the stove turned on, misusing electrical appliances?

---

*A new resource providing some respite time to family caregivers and in-home help, is called Video Respite™. These videotapes are specifically geared to maintaining the attention of dementia patients.

Time and energy

1. Does your EFM require someone available at all times to provide care?

2. Must bed linens and clothing be changed so often that care becomes an excessive demand?

3. Do you have responsibility for the care of others, such as young children or other family members, which will result in divided loyalties and work overload?

Family considerations

1. Does your EFM regularly interfere with the running of your household?

2. Will the loss of privacy create conflicts with other adult and teenage members of the household?

3. Is there strife between younger family members and the EFM?

Emotional considerations

1. Has your EFM become emotionally explosive, verbally abusive, threatened or engaged in violent behavior?

2. Does your EFM accuse people of stealing money or trying to physically harm them?

3. Will you become cut-off from friends and relatives because of your EFM's demands?

4. Will you have to give-up interests and activities that are important to you?

Situational considerations

1. Is it necessary for the family to change homes or move to another community, making continued care unrealistic?

2. Have financial demands made employment or working longer hours necessary?

3. Have additional family member emergencies created conflicts, or competition for your time and energy?

4. Has a supportive family member moved out of the household, increasing the burden on you?

The more times you answered "yes" to the questions, the greater the likelihood that caring for your EFM at home will be unduly burdensome and unwise.

Remember, taking the step of bringing a frail or ill older person into a nuclear family situation is like throwing a large rock into a tranquil pond. The waves that are created can upset the peace and tranquillity of your personal "ecosystem."

Placement in a retirement hotel

Retirement hotels offer board and care for seniors who may or may not be able to take care of all their needs, providing excellent care in a safe setting.

While a board and care home is usually a single-family residence, a retirement hotel usually cares for between 40 and 200 residents at a time. Retirement hotels may or may not be licensed.

As the name implies, the setting of a retirement hotel is residential, but more commercial than the home-like setting of a 6-bed board and care. However, such hotels are not institutional, like nursing homes. Residents do not think of themselves as institutionalized or "put away."

Many of the facilities will make sure the residents are eating right and their basic needs are cared for in a hotel-like atmosphere.

Some older people thrive in a retirement hotel setting. The environment allows for socialization in a nice atmosphere. It's good to have relationships with peers who understand the indignities of old age, such as waking up with aching joints, and who can commiserate together. Residents find it highly enjoyable to participate in the recreational activities that most hotels provide, such as exercise classes, crafts, card and board games, movies, music, singing, parties, lectures, and special trips.

The level of care offered by retirement hotels varies. Many are licensed. When looking for the right one, make sure you match the level of care offered with the specific needs of the older relative.

You should also be aware of the minimum physical requirements that the hotel insists its residents meet. Your EFM will be asked to leave the facility if they fall below those minimum standards.

You may choose to use the services of a private geriatric care manager who will know the hotels which match the needs and right services for your EFM. This saves you a lot of time, bother and heartache. Ideally, you only want to go through the painful process of placement once.

Because it is of such import, I repeat that some retirement hotels are licensed and others are not. Those that are licensed must provide assistance with hygiene and medication. They allow walkers and perhaps wheelchairs. Retirement hotels that are not licensed may be pleasant and attractive, but most are strictly hotels.

Competition from small board and care facilities has caused many retirement hotels to tout themselves as **assisted living facilities**. They invite residents who require more supervision and care. Assisted living facilities provide more personal care and different levels of care, but the cost increases as more services are needed.

An assisted living facility might be an especially good placement option for a long-term married couple who have different needs of care, but don't want to be separated (i.e., one has short-term memory loss, the other has a heart condition). Or in another scenario, the caregiver spouse gets ill and needs care too.

Retirement hotels often offer **respite care**, so that a spouse or other caregiver can leave the patient there temporarily. This is a valuable service if a caregiver has to travel for work or pleasure, or needs relief because of exhaustion.

Placement in a small board and care home

Small board and care homes (also known as **licensed residential care homes**) are a relatively new phenomenon in the care of elderly people. They are typically single-family homes, much like yours or mine, which are licensed by the state to house and care for a small number of senior citizens, usually no more than ten. Check with your state regarding its licensing requirements for small board and care facilities.

These homes provide an excellent alternative to living with a relative. Benefits to the elderly person, and to the family opting for a board and care facility, include:

Social
Older people often get a great deal of social satisfaction from living together in small board and care homes. They have the opportunity to interact on a daily basis during meals and other activities, and enjoy sharing memories with each other.

Because board and care homes are so small, it is important to find one where the staff speaks English. Unfortunately, for non-English speaking elderly, it's very hard to find a board and care where their native language is spoken, but it's worth searching for.

Elderly residents generally receive excellent custodial care, and feel comfortable living with their peers in a homey environment. Visits by family members are encouraged, which all seem to enjoy.

Residents who need more activities than their small board and care can offer, may also be taken to a senior center, an adult day treatment program, or an adult day-care center.

The combination of a small board and care home, along with involvement in an appropriate community program, provides more stimulation, adding to the already good care at the residential home.

Health
Since the setting of a small board and care facility is a home, not a hospital, residents tend to be less depressed and enjoy life more, despite chronic health concerns.

The owners of the home and their staff are there to assist with personal care, medication management and food preparation, in a familial, rather than an institutional atmosphere.

Economics

Board and care homes provide excellent care at a far lower price than nursing homes, because skilled nursing care is not provided in-house. Rather, it can be provided by outside *home-health agencies*. For instance, if the patient needs insulin, a home-health nurse can come by each day to give the shots.

Lower costs not only save Pop's estate, but since families often have to assist with nursing home expenses, it also saves the bank accounts of the EFM's children.

Moreover, if the EFM is forced to rely on Social Security and SSI, those limited funds will go further buying quality board and care, than buying quality nursing home care.

On the other hand, Medicaid will not pay for a residential home, while it will pay for care in a skilled nursing facility.

Warning: I have found that some small residential homes for the elderly, which rely exclusively on clients who pay with SSI or Social Security, skimp on the quality of care. Financial pressures on under-financed residential care homes can lead to neglect or abuse.

Family happiness

I am convinced that the families of EFMs feel much better about placement in a quality small board and care home, than placement in a nursing home, when there is a choice.

There is the joy of seeing Grandma enjoy herself in a home like the one she used to have. There is the security of knowing that medications will be taken on time, in the proper dosages; that there will be three hot, nutritious, tasty meals a day. And, there is far less guilt.

Placement in a life-care home

Life-care homes (also known as continuing care retirement communities, congregate living, or congregate housing) usually offer elderly residents three types of contracts:

1. All Inclusive Care guarantees catastrophic nursing care and long-term care for seniors, no matter what their physi-

cal condition is now, or what it becomes in the future.

2. Modified Care offers some nursing services and a specified number of nursing days, with fees for uncovered services.

3. Fee-For-Service requires residents to pay for nursing care as needed, and may require them to have long-term care insurance.

Most of these facilities are run on a non-profit basis by religious organizations, or by corporations loosely affiliated with religious or fraternal groups.

Upon entering a life-care home, an EFM who is fully capable of all physical and mental functions is placed in a small house or apartment, similar to independent living. If their condition deteriorates, the EFM will be moved to an intermediate care facility, similar to a retirement hotel, or if necessary, the life-care home's skilled nursing center.

A downside to these life-care homes is cost. They can be quite expensive. In order to be admitted, your EFM usually has to be in generally good health.

If you are interested in a life-care home, check out its administration, corporate structure, and financial stability, which should be as solid as possible. Remember, the facility has to continue in existence for the life of your EFM.

For more information on life-care homes, contact: American Association of Homes for the Aging (*see Appendix G*).

Placement in a nursing home

The remaining option is the traditional **convalescent** or **nursing home**. Most nursing homes are specifically designed to care for those who need skilled nursing care - for example, the use of *catheters* or *tube feeding* - and for those who are totally bedridden. Many nursing homes also specialize in rehabilitation.

Because of serious physical disabilities, such patients cannot care for themselves and no longer meet the criteria for board and care homes. Usually, they are old and frail, although younger persons who have suffered traumatic injury or illness sometimes find themselves "housed" in a nursing facility.

On the positive side, many people don't realize that a nursing home can serve as a bridge back to the community-at-large, or back to more independent living at a retirement hotel/board and care home.

Nursing homes conjure up nightmarish images. There are several reasons why people may dread the thought of placement in a nursing home...

The atmosphere

Even the most delightfully furnished and well-maintained nursing home can be a thoroughly depressing place to visit, let alone live in.

Most (but certainly not all) patients arrive at the nursing facility on a one-way ticket, and never will permanently leave during the rest of their lives. The "feel" of the place may be that of a warehouse, where old people are housed while society waits for them to die.

It would be enormously helpful if less-caring staff members, administrators, and owners of nursing homes would spend one full day in a wheelchair, like the patients at their facility, to get a real feel for what daily life is like (*see Appendix A*). Physicians could also benefit from this sensitization. (It might be a useful course in medical school.)

Of course, not all nursing homes are just warehouses for the aged. Many work exceptionally hard to keep their residents not only clean and comfortable, but cheerful as well. They provide recreation and other activities to keep patients' minds and souls occupied, engaged in life as much as possible. And they hire staff who really care.

One of the care manager's key jobs is to find these better facilities.

The costs

A quality nursing home is expensive, typically running in excess of $3,500 a month. (In New York City, the monthly cost can exceed $5,000!)

Under current regulations, **Medicare** will sometimes pay

for nursing home care, for a brief period, if the patient is there for *rehabilitation*, and is *making progress*, in order to become healthy enough to move into another living arrangement. **Medicaid** (called **Medi-Cal** in California), the state and federal jointly-funded health care program for the poor, only kicks in when a patient is impoverished. The government provides little or no assistance with costs, until the estate of the single elderly person has been almost completely used up, then Medicaid becomes available. If the patient has a spouse, Medicaid allows them to keep approximately $70,000, but they must spend all the rest of their savings down to that point. These rules make it most difficult for the middle-class who need Medicaid..

At one time, people could rather easily "shelter" some assets when being considered for eligibility by Medicaid. That is no longer true. According to **Barbara Bergstein**, a dedicated elder law attorney and partner in the firm of Burgh, Balian & Bergstein: "The government has clamped down on abuses in the Medicaid system by severely penalizing non-exempt transfers of assets."

In plain language, this means that Medicaid no longer permits eligibility for benefits, even when the EFM qualifies, if money has been sheltered incorrectly.

The primary change in the law has reduced the ability to preserve estate assets for one's family. Under the prior law, an individual who wished to give away his/her assets to family members and apply for Medicaid, would be penalized for no more than 30 months from the date of transfer. The transfer period was the same whether the gift was directly made or made to a trust.

Under the new 1993 law, the federal government penalizes the perspective medical beneficiary by the use of "look back periods." Gifts made directly to an individual are subject to a **36-month look back period**. This means that if the elderly individual transfers assets as a gift to a family member within 36 months of applying for Medicaid benefits, the amount of the gift will be carefully scrutinized by Medicaid.

Furthermore, if the gift is made "to" or "from" a trust, the look back period is increased to 60 months. Because many elderly people wish to avoid probate proceedings at death, they establish living trusts. Gifts of assets from such trusts will be subject to the **60-month** look back period.

The key in transferring assets is to make the transfers well in advance of these periods. For example, if an elderly person transfers money to her children on January 1, 1996, in February of 1999 she would finally be able to qualify for Medicaid without being subjected to the 36-month look back period.

Here's how the system currently works: Assume that you have "given" your grandchildren $300,000 by establishing an irrevocable trust in their names. Also assume that the average monthly nursing home fee in your community is $3000. Medicaid will divide the amount of the gift by the average fee, to determine the amount of time that you will not be eligible for Medicaid. (The $300,000 gift, divided by a $3000 average monthly nursing home fee = 100 months of ineligibility.)

Still, all hope is not lost. While the laws in each state will vary (Medicaid is jointly financed by the states and the Federal Government, but administered by the states), there are certain uniform rules now in effect that allow some property to be kept, even if a loved one's nursing home expenses are paid by Medicaid:

• A Medicaid beneficiary who owns a house can transfer ownership of that house to their spouse or certain relatives, and still retain Medicaid eligibility.

• The spouse who remains at home may be entitled to a "monthly maintenance-needs allowance" from the income of the spouse in the nursing home. Each request for such an allowance is determined on a case-by-case basis.

Of course, what the government gives with one hand, it often takes back with the other... A downside of the new law allows the government to consider the property of the spouse who does not receive Medicaid (excluding the home) in determining continued eligibility. This is known as the spousal "deeming" rule, under which one spouse's income and property are deemed available to support the other, even if the property was owned before the marriage.

There are a myriad of other rules you need to know about if your loved one is heading for a nursing home, to be financed with Medicaid funds. I urge you to consult a lawyer in your community who practices elder law.

Excellent referral sources include: National Academy Of Elder Law Attorneys, National Association Of Professional Geriatric Care Managers, and your local Bar Association.

Considering these financial facts of life, and since better nursing homes often refuse to sign agreements with the government to accept Medicaid patients, it often falls upon the family to pay for expensive nursing home care.

Families may try to get around the financial bind by purchasing **long-term care insurance** (also known as convalescent home or nursing home insurance). It defrays part of the cost for a limited period of time (usually two, four, or six years). Some policies also cover home care.

Be sure your long-term care insurance policy is one of the newer, better policies. Older policies used to have clauses which severely reduced coverage. Some negative points you may need to watch out for are:

• It may exclude from coverage the very illnesses which are the principle reason to of enter a nursing home, such as Alzheimer's disease.

• It sometimes excludes all nursing home placements that do not follow a hospital stay...a great many cases.

• It can be very expensive, costing in excess of $300/month ($3600/year).

• It must be purchased *before* it is needed. Otherwise, the insurance company will not issue the policy because it will claim the nursing home placement was caused by a pre-existing condition which then relieves the company of responsibility.

Do think about purchasing a nursing home insurance policy for yourself or a loved one, but be careful! Know what you are buying, and what it does not cover.

"Financial planning has become an important issue because people are living so much longer," according to **Neal E. Cutler,** of the Boettner Center of Financial Gerontology at the University of Pennsylvania, an expert in the important new field of elder financial planning.

It is essential to consult a certified financial planner who is knowledgeable about *elder financial planning,* not just any insurance salesman, banker, stock market broker, or accountant.

A few states, such as California and New York, have established what is called a **Partnership for Long-Term Care.** This is an alliance between the public and private sectors, designed to make lifetime protection an affordable option. Private insurance coverage will cover the first part of long-term care, with Medicaid picking up coverage later on.

What is unique about the Partnership concept is that the amount of care paid for by the private insurance policy, translates into assets "protected" from Medicaid eligibility requirements, dollar-for-dollar. For example: If you receive $10,000 in insurance benefits and then apply for Medicaid, your $10,000 savings account will not count against you in determining Medicaid eligibility. This means more money can be kept in your pocket or left to your kids, even if you go on Medicaid.

Since laws are constantly being changed, according to the political and economic climate in America, always first check with an elder care lawyer, certified financial planner, and experienced insurance agent before determining your long-term plan of action.

For more information, contact the Department of Insurance or Department of Health in your state. (In California, contact: California Partnership for Long-Term Care.)

The guilt

Of all placement decisions, placing a beloved EFM in a nursing home is the most emotionally disturbing to caregiving families. Many families will literally sacrifice health and home to keep their relatives out of nursing homes.

People are often so wracked by guilt that they don't see the positive side to a nursing home placement. Often, a nursing home acts as a bridge back from the brink of ill-health, to independent or semi-independent living.

Even when that is not possible, a good nursing home provides an environment where frail older people can live their remaining time in comfort and dignity. Such nursing homes attempt to improve their quality of life through good care and nurturing attitudes.

If you find yourself going through a tough case of the "nursing home guilt blues," join a family support group that can assist you through this rough period. There, people who are going through the same emotional trauma and guilt that you may be suffering, get together to discuss the hard times. At the meetings, you will find information, companionship, and the valuable realization that you are not alone.

Organizations providing valuable information include: Alzheimer's Association, American Association of Homes for the Aging, American Health Care Association, Older Women's League, and National Association of Professional Geriatric Care Managers (*see Appendix G*).

Choosing the right facility

Once the decision is made to place an elderly family member, what do you do next? Of the hundreds of facilities that may be available near a large city, which is the right one for your EFM and your unique situation?

Left on their own, some caregivers use the Yellow Pages. Some people will use brochures listing facilities, but be aware that in most of these guides, any facility, regardless of quality, will be listed if it pays for an ad.

Some people are comfortable using a list, and looking on their own. However, when you're too busy to personally spend months carefully evaluating facilities, when you live out-of-town, and especially during a crisis, many family members desire and seek out professional guidance.

Geriatric care managers have already checked out and evaluated your local retirement hotels, board and care homes, and nursing homes. They determine which cater to more independent seniors, and which emphasize care for those unable to mentally and/or physically fend for themselves.

Geriatric care managers like to use what is called the *Goldilocks concept:* knowing which "home" has porridge and a bed that is "just right." They direct you to the best facilities, according to your EFM's individual circumstances and needs. Within a brief period of time, GCMs do what it would take weeks or months of diligent research to find out on your own.

Not only that, GCMs periodically "take the temperature" at the facility you select, holding it accountable to you. They maintain contact with administrators and staff, keeping tabs on new owners and new policies, and check on any changes for the worse in the nursing home. If anything is awry, they try to solve the problem.

That being said, the following matters should be brought to your attention:

• Retirement facilities, and board and care homes do not accept people who are bedridden. If your relative is virtually bedridden, the two remaining options are a nursing home or caregiving at home.

• Unless family members can either afford professional assistance, or have heroic strength of character as well as physical strength (to lift the patient from a wheelchair onto a toilet, in and out of bed, etc.), then the remaining choice will undoubtedly have to be a nursing home.

• If your EFM is mentally competent, it is vital to involve him or her in the placement decision-making. It's not only the polite and respectful thing to do, but our laws are unequivocally strict when it comes to preventing forced institutionalization.

• If your EFM opposes placement, but placement is necessary for physical or mental reasons, you may have to bring an action in court to compel that it be done. But I urge you not to take this step lightly. Not only is this approach expensive, it is emotionally traumatic, and can divide and embitter a family. With so much at stake, it is obviously best to deal with the disturbing question of placement early, rather than late.

• If a nursing home is likely to be the ultimate destination of your EFM, plan the timing of the placement carefully. Here's why: As I described earlier, many of the best nursing homes may not accept patients who are or will soon be on Medicaid, since the compensation they receive from the government is much lower than what they charge private patients.

• Nursing homes which do accept Medicaid patients often have a long waiting list. By placing your EFM early, or at least putting them on a waiting list, you may be able to avoid a facility that doesn't come up to your high standards.

Some of the most heart-warming success stories during my career as a care manager, have come from helping families through the ordeal of placement. Yes, there's life after placement...

CHAPTER 6

"Success Stories:" Case Histories of Successful Placements

We have beheld the magic of flowerdom:
The bud to enfold this rare beauty awaits a perfect time
For a butterfly blossoming.
Two flowers atop a sturdy stem stand with queenly pride.
PINK AMARYLLIS
You have stilled us and thrilled us with wonder
And taught us to ponder
On lessons of Infinite Truth.

- Nita Yore Kelsey,
(written in her 90's)

Many families see placement as the next-to-the-last-nail in their beloved parent's or relative's coffin. After all, they reason, Dad can't live alone anymore, and what opportunities for joy and fulfillment will there be in an "old folk's home?"

On the other hand, after facilitating thousands of placements, I don't see placement as an ending, but as a beginning...an opportunity not only to extend the years of an older person's life, but also to maximize its quality.

Moreover, a well-aimed placement can actually benefit an older person in resisting their decline, so their potential for a higher level of achievement and a more fulfilling life can be reached.

But don't take my word for it. Let's dig into my files, where

families just like yours have been able to get through their placement crises, improving the situation for young and old alike...

Molly

Molly wasn't the most pleasant older person around. She
was rude, caustic and crabby. Yet there was cause. At 92, she
was nearly blind, had a pacemaker, and needed a walker and
hearing aid, but refused to use them. As a consequence, Molly
usually felt bad, which caused her to treat others even worse.

Molly wouldn't admit that her health was in serious decline. Such an attitude can be admirable. It can also be self-
destructive, when not "giving in" means refusing desperately
needed care.

Molly had definitely moved into this vast arena of denial.
In order to help the feisty old lady, her family and I first had to
overcome her manipulative tactics. We all wanted to provide
Molly a safe, healthy foundation, from which she could stabilize and grow. A positive living environment would give her
an opportunity to plant some quality seeds of life.

What Molly really needed was to be placed in a small board
and care home, where experienced staff would give her an
abundance of TLC, without taking her verbal abuses personally. The caregivers had to be kind, but firm, making sure she
did what should be done to protect her well-being.

The plan was a good one, but there was one major stumbling block: Molly refused to cooperate. She insisted on staying in her one-bedroom apartment.

Finally, Molly had to admit that living alone wasn't such a
good idea after all and she decided, on her own, to move into a
retirement hotel. Not unexpectedly, it didn't work out. Her
physical troubles and, shall we say, difficult demeanor, caused
the facility to "ask" her to leave.

Molly's daughters, Joan and Barbara, were in despair. They
were afraid that the only place which would take their mother
was a nursing home, because Molly was unwilling to take the
physical therapy required to keep her ambulatory. All she
wanted to do was lie in bed and be mean to people. Had she
been given her way, a nursing home would soon have been the

only option.

Joan called and asked me to pull a rabbit out of a hat for her mother. We had to find the right button to push, in order to save Molly from wasting the remainder of her life.

Under normal circumstances, this wouldn't have been complicated. Joan and Barbara loved her and were supportive, despite Molly's constant complaining and lashing out at them. She also had grandchildren nearby, almost always a source of joy for older people. But Molly was unable to count her blessings. She became her own worst enemy because of fear about her losses, and stubborn unwillingness to do whatever was necessary to overcome her plight. Molly was effectively shaping a classic self-fulfilling prophesy: her own actions and inaction were creating the exact conditions she feared most. In other words, Molly was making herself into nursing home material.

As a professional geriatric care manager, I make it my business to know the strengths and weaknesses of the facilities in the area, so I can find the right one to match each patient's individual needs. This is the art of placement: finding a home which will not only provide food and shelter, but also maximize the quality of a patient's life. A good placement definitely has a win-win outcome.

In considering Molly's special needs, one particular small board and care home came to mind. The dedicated owners of this facility had an excellent track record working with more difficult clients who seemed destined for nursing home care, due to depression or refusal to do the best they could. Operating their home was not just a business, but a joy. They considered their elderly patients "part of the family."

Luckily, the home had a vacancy. I knew that the board and care owners were grieving over two residents who had recently died. The timing was right to make the placement, for both Molly and the home. If Molly moved into the home, there was a chance she could still turn her life around, but how to get her there? That was the rub.

Joan and Barbara were used to upscale neighborhoods. This home was in a nice clean neighborhood, but it was definitely not upper-crust. My first task was to convince the daughters to place their mother in a board and care home where the cars in the driveway were used Toyotas, not new BMWs.

I told them the truth: Love, care, and experience in creating a good quality of life for the patient, are more important than the view from the porch. After the daughters agreed to meet the wonderful family who ran the rather earthy-looking home, they finally understood what I was talking about. To their credit, they agreed to try the placement, despite any misgivings.

Reluctantly, Molly moved in. She required a lot of attention from the owners, who, fortunately, had more than enough heart to give. To the daughter's amazement, and perhaps Molly's too, the placement literally changed her life.

Barbara wrote to me: "Everything has worked out beautifully. My mother looks radiant. After all the apprehension and fear, she's finally happy. Everybody at the home is friendly. The few times she feels lonely, my mother simply calls up all the '800' telephone numbers to chat with 'the nice people,' and she gets a mountain of free information and catalogues in the mail.

"She keeps telling me what good people they are, and about all the wonderful care she's getting. I can't believe it, coming from my mother! You did a very, very special thing, and I want to thank you."

That is what makes my work so worthwhile.

David

David was a retired physician in his 70's. As a teenager, he lost most of his family in World War II. David spent a successful life as a respected healer, and was also a good provider for his family. But life turned sour when David's wife died.

Virginia's death devastated the entire family. Sally, their daughter, had been uncommonly close to Virginia and required therapy to move beyond her grief. But it was David who was especially hard hit. Not only had he lost his beloved mate, but he lost his emotional anchor in the world.

David always exhibited a touch of despondency in his private life, and it was Virginia who kept it under control. Now, with his wife gone, David soon began to slip into inappropriate emotional behavior.

He became extremely paranoid and depressed, developing symptoms similar to early dementia, such as forgetting to eat and refusing to get dressed in the morning.

Sally rode to the rescue. Fortunately, David's medical practice had been successful. Lack of money was not a consideration limiting the family's options,* so Sally hired help to care for David in his large rambling house.

She started with one person, four hours per day. Within a few months, Sally hired live-in help to assist her dad 24-hours - one person five days a week, and a relief person on the weekends.

You might have thought that the helpers made Sally's life miraculously easier. They didn't. Hiring outside help can be useful and necessary, but it is not a panacea. In fact, it can create it's own problems.**

Sally discovered to her shock that she now had to train, supervise, and monitor not only her own family and her Dad, but even the hired caregivers, who had their own personal prob-

---

*I can't take away the problems, but money certainly provides more options... "Money can't buy happiness, but it can buy away a lot of unhappiness."

**Hired in-home caregivers can be extremely sensitive and compassionate, or they can be bossy, always complaining, competing and arguing with each other; some may even steal things. EFMs may not be saints, either, and have been known to abuse hired help until they quit and flee...one after the other.

Even if a family can afford home-care, they still need a geriatric care manager's professional advice on how to find, train, and supervise the employees. Certainly in the beginning, home health care workers should be carefully evaluated to determine if they are trustworthy, responsible, and diligent about reminding the patient to take medications on time and in the right doses. In addition, workers should be cheerful, providing good companionship, and committed to your EFM's care and well-being.

lems and needs. To make matters worse, the helpers all found her father very hard to deal with.

Placement in an alternative living facility is relatively easy: there's a large staff to do the minute-by-minute work. Having your elderly family member live at home may be the hardest way to go: You are the primary staff.

Sally had to continually deal with crises caused by David. Every chance he got, he verbally abused the live-in caregivers with his razor-sharp tongue. As a result, Sally seemed to always be on the phone with workers, who either threatened to quit or did quit because of David's cruel and unfounded personal attacks.

This put tremendous pressure on Sally. She was still mourning the loss of her mother, and now her father was making life miserable for everyone he came in contact with. Moreover, Sally had a husband and three children of her own to care for. She was near her breaking point.

The pot finally boiled over when David's paranoia grew to the extreme. Having brushed against the terror of the Holocaust in his earlier years, paranoia soon convinced him that the "Gestapo" (in reality, his hired caregivers and every stranger on the street) were about to poison or kill him.

All of this caused one home health aide to quit without any notice. Sally was frantic. She had her hands full with her own household, so she called me.

A board-certified geropsychiatrist was essential to stabilize the situation. David's behavior was way over the line, and medical intervention was an absolute necessity.

David wasn't eating or sleeping, and he was hallucinating. I advised Sally and her husband to get David to the geriatric psychiatry unit at the hospital as soon as possible.

The geropsychiatrist cleared the decks for David, considering him an incoming emergency case. Placed in an excellent hospital psychiatric unit, David began receiving therapy and medications for his paranoia and depression.

At first, Sally found it impossible to accept that her father needed psychiatric help. But, after some deep soul-searching, she came through and was able to convince her dad to go along with the mental health treatment.

Half-way through the grueling weeks of David's hospital treatment, Sally almost cracked. One time, Sally came to see her father and found him sitting by himself in a corner with his head on his chest. This was more than she could bear.

Sally blew-up, screaming at the nurses about David's care. She even yelled at the geropsychiatrist, calling him a "quack," and threatening to take David out of the hospital. Clearly, a crisis was at hand.

The hospital staff were really miffed at the way they had been treated. I explained to them, "She feels guilty, sad and angry. Sally is losing her father, without having had time to grieve for the recent loss of her mother. She's entitled to her feelings in dealing with all the stress."*

If Sally took her father taken out of the hospital, she would be back to square one, without the professional help she needed. David would be back home, where everyone was the Gestapo... crazed, out of control, demented. She would suffer terribly from stress and guilt.

If Sally gave it some thought, instead of immediately reacting, she'd realize that the hospital was the right place for her father at that time, because it could give him proper treatment.

Luckily, Sally's husband, Phil, was far less emotional. We all had a long talk, and convinced Sally not to quit half-way home. We helped her realize that she was becoming a "candle person"... someone who tries to burn her flame at both ends, but only succeeds in burning-out the center, so that the whole candle gives way.

So, Sally calmed-down and allowed her father's treatment to run its course, which fortuitously, succeeded in stabilizing the old man. His paranoia slipped away, he stopped seeing things, and even his depression responded to treatment. While David wasn't turning cartwheels, at least he was back in the

---

*It's okay to have such strong feelings, even if they're illogical, especially when faced with powerful emotional crises. Feelings are not right or wrong.

land of reality with a family who loved him deeply.

Unfortunately, David's physical condition deteriorated at this time. His diabetes worsened and he remained cantankerous. It was decided that he could no longer live at home, or even in a retirement hotel. A small board and care home was also ruled out, because David's personality made his chance of fitting into a 6-bed home "iffy," at best.

The patient's unique personality should always be a major factor in determining placement. In this case, a nursing home was better than a board and care. Since he was a retired physician, David actually felt more at home in such an institutional setting, where people called him "Doctor" and he could interact with so many "doctors and nurses." It was crucial to his successful placement.

David could afford the best. So, I scoured the community with three main goals in mind:

1. To find a nursing home close to Sally, so she could visit her father on a regular basis.

2. To find a home in which the patients were relatively alert and active. David needed nursing home assistance, but not just any nursing home. Because of his strong personality and level of awareness, he needed a facility where a high proportion of residents were capable of meaningful interaction...a place where David could have good relationships with his peers.

3. To find a home that was well-maintained by professionals, offering the highest quality of service for its patients.

It was very gratifying when all the pieces fell together. I was able to find a nursing home that fit all three criteria to the letter. As of today, Sally's family crisis is completely under control. Her father lives close enough, so she can visit him nearly every day, taking him home for dinners and holidays.

Sally stopped burning her candle at both ends. Her emotional and physical state has improved, as well as her marriage.

And David is doing well, too. Oh, he abuses the nurses now and then, with a string of curses that could wake the dead, but they take it in stride and go about their business.

Manny, Moe & Jackie

Of all of my placement success stories, this is one of my favorites... Manny and Moe are brothers. Manny was the smart one who had a real business head and succeeded in the grocery field. He could be called the patriarch of the family.

Moe, on the other hand, was a little simple. He had a heart of gold, but simply didn't have the business sense to make a great financial success in life. Still, he was deeply loved by Manny, who always made sure that Moe had a job.

Manny was married to Jackie for over 60 years. She and Moe got along famously. When Moe's wife died a few years back, the natural thing for Manny and Jackie to do was to invite him to live with them.

The three were a perfect fit. They went everywhere and did everything together. But there were storm clouds on the horizon: Moe and Jackie, both in their mid-80's, began to show visible signs of wear. They became less able to get around physically and began to experience loss of memory. Yet, as long as Manny was healthy, things held together.

Finally, Manny, who was three years older than Moe and Jackie, had a stroke which left him physically unable to do more than the simplest task. For a while, Jackie tried to keep hearth and home together, but soon found that she simply didn't have the capacity to be a caregiver for Manny, let alone assist Moe, too.

That was the state of affairs when Manny's daughter, Phyllis, came to me. She was heartbroken. Oh, she might be able to bring one of the trio into her own home, but that would mean splitting them up. She just didn't have the heart to do that.

I decided to try a retirement hotel first. Two of the three were reasonably fit, and even Manny could shuffle along on a walker. Manny and Jackie could live in the same room. We found a place that put Moe right next door to his brother and sister-in-law, since they were so close.

Then, another crisis arose: Jackie took a fall and nearly broke her hip. She wasn't a candidate for a nursing home, but she couldn't assist Manny any longer with his physical needs. Besides, her forgetfulness caused worry that in the middle of the night, she wouldn't remember her physical limitations and might really hurt herself.

So, a "companion" was hired to assist Manny and Jackie at the retirement hotel. And it worked well, except for one thing: the cost.

Retirement hotels may not cost as much as nursing homes, but they are not cheap. Add to that, the cost of a nearly full-time companion, and you can see that Manny and Jackie were quickly pouring their nest egg into an omelet maker.

Manny's daughter called and asked what could be done. She knew her folks couldn't afford the fees for both full-time help and the retirement hotel. There was also her Uncle Moe to think about. She adored him, and couldn't bear the thought of moving Manny and Jackie, while leaving Moe at the retirement hotel.

I suggested a small 6-bed board and care home. The price wouldn't be much more than a retirement hotel, but the level of care would be greatly increased. The only complication was finding one that would take all three.

As things turned out, we were back in luck. A brand new home was opening in the community. The owner was an experienced, capable, caring person, who would serve the trio well.

Manny, Moe and Jackie became the first tenants to move into the lovely small board and care home. As such, they took on a pride of ownership as if it was their own home. When others moved in, the three considered them "tenants," and were quite elated about "all the money" they were making.

When last I checked on Manny, Moe and Jackie, they were doing remarkably well. Jackie was getting along fine on a walker. Manny had regained some, but not all, of his physical abilities. And Moe was as happy-go-lucky as ever.

Although all three were content and their lives had quality, I noticed there was still an important missing element. Manny, Moe and Jackie needed more mental and social stimulation.

We successfully arranged to have them transported to a senior center three times a week, where they could get out and have a good time. Gin rummy, anybody?

Anna

When Dorothy, of *Wizard of Oz* fame, found herself in a strange and magical land, she learned the great truth: "There's no place like home." For the families of those who are in the winter of their lives, this truth frequently has even deeper meaning. That's why so many elect to take on the heavy responsibility of caring for an aging parent or other relative in their own homes, rather than placing them in care facilities.

One such story is that of Anna, who came alone to America when she was only 15. Being of strong immigrant stock, Anna soon was working in a bakery and sending money to the old country, so the rest of her family could come across the sea to "the promised land."

Life wasn't easy for Anna. She married at an early age and soon had two children, Antoni and Julietta. Her husband was a gambler and philanderer, who spent a lot of time away from the family. Still, together they sought to fulfill the American dream by bettering their lives and those of their children.

Life got even tougher in the 1920s. Anna's husband died unexpectedly, just at a time when he was beginning to achieve some business success in his New England factory town.

Suddenly, Anna had two mouths to feed, with no visible means of support. This was the time before Social Security or any government-funded safety nets.

Anna reached into her "toughness reserve." She sold the industrial building her husband owned, and made enough profit to open a small beauty shop.

Never remarrying, Anna successfully raised her two children. The close-knit family wasn't rich, but it got by, even during the depths of the Depression.

In her later years, Anna lived in California. Julietta shortened her name to the more American "Juliet," married a wonderful man named Larry, and had a rambunctious son, Toni Jr. Anna moved-in with them to help care for the little boy while they worked. She even managed to continue operating her beauty salon, and saved enough to travel extensively.

Eventually, sparks flew between Juliet and Anna, and soon Anna moved into her own apartment. The cause of their rift can be summarized by the annoying, but memorable TV commercial, when a harried housewife wails, "Mother, please! I'd rather do it myself!"

This setback in their otherwise intimate relationship didn't last long. Soon, mother and daughter were working together again in Anna's shop. Eventually, Juliet took over the business.

Anna continued to live independently until Christmas of her 86th year, but she was growing increasingly "afraid." After a minor auto accident, Anna suddenly became scared to drive...this from a woman who had bravely traveled alone to places like Italy, Russia, and Australia.

Anna began to demand daily visits from Juliet, fearful about some stranger mugging "an old woman in her own home."

Finally, when her family left after a visit for Christmas dinner, Anna fell and couldn't get up. She didn't have an emergency response system, so she ended up spending the entire night on the cold bathroom floor, futilely calling for help. But nobody heard. Juliet found her the next morning.

This truly disturbing experience broke Anna's once fiery spirit. Anna was now terrified of living alone. She became incontinent, not due to a medical condition, but because she was afraid to walk unassisted to the bathroom.

As Anna grew more fearful of walking, her ability to do so deteriorated. Soon, she was using a cane, then demanded a walker, even though she didn't physically need one.

At this point, Julietta had to make a hard decision: either place Anna in a residential facility, or bring her home. Larry, was adamant: "Ma," as her son-in-law affectionately called her, "is not going to a nursing home or any other institution!"

The family all agreed, so Anna "came back home" to Larry and Julietta's house, where she felt she belonged.

People who take on the responsibility of caring for an elderly relative must be cautioned about all the pressures and tensions that performing this loving task will generate in the family. Anna's case was no exception.

I told Juliet that she could expect to find her nerves fraying and her temper flaring. She would also experience the loss of her own freedom, while she was caring for her increasingly dependent mother.

Unfazed by these predictions, Juliet reasoned that she had already given up her freedom to raise her son.

I pointed out that the freedom "lost" while bringing up a child isn't really a loss, but a joy. Parents sacrifice a lot out of love. Yet they are often deeply rewarded as they watch their children grow, slowly releasing childhood and discovering the independence of adulthood.

Sadly, though, when caregiving an elderly person, the same joy and rewards do not always exist. On the contrary, there is a great deal of emotional pain associated with being forced to watch a once vital, powerful loved one slowly fade away.

But Juliet and Larry were game and insisted on giving themselves the opportunity to help Anna. They wanted to be able to look back upon this emotionally difficult time without regrets, knowing that they had done all they could to return the love, devotion, and financial assistance they received from Anna through the years.

They were right. Anna lived with Juliet and Larry during the last two years of her life. She grew more and more frail, yet she thrived in the bosom of her family. Anna especially loved the visits from Toni Jr., her handsome grandson who remained the apple of her eye.

Toward the end, Juliet found herself lying in bed next to her mother, singing old Italian children's songs and reminiscing with her mother about the past.

The time came for Anna to die. As often happens when a person is close to death, she held on until Toni Jr. returned home from Europe, where he had been studying architecture. Anna relished the emotional reunion. That night, she suffered a stroke and passed away peacefully in her sleep.

And the family? They live with all their fond memories of Anna. They feel a warm glow knowing that they did, in fact, repay Anna for all the sacrifices she made for them during her long and productive life.

Was the caregiving easy? No. Juliet sacrificed many of the dreams she and Larry had planned to do in retirement, including an around-the-world trip.

But looking back on the caregiving experience, Juliet wouldn't trade it for all the vacations in the world: "I never felt closer to my mother than during the last years of her life, and she never felt closer to me."

Juliet is also blessedly free...free from guilt, free from bitterness, and free from the self-recrimination that many children experience when a parent dies. It is a gift, one that Anna would gladly approve.

Christopher

A common misconception that people have is the myth, "once placed, always placed." Placements are often permanent, but sometimes they are temporary, enabling the older person to get back on their feet.

One example of a temporary placement is that of Christopher, a successful owner of a manufacturing company. Despite the fact that he was nearing 80, Christopher remained in complete control of his business. But as often happens to older people, when things begin to go wrong, they soon turn catastrophic.

First, Christopher's wife died. Then, his sister's husband died. As if that weren't enough, Christopher's sister was diagnosed with cancer. Christopher brought his sister home to care for her as she slowly faded-away.

About six months after his sister died, Christopher suffered a serious stroke. Such a circumstance is relatively common: the stress of multiple losses often leads to a serious or fatal illness in the elderly. Christopher was hospitalized, but ultimately returned home with around-the-clock private nursing care.

I was approached by Christopher's children when he failed to make progress in regaining optimum health. The cause seemed to be depression, which robbed him of the will to strive for improvement. Christopher became steadily more reclusive and withdrawn. Even Kathy, one of my compassionate staff social workers, was unable to break through his emotional barrier.

After much discussion with the children, we tried to persuade Christopher to move into an upscale retirement hotel, where he would receive good care and have the company of his peers to keep the blues away.

We showed him several such places. At first, Christopher was adamantly against the idea. He would not move, despite the fact that he was miserable living at home, with only hired caregivers for company.

Finally, Christopher agreed to move into a retirement hotel. His spirits picked-up markedly there, and soon, his physical abilities improved as well.

Before we knew it, Christopher was reinvesting time into his business and seemed to have regained his interest in the world. Except for some minor physical impairments, Christopher was as functional and capable as he had been before the stroke.

Then, Christopher made an unexpected decision. He wanted to move back home. Since he was well-enough and capable to make intelligent choices, there was nothing to do but accede to his desires. So we watched with some trepidation, as he moved back into his huge house. He looked like a lonely king in charge of a vast palace.

Christopher was fortunate. He was financially able to keep a home that he was not living in.* The family had temporarily rented it out, making sure it was maintained, so all was in order when Christopher made his decision.

---

*If you can afford to keep your EFM 's home, don't sell it yet. The knowledge of still having their home to return to makes an aging person feel much more secure.

If you face similar circumstances, and are able to maintain your EFM's home for a period of time while things sort themselves out, you may be doing yourself and your loved-one a favor. When an old person knows there is a home to go back to, she/he will feel more in control and at the helm of life. This, in turn, can make the emotional and psychological difference between overcoming misfortune or giving in to it.

With pleasure, I can report that Christopher knew exactly what he was doing. Since returning home, he has thrived. True, he's slowly letting others take control of the business. But his lawyers, stock broker, accountant, and business executives all maintain steady pilgrimages to his house, where he now has his office and holds court.

So, what does this prove? Well, for one thing, you may not be able to teach an old dog new tricks, but then, you may not need to!

CHAPTER 7

Mind Over Matter...
Mental Diseases of the Elderly

One of the least recognized aspects of dealing with the elderly is the extent to which psychological or emotional disease can deprive seniors of their vitality, their health, and even their lives.

In fact, it is safe to say that the misdiagnosis, or the failure to diagnose, mental disease in seniors frequently works like alchemy in reverse, turning years that could be "golden" into cold, hard, lifeless lead.

This is a tragedy. Mental afflictions that attack seniors can often be effectively treated by a geriatric psychiatrist. With treatment, seniors who seemed to be going down for the count can get off the mat to lead quality lives of fulfillment, enjoyment, and substantial independence.

If your EFM is in a **managed care plan** (such as an HMO), find out whether there is coverage for psychiatric help, how much will be paid, and for how long.

When patients are treated by the right professional, families can avoid debilitating their own energy while caring for the seniors. Instead, families can enjoy the love and happiness of family interaction with their parents, grandparents, or other beloved relatives.

Perhaps the most common "attack of mental disease" is depression...

DEPRESSION

Depression is a serious, chronic illness of the brain, which may result from biochemical, genetic, psychological, and/or environmental causes.* There are two forms of depression:

1. Appropriate depression that we all go through, which is intensified in the elderly.

2. Major depression, a destructive disease which is usually treatable.

Depression, With a Small "d"

Small "d" depression occurs in reaction to all the losses in old age: the loss of spouse or loved-ones, the diminution in physical ability, the loss of feeling needed at work or at home, the awareness that death is approaching. This form of depression can be called "the common cold of old age," since sooner or later, nearly all elderly people suffer from it.

That is not to say that small "d" depression should be shrugged off, as if it were only a slight sniffle. Sensitive help is needed to assist an old person through these distressing periods and into a renewed life. This can be done in several ways, including: grief therapy, psychotherapy, anti-depressant medication, involvement in new activities, reminiscence, life review, and using the healing quality of time.

Such "down periods" should *not* be thought of as a disease, but as a natural part of the aging experience...

It is not wrong for an old person to cry and feel bitter or angry when their spouse dies. Cry! Grieve! Show emotions! Only by releasing these feelings can healing begin.

It is not wrong for an old person to feel like taking time-out from life while learning to deal with such losses.

In short, it is not wrong to grieve for the loss of their beloved, and the old ways, while new ways of living are slowly adopted and "integration" occurs. The goal is to reach a state of acceptance which is healthy.

One of the big mistakes we make as a nation, concerning depression with a small "d," is that we put great emphasis on rushing to get over it. For some reason, we disdain expressing what are thought of as "negative" emotions.

Thus, while it may be acceptable to cry at a funeral, far too

---

*Depression must be distinguished from "the blues," and feelings of sadness or disappointment.

frequently we urge those in grief to turn away from their feelings as fast as possible. We even actively shun those who cannot do so within our arbitrary "acceptable" timetable. Such pressure to eliminate healthy, natural feelings can lead to deeper grief, and even mental illness.

If you suspect that an elderly person you love is suffering from small "d" depression, get involved. Here are some tips:

• Help your EFM get back into the activities they enjoyed before becoming depressed. Encourage them to get "back in the saddle again." Give them things to look forward to, and a purpose for their life.

• Treat them to a creative hair stylist and suggest trying out a new cut.

• Buy them a new outfit, and make sure they are well-groomed. Looking good inspires feeling good.

• Get them an inexpensive computer. Teach them how to play computer games, and how to make new friends around the world on the BBSs and Internet.

• Exercise. Go for walks together. If your EFM is able, go fishing or play a round of golf.

• Share good feelings and good times. Take them to a comedy movie or a theater musical. Tell jokes. Play.

• Have real conversations. Encourage talking about their feelings. Let them cry on your shoulder.

• Make sure your EFM eats regular, nutritious meals.

• Discourage alcohol consumption.

• Tape their life story, or let a professional do it, as a legacy.

• Without being preachy, encourage your EFM to count their blessings... family, nature, life.

• Obtain professional help, or urge them to join a support group to get through their emotional valleys.

Healing takes time. But if you take the time, make the effort, and have enough love to stick with it, chances are that small "d" depression will be vanquished. The sun can shine for your elderly loved one, once again.

This brings to mind a recent case...

Cicely

Cicely was referred to me by her concerned physician, because she had been unable to break-out of her grief during the three years since her husband of thirty-four years died. Self-educated, Johnny, had worked his way up from manual labor to owning a factory. Through thick and thin, he remained a faithful husband, devoted father, and rock of strength in the close-knit African American family.

Cicely had found true fulfillment in the traditional, and often courageous roles, of wife and mother. At first she worked for the post office, also doing her share of volunteer work and political organizing. When Cicely had twin girls, Charlotte and Lisa, she decided her first priority was to raise a healthy family and keep it together, no matter what.

She did. Cicely kept the kids out of trouble, but now they were grown, building independent lives of their own...and her beloved husband was gone. Sadly, this strong, devoted and loving woman came to believe that "nobody needs me." Such depression is quite common when a spouse of many years dies.

The biggest stumbling block that Cicely faced, ironically, was the guilt she felt for grieving "three whole years." She felt weak in character and deficient as a person, because she had been unable to reconcile with Johnny's loss. Despite her pain, she had not done her "grief work."*

Her well-meaning friends tried to cheer her up and told her "to look on the bright side." What bright side? They strongly suggested that Cicely should have been able to re-adjust to life within the "usual" year's time.

I had to convince her that even three years of mourning could not make up for such a loss. It didn't reflect poorly on

---

*Grieving takes many forms, and there are various "socially acceptable" lengths for the process in different cultures. In some emotionally repressed cultures, outward expression of grief or talking about it isn't generally accepted, despite the most basic psychological need to let feelings out. But grief must be confronted, or it may never stop.

her character at all, rather, the grief showed her depth of devotion to Johnny. After some time, Cicely was finally able to accept that her "lengthy" grieving was one way of dealing with the tremendous loss. This acceptance of her valid feelings finally allowed Cicely to believe that she had the personal strength to create a positive new life.

Cicely decided that the best thing for her would be to use her skills as a caring nurturer to assist others in need. She volunteered at a local convalescent home as a companion/friend to several other elderly residents, some younger than herself. Cicely felt useful again. Her life had importance. She was needed.

Cicely successfully took control of her own life. Recently, she decided to move into a smaller apartment and is in the process of building a social life. Cicely finds great joy spending time with her children and grandchildren, who all truly love her.

The moral of the story? Each of us has to accept our own unique timetable for overcoming devastating losses and rebuilding our lives. Whenever we are ready to move on, we will, doing what it takes to get the job done...with a little help from our friends, and a therapist if needed.

Depression, with a capital "D"

Major depression, with a capital "D" (as opposed to small "d" depression), is the most serious presentation of mood disorder in the elderly. Often triggered by chronic stress, it strikes seniors and their caregivers with alarming frequency. It can affect a person's whole system, like diabetes or cancer. And like many chronic illnesses, major depression is also ignored until it hits full-force, leaving the victim devastated.

Untreated major depression is a leading cause of suicide... deaths which would not have occurred had the condition been properly diagnosed and combated.*

According to **Barry Friedman, M.D.**, a Board Certified Geriatric Psychiatrist** in Beverly Hills, who is experienced in working with the elderly, the following are the most common symptoms of major depression (also called clinical depression). If your elderly loved-one suffers from one or more of these, see a doctor and/or geropsychiatrist for diagnosis and treatment:

- Depressed mood
- Hopelessness
- Loss of energy
- Decreased appetite and weight loss
- Psycho-motor retardation (mental and physical slowing)
- Feelings of guilt
- Refusal to do activities that used to bring great pleasure
- Symptoms of dementia

Other symptoms of major depression include: inability to concentrate or make decisions, chronic physical symptoms not caused by disease, continuous anxiety, unexplained fatigue, loss of interest in friends, and constant thoughts of death.*** Depressed individuals may stop bathing, no longer change their underwear, and generally allow their hygiene to deteriorate. They often have altered sleep patterns, including early morning awakening and insomnia.

Interestingly, a minority of victims of clinical depression may suffer the reverse of these symptoms. For example, rather than having problems getting enough sleep, the depressed person may sleep up to fourteen hours a day. Rather than refusing to eat, the depression person may eat to excess and gain

---

*Left untreated, about 15% of seriously depressed people commit suicide. The highest rate of suicide is males over age 65. While women tend to take pills and frequently don't succeed, men use guns and do succeed, or they jump to their deaths.

**Board Certified in Psychiatry, with Additional Qualifications in the new specialty of Geriatric Psychiatry.

***If symptoms continue for more than a couple of weeks, the EFM should be evaluated for depression. Over 80% of serious depressions can be helped with a combination of psychological therapy and antidepressant drugs.

weight.

In any event, if your loved-one's personality significantly changes in any of the above ways, be sure that they receive medical attention. According to Dr. Friedman, you may have to insist on treatment, since many mentally-ill elderly will not seek it out on their own.

Elderly patients suffering from any form of depression can be misdiagnosed as having dementia. When depression mimics dementia, with symptoms ranging from forgetfulness to personality changes (as in Alzheimer's disease) it is termed **pseudo-dementia**.

Misdiagnosing pseudo-dementia (depression) as real dementia can result in a patient warehoused in a nursing home, with "Alzheimer's" written on their medical chart. Often, little or no treatment will be given, since many forms of dementia are considered uncurable.

Depression, even when it is misdiagnosed as pseudo-dementia, is treatable. However, many people - including some medical doctors - do not know this. It is tragic when treatable depression isn't treated.

In the same way that some retirement hotels ignore signs of depression in residents, depression may also go untreated in patients at nursing homes, because visiting psychiatrists often come to nursing homes monthly and are unable to monitor the daily effects of medications.*

An elderly patient is appropriately started off with a low dosage of anti-depressants to test their reactions, but that initial level of medication might never be raised to a useful thera-

---

*The possibility of pseudo-dementia occurs both in nursing homes and outside of them, wherever a patient is taking medications. One reason is that the some drugs cause symptoms which imitate dementia. Blood pressure medication, for instance, may cause depression. Always consult with your EFM's physician about the possible side-effects of medications, and keep an eye out for any negative or unexpected reactions.

peutic dose. The patient may be left with possible side-effects, yet without the benefits.

Such a common sad situation is one important reason why you should consult with a **geropsychiatrist** who specializes in depression, dementia, and the unique problems of the elderly.*

There are too many elderly who could be living fuller lives, wasting away at home, board and care facilities, and nursing homes because of undiagnosed, and therefore, untreated small "d" and big "D" depression.

Depressed patients really need an advocate to get the right medical assistance in our increasingly complex health care system. One case which, without proper guidance, could easily have become a tragedy, was Rachael...

Rachael

Rachael is one of those zealous Brooklynites that we have all run into from time-to-time. She was born in Brooklyn, raised her family in Brooklyn, and by god, she hoped to die in Brooklyn!

Rachael's daughter, Jenny, had married and left the old neighborhood, moving with her husband to Thousand Oaks, a suburb of Los Angeles. Jenny contacted me when she heard me lecture on caring for aging parents and planning for long-term care. The problem: Rachael's husband had died. Jenny was concerned about her mother living alone.

After giving her a little advice, Jenny went on her way. About six months later, Jenny contacted me again. Rachael had suffered a serious stroke.

The call wasn't because Rachael had become completely dependent. In fact, she had received excellent medical care and experienced a good recovery. But Jenny didn't want her living alone in Brooklyn, where there were no relatives left to pitch in.

There was more to the story... Jenny was concerned that her mother seemed terribly depressed. Rachael was a woman who

---

*For a Board Certified geriatric psychiatrist, call your medical society.

always had a strong tendency towards small "d" depression. Now, the physical limitations dictated by the stroke, added to the loss of Rachael's husband, apparently resulted in what looked like big "D" clinical depression.

So Jenny decided the time had come to bring Mom to California. We discussed the situation, and after some persuasion, Rachael agreed to live with her daughter.

Unfortunately, life in Jenny's household didn't work well. Rachael and Jenny had never resolved their early conflicts, and living together did not improve the quality of their interaction.

To keep their relationship from reaching crisis proportions, Rachael agreed that, at the end of the month, she would move into a small board and care home not far from Jenny.

Just before the move, without warning, Rachael deliberately took a lethal overdose of medication. The loss of her husband, the loss of some physical abilities, the loss of her beloved Brooklyn, along with her reluctance to live in a board and care home, were more than Rachael could take. Luckily, Jenny discovered the suicide attempt and called the paramedics in time to get her mother to the hospital, which saved her life.

Rachael recovered physically in the hospital, but she became totally passive, refusing to eat and generally withdrawing from life. Since a board and care home was no longer an option, Rachael had to be placed in a nursing home.

That's when Jenny asked me to assess the situation. I was convinced that Rachael could better benefit from an in-patient stay at a geriatric mental health facility, and she was admitted to such a unit.

Rachael significantly improved due to her stay at an excellent geriatric/psychiatric unit. She was given carefully-monitored anti-depressant medication, intensive psychotherapy, group therapy, and excellent physical care. In addition, the behavioral structure she received in the hospital made it easier for Rachael to get back on an even keel.

Now Jenny was faced with the question of placement again. It was clear that Rachael did not belong in a nursing home. We wondered how she would react to a board and care home...after all, the thought of living in one had been one of the straws that had broken Rachael's back psychologically.

But this time, things were different. The "new Rachael" was involved in the decision-making process to choose her own home. This time, she settled quite comfortably into a board and care home near Jenny.

Unfortunately, this happy ending was not final. After an entirely pleasant year at the board and care home, Rachael began to experience some unusual, persistent symptoms of dementia over a period of a few months.

Jenny became worried and called the geriatric psychiatrist I had referred her to, the one who successfully treated Rachael previously. He was on vacation and another psychiatrist was covering for him. The new doctor re-hospitalized Rachael. Concerned about her mother's care, Jenny again called me.

I was shocked and surprised by Rachael's poor condition. She repeatedly spit-up her food and resisted the nurses' attempts to care for her. Rachael was extremely confused and appeared to be demented, which was most unlikely, since the onset was too sudden.

The new psychiatrist had a CAT scan done to rule-out a brain tumor, which could cause such sudden behavioral changes. She didn't have a brain tumor. So the psychiatrist put her on medication often given to dementia patients, and gave her a discharge date, along with the recommendation that Rachael be placed in a nursing home.

I was appalled. Rachael was salvageable. Since I didn't know this particular doctor or the depth of his experience with elderly patients. I advised Jenny to contact a trusted geropsychiatrist for a second opinion.

As an assertive caregiver, you should never be shy about seeking a second opinion if you have any doubts about the treatment being given to your loved one. Having a strong advocate is essential for your EFM, especially if it is believed they have dementia or depression.

This is particularly true for some HMOs and other managed care plans,which may be reluctant to spend the time and money needed to fully assess and treat these conditions.

Fortunately, getting the second-opinion was a good idea

because it yielded gold. Rachael's reviewing geropsychiatrist felt that more should be done before giving up. Rachael was immediately admitted to another hospital's psychiatric ward.

Her new psychiatrist felt strongly, as I do, that <u>we should never write people off because of old age</u>. He dug deeper into the case, consulting with an excellent internist, in order to rule-out any medical cause for Rachael's behavior, no matter how remote.

The internist hit the jackpot. It turned out that Rachael was suffering from a disease known as *hyperparathyroidism*, a treatable condition.

So the correct conclusion was reached that Rachael was not demented, which is hardly surprising, considering her medical history of depression. She was referred to another physician, expert at treating the malady. Once again, Rachael was "brought back to life," a richer life of quality and satisfaction.

I rejoice in both of Rachael's major recoveries! But I wonder how many of our fathers and mothers are lying in nursing homes...when, with a little extra effort by those entrusted with their care, they could be living cheerful, even vigorous lives?

Rachael's case illustrates a vital point which cannot be over-stressed: It is essential that those who diagnose and treat the elderly be knowledgeable, trained, and certified in the diseases and conditions of old age.

This truth is as important as bringing your sick baby to a pediatrician, not to a chiropractor, orthodontist, or veterinarian. Elderly people react differently to disease than do younger people. Their treatment can differ both as to kind and as to method.

If your EFM's care seems to have hit a brick wall, be sure the doctors have expertise in geriatric medicine. If they do not, insist on a second opinion with a doctor who does.

It should be noted how successful the new medications often are for the treatment of depression. Massive strides have been made in psychopharmacology.

According to Barry Friedman, MD: "Many new psychiatric medications are now available, and more are in the process of being developed. Some of the newer anti-depressants and anti-psychotics are particularly suitable for the elderly patient, as they have far fewer and less troublesome side-effects than their predecessors. When used correctly, they can make an enormous difference in a suffering elderly person's life."

Discuss the issue of medications fully with your doctor, to assess the side-effects and to determine whether they will be beneficial.

PSYCHOTIC REACTION TO DEMENTIA

The second significant mental affliction that can strike a previously symptom-free elderly person, is a psychotic reaction to dementia. It is a symptom of dementia, not a separate disease. The victim undergoes severe changes in behavior and personality...so severe that they become actively psychotic.

The fact that a dementia patient can become psychotic is a doubly cruel blow. Dementia patients are already sliding down a slippery slope to eventual oblivion. Not only do they suffer from loss of memory, becoming less able to perform even simple tasks, they often progressively lose their overall health.

Then, BAM! They get hit with psychosis. Now, the caregivers have a two-track ordeal: the dementia and the resulting psychotic symptoms.

Perhaps the psychotic symptom is severe **paranoia**. In this scenario, a formerly loving mother may become convinced that her beloved daughter is poisoning the soup. As a result, she refuses to eat properly and may become violent towards the "poisoner," as she engages in active "self-defense."

How emotionally painful it is for the caregiver to suffer such accusations...especially when she is giving so much and loving her parent or elderly family member with all her heart.

At other times, the psychotic reaction may express itself through **hallucinations**. Sometimes, these hallucinations can be harmless, such as having a benign imaginary "friend."

Unfortunately, the hallucinations often take a malignant turn. Dementia patients may become terrified of the visions they see. This can lead to violent reactions, directed at themselves, their caregivers, or even strangers on the street.

For example, one patient broke her husband's arm with a lamp, imagining he was an intruder: She stared right at her husband and didn't recognize him.

In another case, a Parkinson's disease patient who developed dementia, called her daughter and swore she saw a stranger in the closet. But the patient said not to worry, because she started a fire and drove the stranger away. The daughter immediately called the fire department, which fortunately arrived in the nick of time.

Equally heartbreaking is the patient who suffers from delusions. A **delusion** is different from a hallucination. The patient who suffers from a hallucination actually sees something that isn't really there. The patient with a delusion is tormented by a false belief.

For instance: An old person may believe the world will end tomorrow, and acts accordingly. Or they may believe that an intruder is speaking through the electrical outlet in the wall... Actions based on delusions can be dangerous to the patient and to others.

It is best not to try talking the delusional or hallucinating patient out of what they think they know or see. Rather, delusions and hallucinations need the benefit of a psychiatrist.

The good news is that, while dementia itself is usually not treatable, psychotic reactions in dementia patients can often be treated, just as they can in non-demented people.

There are, however, a few things you need to know about the treatment:

Administering anti-psychotic medication

A psychiatrist usually administers anti-psychotic medication. When a dementia patient becomes psychotic, the treatment often involves a combination of anti-psychotic medications along with psychotherapy. (If memory loss is too severe, psychotherapy is not useful.)

The drugs used are intensely powerful substances which can have profound side-effects. Moreover, the drug dosages must be carefully adjusted and monitored to meet the needs of the individual patient.

Selecting the right psychiatrist

It must be re-emphasized that all psychiatrists are not equally adept at treating elderly patients. Some primarily treat young people or adults, while others specialize in treating geriatric patients. The dosage of an anti-psychotic medication that might work well for a man when he's 40, may be much too strong for the same man at age 70, not to mention at age 90.

Not only that, but an older person is far more likely to be taking medications to treat other physical conditions. So there is a greater than average possibility that the psychiatrist's prescriptions will adversely react to the internist's prescriptions.

Treatment in a psychiatric hospital

When a dementia patient becomes psychotic, as a symptom of the overall illness of dementia, their actions frequently become so anti-social and destructive to self or others that they must be hospitalized. Usually treatment takes place in a psychiatric hospital or in the psychiatric unit of a medical hospital.

Medications used to combat depression and psychosis often have such strong side-effects that, ideally, the patient should remain in the safe confines of the hospital. In this way, doctors can make sure that drug reactions do not pose a danger to the health of the patient. These side-effects can range from minor irritations to life-threatening problems.

Note: Monitoring the physical reactions of the patient to the drug treatment is vital. Indeed, it can be called the cornerstone of treatment, because side-effects can be detected and the efficacy of the treatment can be fine-tuned.

It is helpful to know that if the patient is hospitalized, they may be put in a wheelchair for their safety, liability reasons, or sometimes for the convenience of the staff, physical therapy may be overlooked. It is especially important that a dementia patient being treated for psychiatric problems have physical therapy, in addition to any medications, because without it, they may forget how to walk.

The treatment is not a cure
The only aspect of Alzheimer's dementia that is usually treatable is psychotic reaction. With the right medication, a geropsychiatrist can treat symptoms such as hallucinations or paranoia, making the patient more comfortable... But the disease itself will continue on its unstoppable course.

Day treatment programs
Day treatment (partial hospitalization) programs are designed for older patients suffering a psychiatric illness. If a psychiatrist has made the diagnosis and prescribes such a plan, day treatment may still be covered by Medicare. This would save the family a great deal of money, as well as providing significant benefit to your EFM.

In addition to the seniors who are attacked by mental afflictions for the first time in their lives, there are also individuals who have had a history of chronic mental disease. These mental illnesses do not let-up merely because the victims have reached the autumn of their lives.

The major pre-existing mental illnesses are schizophrenia, bipolar disease (popularly known as manic-depressive), obsessive-compulsive disorder, and panic disorder. Such diseases frequently affect their victim for many years before a geriatric care manager meets the patient. With treatment, about 80% of people with bipolar disorder and panic disorder improve, 60% of patients with schizophrenia and obsessive-compulsive disorder improve, and 65% of those with major depression improve.

SCHIZOPHRENIA

Doctors and researchers have not been able to determine what causes this tragic affliction. That is unfortunate, since the disease cuts a swath of devastation in the lives of its victims and their families.

Schizophrenics have little or no touch with reality. Instead, they will hear voices, see visions on occasion, and suffer profound delusions. These symptoms often make it impossible for the sufferers to relate to people and the environment around them.

The voices or other impulses generated by this disease often compel the sufferer to act-out in totally anti-social ways. This can result in verbal or physical violence against others, as well as self-destructive impulses.

Even if the schizophrenic resists the impulses, the voices often will increase their "yelling," tormenting the victim until the commanded deed is done. Schizophrenics used to spend much of their lives in mental hospitals. However, with current medications, there is real hope.

BIPOLAR DISEASE

The bipolar patient may be either manic or depressed, and may alternate between the two states. Bipolar disease exhibits its symptoms in an emotional roller coaster ride.

When a person is manic, they feel on top of the world and omnipotent. The disease can worsen to include delusions of grandeur, and the belief that the victim is super-human, or even a god. Manics have been known to try feats of daring-do that landed them in the hospital, or worse. They have also been known to go on $50,000 shopping sprees, believing that they are among the super-rich.

Clearly, such behavior is destructive to self and family. Frequently, manic patients need to be hospitalized and stabilized with medication.

Bipolar patients may suffer severe depressive cycles, at which times they are unable to function at all. They may be self-destructive and suicidal. At these times, hospitalization is also essential.

The intense mood swings of the manic-depressive can frequently be controlled with medications such as lithium. The victim often misses the manic high, so there must be continuing vigilance to make sure they stay on their medication.

By the time patients with schizophrenia and bipolar disorder reach my door, they have been burned too often, so they're usually willing to cooperate in controlling and managing their disease.

Just as an elderly patient with a physical illness needs different care than the same person might have needed when thirty years younger, so too does the elderly patient with chronic mental illness.

As the mentally-afflicted person grows older, a geropsychiatrist should be consulted to make sure that levels of medication continue to be appropriate, and to evaluate whether the patient would benefit from a partial hospitalization program.

Henry

I can't leave the topic of mental illness without briefly describing a case I handled five years ago, working with a schizophrenic patient and his family.

80-year-old Henry had experienced schizophrenia during his entire adult life. Fortunately, it was a mild case, so he had not exhibited any violent or self-destructive tendencies.

Henry was also lucky because he was truly loved by his family, his siblings, and their spouses, all of whom tried to take really good care of him. When his condition worsened, he would be hospitalized; and then when he got better, he would be released to a secured nursing home.

At the time I first met him, Henry was doing reasonably well, living in a large retirement hotel. However, unexpected stumbling blocks caused the family to consult a geropsychiatrist, who referred them to me.

It seemed that Henry was causing disruptions at the retirement hotel. Not that he was harmful to himself or others... It was just that when he had to urinate, he would use the bushes in front of the hotel.

Frequently, he sat in the lobby having long conversations, and using broad gestures, with an invisible person. That might have been funny in the movies, but the retirement hotel did not wish Henry to remain there.

The psychiatrist didn't feel it was necessary to hospitalize Henry because of these fairly mild symptoms. And the family didn't want to place him back into a nursing home. They wanted him to be able to live as normally as possible.

I found a comfortable 6-bed board and care home. The owner was accustomed to managing elderly people who had habits or tendencies that embarrassed others. She learned to cook Henry's favorite dishes, which indirectly endeared him to the other residents, who loved the food too. Two residents brought their dogs, which were enthusiastically adopted by the entire household. Henry loves the pets.

Henry adjusted very well, and has lived in his new home for five years. His dedicated family are thrilled, because they get to visit often and see him cheerful again.

SOME FINAL THOUGHTS

There are two more points I want to emphasize in this chapter. One concerns the treatment of mental illness in the elderly: Beware of the *"it's only old age"* syndrome. It's an unfortunate informal diagnosis that many doctors give, when they are not trained in gerontology.

You know the scenario: You bring in your spouse or parent who is becoming forgetful, or perhaps is suffering a change of personality. The patient is 80-years-old, so the doctor may shrug and say, "Sorry, there's nothing I can do. What can you expect at age 80?"

Because of this mistaken ageist attitude, many patients are abandoned by the medical profession. Instead, they could be receiving treatment that might substantially cure them or, at the very least, give them a higher quality of life.

The second warning is this: *Beware of the "easy" psychiatric diagnosis.* Sometimes, a doctor may rush to judgment when an elderly patient acts troubled, giving a psychiatric diagnosis before making sure that the cause is not physical.

Such was the case with Pearl...

Pearl

Pearl had lived her entire life in the Midwest. After the death of Pearl's husband, her daughter, Nancy, contacted me. She needed my assistance with moving Pearl from a nursing home in Michigan to one here in California. Once that was accomplished, I assumed the case was over and wished the family well.

My assumption proved to be incorrect. Nancy noticed that her mother was unquestionably acting strange. The old woman's personality had undergone a marked change: she became cranky, moody, combative on occasion, and extremely troublesome to be around.

Nancy suffered severe headaches after each visit with her mother at the nursing home, so she called me to discuss her painful reactions.

Due to my illness, I wasn't able to visit Pearl personally, but sent my trusted assistant, Martha, to assess the situation. Martha's report disturbed me a lot.

Pearl wouldn't look at Martha when talking to her. This wasn't merely the annoying tendency some people have to look at the other person's forehead during a conversation. No, Pearl's conduct was much stranger than that... She conversed with her back to Martha.

The facility's staff, where Pearl lived, requested that Nancy move her to a locked psychiatric nursing home nearby. They advised that it would be a more appropriate place.

I asked Nancy to get second opinions from a geropsychiatrist and a geriatrician. After a complete work-up, including an MRI, Pearl was diagnosed with a brain tumor. Her symptoms were due to physical, not mental illness.

The proper treatment of a person with a brain tumor is far different than just placing her into a nursing home for psychiatric patients and throwing away the key. This grave error could have come to pass in Pearl's case.

Now that Pearl is receiving the appropriate medical treatment to reduce the size of the tumor, her personality has stabilized. Ironically, she has become one of the nursing home's favorite residents, rather than one of its outcasts.

Pearl certainly feels much better and enjoys her daughter's visits, as well as the social activities of her care facility. Oh, and one more thing... Nancy doesn't suffer those terrible tension headaches anymore. Now she volunteers her time as an ombudsman in homes for the elderly.

There are two key points that Pearl's case teaches:

1. Don't accept any diagnosis until you have satisfied yourself with a second and, if necessary, a third opinion.

2. Don't give up on trying to improve the quality of life for your elderly loved-one, simply because of their age...because of the frustrating medical bureaucracy...because they are in a care facility...or even because they are dying.

CHAPTER 8

God Helps Those Who Help Themselves: Empowering The Caregivers

There are a number of families who cannot afford to retain the services of a professional geriatric care manager for an extended period of time. Many have to care for both their children and their parents. Others are already senior citizens, who may have limited resources.

It is not uncommon to have a 70-year-old client inquiring about a 93-year-old parent. In fact, I recently just had my first second-generation placement.

Ten years ago Leona, then in her early 60s, retained me to assess and place her mother Gertrude, who was in her 80s. Now, Leona's son, Chuck, recently hired me to do the same for Leona.

Still, many people simply don't earn sufficient incomes to pay lawyers, doctors, or care managers during the many months and years that older people often require personalized care.

Fortunately, such people don't have to completely fend for themselves. An unusually valuable service that professional care managers can provide clients, at a reasonable cost, is to teach them how to render their own **care coordination**.

After meeting with you and the patient, a care manager will develop a care plan which you can implement yourself. They will instruct you how do it, and will be there for needed support.

HANDLING THE CASE YOURSELF

In many instances, doing it "your way" can work-out best for all concerned. Learning the ins and outs of managing your loved-one's care, is a profound gift to them. You will almost surely look back on your time as a care manager with great pride.

This is not to say there won't be turbulence, anxiety, and even anguish. In all likelihood there will be. But such obstacles are a natural part of life and, if handled correctly, can bind a family rather than tear it apart.

Educate yourself

In order to be a good care manager, it is crucial to educate yourself concerning the real trials that your EFM is facing...physical, mental, and emotional.

For example, if your senior is suffering from a physical malady, such as cancer, you need to know the following:

- What kind of cancer is it?
- Who are the doctors in your community who can render the right specialized medical care including pain control?
- What are the treatment options?
- What side-effects of the treatment can be expected?
- How will these side-effects change the living requirements of your senior?
- Will these changes require additional services that will have to be procured and paid for?
- If so, which agencies in town are the best to provide such services?
- What long-term planning needs to be done?

It's not easy

Being a care manager is a demanding, challenging task. It takes time, effort and dedication. You have to be willing to go out and find the answers, no matter how many doors you have to knock on.

There are an abundance of books, articles, organizations,

and professionals to assist you in developing the skills you will need to be a top-notch care manager for your loved-one.

In the course of managing their care, you may come face-to-face with the fact that proper care is too formidable a job to do at home. Placement may be necessary. You may have to deal head-on with the daunting task of finding an alternative living arrangement.

If you are considering placement of your elderly family member, carefully examine all the issues in depth before determining what kind of placement is needed. Read the case histories in this book to find out how families just like yours were able to deal with this onerous, painful situation.

It is human nature to wait until a crisis before confronting an extremely difficult emotional decision, such as placement of an EFM. In fact, many clients do not call me until their caregiving situation has reached the panic stage. While this is psychologically understandable, it is not the most effective approach to problem-solving.

If at all possible, consider investigating and making a placement decision *before* the inevitable crisis hits, when you still have the luxury of time and a number of options.

As I mentioned, the best way to learn to manage the care of your elderly family member is to hire a professional geriatric care manager who will teach you the ropes. They will expedite developing your individual management plan and getting it off the ground into action.

Let me illustrate how my clients handled completely different situations...

Jane

Jane is a case in point. She came to my office with a unique predicament. Margaret, her deaf mother, was in real need of assistance, and Jane was one of the few people who could provide it: she knows sign language.

Margaret was slightly demented, with psychological disorders and difficulty communicating, stemming from her deafness since birth. To complicate matters, Jane had a hectic, productive life of her own. She was a teacher for the deaf, and a foster mother of three deaf children. Needless to say, her hands were full.

Moreover, Jane had mild cerebral palsy, which presented many hurdles that she successfully overcame.

Like many of my clients, Jane had always been a person who put other's needs ahead of her own. With therapy, she finally identified her own needs and had gotten her life right where she wanted it... Then, along came Mom, threatening the equilibrium that Jane had so painstakingly achieved.

Margaret had become greatly dependent and demanding, hanging onto her daughter like a toddler, afraid of being alone. Jane was terribly guilt-ridden, because she resented the time she would have to give to her mother.

Jane wanted support. Although she could afford my professional services on a regular basis, she really didn't need them. All she needed was some training in being her mother's care manager, which I provided.

Now, one month later, Jane is elated. She has learned how to care for Margaret in a way that does not destroy her own identity. She has also learned how to access community resources and get other family members to lend a hand.

As Jane recently said, "I can take care of Mom and still have a life."

Peter and Steve

Peter and Steve had lived together for over forty years, longer than most marriages. As life-partners, they had vowed to take care of each other through thick and thin, but Steve contracted AIDS. Both men were in their 60's, still in the prime of life. They knew the reality of the dreaded disease, because AIDS had already claimed the lives of dozens of their friends.

Steve was becoming demented during the last stages of AIDS. Peter didn't know what to do. Although he loved his partner and would never leave him, Peter's job and health were suffering greatly. He was continuously receiving emergency calls from Steve on his beeper, and couldn't get anything else accomplished.

Determined to handle everything himself, "like a loyal partner should," Peter was on the verge of falling apart. After consulting me for a bit of advice and hope, Peter realized he needed help and accepted the idea of calling a home care agency known to be experienced with the care of AIDS patients. The agency send a calm, competent person to be with Steve, giving Peter much needed relief.

The assistance worked wonders for their relationship. Peter was able fulfill his responsibilities to Steve and to his own life. No longer did undercurrents of guilt, pressure, fear, resentment, and blame separate them. The couple, united as never before, were able to enjoy their togetherness... Life goes on.

Where to begin?

As I have continually stressed throughout this book, it is vital that your elderly family member be treated like an individual, rather than as a "generic old person."

Many doctors, social workers, and others who deal with older people on a regular basis, can become jaundiced in their view of seniors' potential to live lives of quality and relative independence.

This tendency is demonstrated by health care professionals who decline to aggressively fight disease...or who throw up their hands and say, "Get thee to a nursing home"...or the HMO that does not adequately monitor the chronic diseases of the elderly.

Assessing the level of care your elderly family member's needs is best done by a professional. But there are important questions you should ask and answer yourself, to pave the way for working on your own:

- **How independent is your EFM?**
  Clearly, the more independent the older person is, the more they will be able to do the activities of daily living, such as

bathing, toileting, and dressing, saving you from the necessity to hire someone for assistance.

- **Is your EFM able to take medications properly?**
  The patient must be willing to comply with doctors' instructions, and able to take the right medications, on time and in the correct dosages. It's not as easy as you think, particularly as forgetfulness and confusion increases. It is often difficult to see tiny pills and manipulate vials so they don't spill all over the floor. If shots are necessary, a steady hand and good vision are essential. Finally, possible drug interactions and negative side-effects must be monitored. Knowing whether or not your EFM is taking drugs properly is difficult, since lack of medication doesn't always produce symptoms until too late.

- **How does your EFM get around?**
  Are they completely mobile? Can they go up and down stairs? Do they need a quad cane, a walker, or a wheelchair? Mobility has a lot to do with the level of care management that is needed, so this concern is of great consequence.

- **Can your EFM transfer easily?**
  Is your EFM a "lift patient?" The level of care that will be required depends on whether minimal or maximum assistance is needed for the patient to get up from a favorite armchair, get out of bed, get on and off the toilet. These can be modified, to a degree, by raising the seats, or buying chairs that help the person to their feet.

- **Can your EFM be responsible for eating properly?**
  Many older persons become ill, or less able to function independently, because they don't eat the right foods. Thus, making sure that your EFM's nutritional needs are met is an intrinsic part of managing their care.

- **Is your EFM able to take care of their living quarters?**
  Doing the daily chores of life is necessary to maintain a

healthy environment. If your parent or elderly relative is unable to keep their home clean and safe, then the need for supervised care will be greater.

- **Does your EFM have special needs that require monitoring?**
Many elderly people require care for chronic medical conditions, such as diabetes. If the elderly person is aware of their problem and independently secures the necessary medical attention, you won't have to provide as much management.

On the other hand, if the elderly person is unable or unwilling to see doctors, follow a special diet, take prescribed medications, and change their lifestyle as required, then your responsibilities become critically important.

Once you and your geriatric care manager have determined the type and amount of assistance that may be required, the next step is to find the people and services to fill gaps in care that your EFM cannot provide for himself/ herself.

Personal emergency response systems

For a person who lives alone, a **PERS** (also called a Personal Response System-PRS, Emergency Response System-ERS, or medical signaling device) could be a life-saver. It is extremely useful when an elderly person falls, gets chest pains, or hears an intruder.

A PERS is a system with a tiny radio transmitter, worn around the neck or wrist, with an emergency button to summon help from a caregiver/friend, or police, fire department, paramedics, ambulance. There is 24-hour monitoring of this alarm system, which goes through the telephone lines and signals for assistance. Most programs require elderly clients to "check-in" daily, otherwise, they will get a callback to see if everything is okay.

A half-million people own or rent a Personal Emergency Response System, and about 200,000 have used it for an emergency. Most users are satisfied, although some have had problems. Since there are over 30 brands on the market, little available product information, and a wide-range of prices, the choice is confusing, so request the AARP's product report brochure on PERS.

Think about how tragic it would be if your elderly loved-one got dizzy, fell, and couldn't get up, or couldn't get out of the bathtub.* Besides suffering the indignity of feeling powerless, they could even die.

If they were fortunate enough to escape injury, the EFM might not remember to tell you, or wouldn't, afraid you'd put them in a nursing home. You would never know the truth.

Now is the time to avoid such a scenario, before a disaster happens. There are quite a number of reliable companies that can provide a PERS. A care manager will have a list of the best systems in your area, or you can consult with a local hospital for information. Whether your EFM will be living alone or with you, a good PERS is a must.

Note: A PERS system is for a cognitively-alert person who knows how to use it. A patient with dementia needs human supervision, not a PERS, because they forget to use it properly.

Home health care and in-home help

Medicare will cover many services, but it will not cover in-home or outside-the-home custodial care.** Home-care is extremely expensive and most families cannot maintain it for as long as it's needed.

Your elderly family member is eligible for in-home supportive services or in-home respite programs through SSI, combined with Medicaid (Medi-Cal), if their assets are low enough.

When your EFM requires medical and custodial services,

---

*In one case, a son found his mother, who had Parkinson's, stuck in her filled bathtub overnight. She was traumatized, but fortunately, she was alive. Another case ended more tragically: an elderly patient without a PERS system had no way to contact help and was scalded to death by water which was much too hot.

**Check for regional difference. For instance, New York's plan is more liberal in paying for such services.

you should interview agencies to select the best one, but keep in mind that hiring through an agency doesn't automatically guarantee quality caregiving.

If you plan to hire someone on your own, rather than going through an agency, the savings can be significant (up to 50%), and you retain the power of being boss. But it's not as easy as it may seem.

First, screen potential employees carefully by phone. Get references and check them out. Then do background criminal, civil, and DMV checks of the finalists. Make sure to obtain a workman's comp insurance policy.

Agree on a clear, detailed plan of care with the hired caregivers and stick to it. Give them a log book and have them keep it up-to-date, accurately.

Sensitive workers instinctively know that <u>each elderly patient must be treated as an individual,</u> not as a generic "old person." Caregivers should pay attention to the EFM, not just to the task at hand.

Hired help need to really listen to patients and also become aware of their non-verbal communication. Things often have to be explained slowly and clearly, frequently repeating them. Whenever possible, EFMs should be given choices and not rushed. Helpers should avoid taking short cuts, and be flexible enough to change procedures. They need to have the generosity of spirit to give EFMs positive feedback, and to avoid looking grim or acting angry. Most of all, caregivers need endless patience.

Perhaps you can train in-home helpers to develop this humane attitude, perhaps not.

As employer, you must realize care workers are individuals too. Try to be sensitive and demonstrate that you appreciate their valuable services. If you do this, workers may relate to your EFM on a more personal, committed basis.

Good hired caregivers are not baby-sitters, and they aren't in the profession just for the money, so the way you treat your helpers is often how they will treat your EFM.

Consider hired caregivers as extended family. Sometimes, they can become even closer than your family. They spend a lot more time with your EFM than anyone else. Include them in family events and photos. Give them a fair salary. (Currently, the average salary is $7/hour, but can range from $6-$15, according to where you live and the individual's qualifications.)

Offer positive feedback and a lot of sincere praise. Remember them on "National Caregivers Week" (November 19-25). You might also enroll your caregivers in stress-reduction or counseling programs, and pay for their time. The cost is very well worth it.

On the other hand, hired caregivers are *not* members of your family. They have families of their own and are human beings who also need care.

If you have good in-home help, you definitely want to keep them. Exceptional caregivers are even rarer. Paying attention to helpers and giving them strokes are essential. If they are going to care for your elderly family member properly, they need to be "watered" like plants. If you personally cannot be around, ask a friend or a geriatric care manager to interact with your caregivers.

Ask a GCM for guidance or a referral to a reliable home health care agency. You may also want your care manager to interview, train, and monitor the employees. Unless you have enough time to do it on a regular, professional basis, you will definitely need someone "to mind the store."

Serious problems

The previous advice is all well and good...provided your hired home health care worker can be trusted. This is when harsh reality may set in.

NBC's "Dateline" did a devastating investigative report,[*] hiring 10 health care workers from various agencies to care for an elderly woman who lived alone in her home. The patient supposedly had Alzheimer's, and needed constant supervision and daily medications. But, in fact, the volunteer "guinea pig" was a member of the **Gray Panthers**, a wonderful senior

---

[*]Thanks to "Dateline" (11/17/95). Copyright © by NBC News, Inc.

ful senior citizen activist group...and she was sharp-as-a-tack. NBC's hidden cameras monitored everything that took place in the home.

Here are the shocking, frightening, infuriating results:
- 3 of the 10 hired caregivers showed up late.
- 5 of the 10 secretively rifled through drawers, handbags, and personal possessions.
- 3 of the 10 actually stole money and jewelry.
- 5 of the 10 made potentially dangerous mistakes giving medications; one worker didn't even write down the instructions and couldn't remember what pills to give.
- Some workers fell asleep, leaving the Alzheimer's patient free to wander out of the home.
- Other workers watched TV all the time, never relating to the patient.
- Several workers made constant telephone calls, which were specifically prohibited.
- One worker even left early, leaving the AD patient completely alone.
- The experienced Gray Panther woman said only 1 of the 10 workers was a good caregiver whom she would hire again, but she was stunned to see a videotape of this caregiver stealing money from her purse.

Currently, 39 states have some licensing requirements of medically-skilled workers...only 10 require licensing of unskilled workers...and as of this date, only a shocking 2 (Florida and Washington) even do background security checks!

In "Dateline's" survey, only 1% of health care agencies did full background checks. Despite the agency's assurances, one health care worker had an easily obtainable record for robbery and shooting someone. When the TV program called back another of the offending agencies, it had already gone out of business.

Obviously, we need strong new laws mandating licensing and background checks, such as those for school bus drivers.

But until our legislators wake-up to the growing problems,

you must take responsibility into your own hands. Be very cautious when hiring from a newspaper ad. Always interview prospective employees outside your home, in a neutral place such as a restaurant. Use agencies which are members of recognized national professional groups that set standards for screening and training.

Even when an agency claims to have done a background check, check out the potential worker yourself. Go to County Records and research their files to find any previous arrests. Even this doesn't guarantee anything, since the potential home health care worker may have an arrest record in other counties or states.

Nothing is foolproof, but one of the best ways to find honest professional aides is to consult with a geriatric care manager who has years of experience with health care agencies and workers. The GCM will know which agencies are reliable, and can interview and check out individual workers.

Community and employer-sponsored programs

If your EFM is able to get around, take care of themselves in a social setting, and is willing to make the effort to participate, a **senior center** could be a godsend. These centers provide recreation and socialization, which help make life worthwhile. There are dancing, concerts, trips, discussion groups, volunteer programs, and classes. Many centers also offer a host of services, among them: psychological counseling, tax assistance, information on Medicare and other government programs, legal, optometry, and podiatry services, either free or for nominal fees. Healthy meals at reasonable prices are often served. A senior center can be an elderly person's and care manager's best friend.

If your ambulatory EFM is memory-impaired, confused, demented and/or frail, a good community **adult day-care center** can be extremely helpful in improving their quality of life, as well as easing family tensions. It provides them with recreation, social interaction with peers, and quality care. Meals are also provided, as well as the monitoring of chronic health con-

There are also many **day-treatment** (partial hospitalization) programs in the community, targeted for depressed patients, or for those who temporarily need psychiatric help. However, they must be cognitively-aware. Their goal is to get the patient back into the community.

Medicare may pay for these programs, but due to the upheavals in federal and state social programs, some programs and services may change. Check out the latest information and your options with the Area Agency on Aging, as well as with a trusted doctor and an elder law attorney.

Professionally run **intergenerational day-care centers** accept adults with progressive dementia, Alzheimer's or Parkinson's disease, and also accepts children, from infants on up. The elderly adults, infants, and pre-school children (up to about age 5) celebrate holidays together and make gifts for each other. Their interaction is shown to be beneficial and extremely meaningful to both groups.

Many companies realize how much stress caregiving puts on employees, decreasing work efficiency and profit. The situation also is very stressful for employers, when they lose key members of "the team." So a few forward-thinking companies provide day-care centers for the elderly, as well as for children.

However, as **Sue Shellenbarger** pointed out in *The Wall Street Journal*, recent studies show that these programs are difficult and costly to administer. Employers are now trying simpler, less expensive methods to help employees cope with the difficult feat of juggling work, family commitments, raising children, and caregiving for elderly family members.* This new approach includes: resource and referral programs, assessments and one-time consultations with geriatric care managers, elder-care seminars, flexible work schedules, long-term care insurance, and working together with GCMs on crisis-planning and care plans.*

The Wall Street Journal (8/2/95), "Work & Family: In Caring for Elders, Sometimes Less Can Accomplish More," by Sue Shellenbarger.

and care plans.*

It is not only forward-thinking, but also very practical and economically feasible, for employers to identify the potentially high-cost caregiving cases early, so they can provide support to key caregiver employees. Such early intervention by an employer often includes paying for a one-time assessment by a professional geriatric care manager. (Assessments typically cost $200-$500.)

General Motors is considering such assessments as part of an elder-care pilot program with the United Auto Workers. In many ways, it is even more vital for *smaller* companies to closely collaborate with their caregiver employees, geriatric care managers, and community agencies, because they have more to lose if a key employee can't handle the caregiving stress.

With the steady aging of our society, more and more employees have EFMs to care for, requiring an enormous investiture of their time, energy, and finances. It is in employers' best interests to help employees reduce stress, so that while at work, they can put more of their energy and focus on their jobs.

Transportation

Many seniors can do pretty well for themselves, but need transportation to doctors, banks, shopping, and the like. This burden is eased in communities which provide seniors with low-cost transportation to health-care appointments. Some also provide such transportation to shopping malls and other community locations.

If transportation services are not available, you will have to improvise. Taxi companies may offer discount coupons to seniors. Volunteer agencies and senior centers often have drivers available, as do churches and synagogues. If you can afford it, consider hiring a private driver ("Driving Miss Daisy").

---

*New studies by **Dr. Dana Friedman** and by **Andrew Scharlach** show that in predicting caregiver stress, the nature of an elder's illness is even more important than such factors as the amount of care provided or the quality of community services.

You can also create a carpooling network of friends and relatives who will drive your EFM to-and-fro, the way neighborhood parents carpool their children to school.

Volunteer services

Don't forget to look into volunteer agencies that may offer valuable services to your family. One wonderful volunteer organization is the **Senior Companion Program,** funded by the Federal government. (Sadly, this priceless program may change, or tragically, even be eliminated, depending on shortsighted governmental budget cuts.)

In the Senior Companion Program, elderly volunteers, whose incomes are below poverty-level, spend twenty-hours a week lightening the load of other elderly folk, regardless of their economic circumstances. They do shopping, letter writing, reading books, and perhaps most important, serve as companion and friend.

If there ever was a "win-win" situation, this is it. Low-income seniors win because they're paid minimum wage, receive daily meals, and gain insurance benefits.

An even more immeasurable benefit is that volunteers experience the thrill and satisfaction of knowing they are needed, and are providing a valuable service to society.

Meanwhile, ailing seniors benefit by having companionship, which makes life more livable and enjoyable.

If you are going to care for a senior, be sure to talk with volunteer agencies in your area about their helpful services.

If Your EFM Can No Longer Live at Home

Many adult children are emotionally unable to place their parents. If you find placement too emotionally draining, it is well worth while to retain a professional to assist you. Together, you will be able to determine the appropriate level of care for your elderly family member, and choose the best one that fits their needs...shared housing, adult foster care, retirement hotel, assisted living facility, board and care home, congregate housing, or nursing home.

If, however, you decide to go it alone, the first step in your search for the appropriate placement facility is to compile a good and long list of the "local talent." This list should be as complete as possible, because you will have the best chance of making a quality placement if you shop around.

Of course, a great many people who must confront the issue of placement have never dealt with it before. They don't know the quality of local facilities, or how to find out this important information.

If this is true for you, contact the American Association of Homes for the Aging, National Shared Housing Resource Center, Administration on Aging, California Department of Aging (*see Appendix G*), or try the following sources of information:

Area Agencies on Aging

The nation has a network of Agencies on Aging, from the federal level down to the local level. You should be able to easily find your local department on aging in the phone book. The agency staff will point you in the right direction as you begin your search.

Senior centers

The people who staff these fine centers are extremely dedicated and knowledgeable. More than likely, they will have a good handle on some of the better placement facilities in your area.

Doctors

Your EFM's physician may be a good source of information concerning health care facilities. Too many doctors, however, don't bother to learn about such issues, since it is normally the function of a social worker or GCM.

Social service departments of hospitals

If your relative has been hospitalized prior to placement, the hospital probably has discharge planners who can give you a list of facilities. Since they work daily with placement issues, they should have a good working knowledge of available choices.

Clergy
One of their pastoral obligations is the responsibility to sustain families through perplexing and emotionally exhausting times. Ministers, priests and rabbis regularly listen to stories from families with crises.

Licensed referral agencies
Some states, such as California, license referral agencies which provide names of quality facilities. The Department of Health should be able to direct you to a **licensed** referral service in your city.

Friends
Many of us know people who have already placed their elderly relatives. If your friends or acquaintances recently faced a dilemma similar to yours, call them. Find out where their EFMs were placed, and in particular, whether or not they are pleased with the way things have worked out. Often, such word-of-mouth referrals can be the best.

Note: Due to frequent changes in ownership, administration and staff, information on facilities must be current in order to be useful.

Professional geriatric care managers
Care managers provide information and assistance on a daily basis, so don't be afraid to ask for their help or to delegate responsibilities to them. It is usually well worth the cost to have professional guidance with your decision-making.

Care managers know about the most critical intangibles in any placement decision: the staff's attitude and skill, and how they relate to the residents:

- Do they treat residents with respect or with disdain?
- Do they have the ability to communicate with residents

- Are they caring, loving and experienced?

The answers to these questions require an ongoing, intimate relationship with the local senior caregiving community. GCMs nurture such relationships.

Professionals aren't overly distracted by considerations which are ultimately irrelevant, such as the aesthetics and luxury of the facility. Geriatric care managers keep their eyes on the cardinal issues:

- Quality of care.
- Cleanliness.
- Ability to meet the EFM's needs as their medical and mental status changes.
- Meals and food service (always a major factor).

Additionally, private geriatric care managers can facilitate the smoothest possible adjustment to the chosen facility for the patient, family, and staff, putting out fires along the way.

NURSING HOME PLACEMENT

"The doctor said my parent needs a nursing home..."

Worse still, is when a spouse needs a nursing home. Husbands and wives have told me that it would be far easier to bury their beloved spouses, than to place them in nursing homes.

Nursing home placement is always the most painful subject people question me about. First, a geriatric care manager clarifies the necessity of such a decision by ruling out alternatives which offer less skilled nursing care. Whenever possible, a GCM tries to keep an elderly person in their own home, or find the right board and care for them.

The more independent your relative is, physically and mentally, the less likely it is that they need a nursing home. But your EFM must pass certain minimum medical requirements (check the specific laws of your state) in order to be accepted (check the specific laws of your state) in order to be accepted into a non-nursing home facility, such as a retirement hotel or small board and care home:

- They cannot be bedridden.
- Patients must be able to turn in bed without assistance.
- They cannot have severe bed sores.
- They must not need a feeding tube.
- They cannot require skilled nursing.

Even if your EFM satisfies these minimum requirements, not all alternative placement facilities accept seniors who need constant attention and heavy care. While some do assist patients within these guidelines, others require residents to be semi-independent.

If other living facilities don't offer enough care for your EFM, or if you can't afford them, then you must consider a nursing home.

How do I choose a nursing home?

Ultimately, many families face the hard reality of having to find a nursing home for a beloved relative. At this point, nightmares run around in the minds of those responsible for making the selection...

They may have heard stories of patients who are allowed to remain in beds soiled by excrement; seniors who developed bed sores because they weren't turned; careless, overworked, underpaid staff who don't speak the same language as the patients.

Although there are many fine nursing homes which provide excellent care, unfortunately, awful conditions do exist in others.

Here are some questions to ask when evaluating prospective nursing homes:*

---

*Many of these considerations are also relevant to board and care homes, and assisted living facilities.

- **Is the home certified to participate in Medicare and Medicaid?**

This is absolutely essential if you plan to avail yourselves of the scarce government benefits available to assist your EFM. Remember, an uncertified facility usually will be ineligible to receive government benefits. You would have to foot the entire bill.

- **Is the home properly licensed by the state?**

Licensing is the bare minimum requirement for any home you are considering.

- **What does the annual state licensing survey have to say?**

Just as people read consumer magazines comparing washing machines and computers before they buy, so too, you should read your State Health Services Department's* licensing reports on each nursing facility. This is a *public document*, thus you have the absolute right to review it.

Most GCMs have nurses on their staff who can quickly evaluate the licensing report or survey, and let you know the results of the government's annual inspection. Such a report lists any citations issued in the last inspection and whether they've been corrected. You can judge whether the citations were serious or numerous enough to rule out the facility. Be sure to differentiate between major defects and minor infractions in the quality of care.

In this regard, look at consequences that may have resulted from the mistakes made by the nursing home. The survey will indicate whether the home has been sued, and if the nursing home was held responsible for any deaths.

Remember, no facility can be perfect, but some will definitely be better than others. A close review of the licensing report is the equivalent of lighting a candle in the darkness.

---

*The Health Services Department is usually listed under "State Government Offices" in the white pages of your telephone book.

- **Does the home provide the special services that your EFM requires?**

Ill elderly patients may need rehabilitation services, IVs, tracheotomy care, special diets, or other special requirements. The home you choose must be able to meet these needs.

For example, if your EFM has a broken hip, you need a nursing home that is strong on rehabilitation services. Hopefully, the home employs physical therapists on staff who are always there, seeing patients daily. Outside physical therapists, hired on contract, may not have the same amount of time to devote to patients, because they must do a lot of traveling between facilities.

Be sure to ask about the staff-to-patient ratio. Ask before you select the home, otherwise you may find yourself having to start the search all over again.

- **Do you like the "feel" of the place?**

When you walk into the home for the first time, notice how you are reacting to the atmosphere of the place. Does the environment seem pleasant, clean and cheerful? Or does it seem dark and dank? Do you smell any foul odors that would make you question the cleanliness of the facility? If the home doesn't pass this initial test, you'll want to look further.

Note: Just because a slight smell of urine may be in the air, it doesn't necessarily mean that the nursing home is unclean or deficient in its care. Many patients have incontinence, and the odor may be due to the time of day you visit. In such a case, return to the facility again at a different time, to see if there's been an improvement.

- **Are the administration and staff serving their patients well?**

When you are looking for a nursing home, take the "official tour," but you should also evaluate the place "unofficially," on your own. When quietly observing the home, note how the staff treats its patients when "nobody is looking."

Are the old people shown respect, courtesy and love? If so, the facility should remain on your list. But if you detect that the patients are treated rudely or arrogantly, with little respect, you will want to look elsewhere.

- **What do the patients and their families have to say?**

The bottom line: It is the patients who really know what's going on in a nursing home. So, when you are checking out a facility, take the time and chat candidly with several mentally alert patients, to get "the real scoop." Listen carefully to what they have to say about the place, interpret what truths lie behind their comments, and compare opinions. Also, question visiting family members. Don't be shy about asking whether they are satisfied with their EFM's care.

Ask about issues of grooming, cleanliness, courtesy and respect. Ask about the recreational and social activities. Ask whether the patients would want to be placed there again, if they have a choice.

Ask. You may just find out that you've come to the right place. Or you may discover some unpleasant things which you would have never detected on your own.

Note: If there are volunteers who assist patients, make a point of talking to them.

- **Are residents allowed to express their individuality?**

Let's face it, nobody likes living in an institutional setting. However, life in such a place can be greatly enhanced if the patients are allowed to express their unique personalities.

Find out whether you and your relative will be able to decorate their living space. Will they be allowed to wear their own clothes? Can they safely have keepsakes, which can be so meaningful, without having them stolen? A facility that encourages individual expression enhances the lives of its patients.

- **Is the nursing home safety-conscious?**

Despite the fact that you want to place your EFM in a nursing home to improve their safety, you'd better be sure that the home is up to the task. The government survey of the home is likely to point out if there have been infractions in safety, but you should personally check to make sure that the home is safety-conscious, not sloppy in their concern for patients.

Are there sufficient ramps and rails to assist those in wheelchairs...grab-bars in the bathrooms...showers with non-slip surfaces? Are there enough easily accessible, fully charged fire extinguishers...clean smoke detectors with fresh batteries...an automatic indoor sprinkler system? Are exits clearly marked, unobstructed, and unlocked from the inside? What is the facility's emergency evacuation plan?

These are very important questions to investigate. Prepare a check-list and take it with you. How a facility handles safety matters directly reflects the care and concern they give their patients.

• **How is the food service?**

When we are old and ill, there are often fewer choices and pleasures left to us. One pleasure that usually remains is eating a good tasting and nutritious meal which is medically appropriate for your EFM, whether on a normal or special diet, e.g.: a low-sodium or low-calorie diet.

Before you select a nursing home, be sure to check out the quality of its food. Eat at least one meal there with the residents. How are the taste, portions, nutritional balance, visual presentation and service? Are plates, silverware, and glass properly washed? Are residents given alternative choices of food?

Is the kitchen reasonably tidy and clean? Does the dish washer keep up with the piles of dirty dishes? Is trash lying around unattended? Are cooks and food servers wearing clean uniforms? Are they careful handling food? Is food left standing in warm areas? Is it exposed to flies?

Ask to see the meal schedule. Are three meals a day served at normal hours? Is the weekly menu varied? Do they serve what is promised? We all like between-meal snacks, so find out whether they are available to patients.

If your EFM is a slow eater, be sure they'll be given enough time before the plate is taken away. In addition, if your elderly relative needs assistance with eating, be sure the home provides such service, and the staff encourages picky eaters. Verify that the nursing home can and will fulfill any special dietary needs.

Licensing may require a nursing home to do many things for health and safety, but does the facility actually do them?

• **What kind of social activities does the home provide?** Ask the activities director what recreational opportunities are available to patients. Many facilities offer games, movies, live performances, religious services, reminiscence groups, escorted trips, and visits from school children.

The schedule of planned activities is usually posted on the bulletin board. However, you will need to investigate whether the announced activities are really being provided, or if events are regularly canceled.

After you have visited a half-dozen or more nursing homes, you will be reasonably prepared to make the final choice.

As the caregiver, you may be visiting your loved-one often, but if you cannot, have someone else visit on a regular basis.

Visiting does a lot for your EFM. First and foremost, it gives them the pleasure of your company, something to look forward to, and helps them feel needed. If there are any two things that most seniors in nursing homes complain about, it is loneliness and lack of a sense of purpose.

Secondly, visiting your relative frequently gives you a more influential role as their advocate. Developing a good relationship with the staff also creates a sense of belonging for your loved-one, rather than a sense of isolation.

The best approach is to act as part of the nursing home team, limiting your criticisms to matters of real importance. Assure the staff that you are working with them, not against them, "for Mom or Dad's sake." And by all means, be generous with your compliments.

Again, visiting regularly is one of the few ways to know whether your EFM is getting the best possible care. If distance or time makes this a hardship, a private geriatric care manager can assist you.

For instance, I visited a 94-year-old man who honored me by telling the story of his amazing life, so I could tape it as a legacy for his family. This gave him a sense of purpose.

The comforting knowledge that a professional will visit when you cannot, relieves you of worry and guilt.

Paying for long-term care

Whatever facility you finally choose, there is going to be a price to pay. Obviously, the more money your family has, the greater the number and the better the facilities there will be to choose from. If you're lucky, you come to the placement table with enough money to pay nursing home costs for awhile.

Nursing homes now charge $3000-$6000/month...$36,000-$72,000/year! Obviously, savings are often not sufficient to last the lifetime of a physically-healthy EFM. Financial assistance for long-term care in a skilled nursing facility is a necessity for most people. When your EFM's funds run out, apply for *long-term* Medicaid (Medi-Cal) benefits.

Medicaid checks under the patient's Social Security number to find out about their assets. The current eligibility standards, in order to receive Medicaid, allow an individual patient to have $2000 in assets; if the person is married, the spouse can keep approximately $70,000.

Families often worry that they will personally be held responsible for nursing home costs. At this time, Medicaid does not check the assets of the patient's family. Since all programs of government assistance to the elderly are currently under attack and subject to major revisions, please be sure to get professional advice from someone who is familiar with the latest changes and potential future change. Check with a qualified elder law attorney, geriatric financial advisor, or geriatric care manager.

If a patient is eligible, Medicaid will pay for a nursing home (unless Congress changes this provision), but the amount is substantially less than the facility's usual fee. This difference may lead some nursing homes to diminish quality and services, so they can still afford to care for your EFM and make a large-enough profit.

If your evaluation of family finances determines that funds to pay for placement will ultimately run dry, be sure to ask the nursing home owner/administrator what their attitude is in such a case. Some facilities will try to avoid accepting potential Medicaid patients, but with legwork, you should be able to find one that accepts Medicaid.

At the present time, if your EFM is in a skilled nursing home *licensed to serve Medicaid patients*, and initially pays with their own savings, the facility cannot legally ask them to leave, even if their savings run out and Medicaid takes over. However, if the nursing home is a private facility that accepts Medicare, but does *not* accept Medicaid patients, then your relative's placement is in jeopardy if their personal funds run out.

The search

The only way you will be able to find out about an individual placement facility's level of involvement with its patients, is to consult with the administrators of various homes. Carefully consider whether or not your EFM meets their requirements, and the nursing home meets yours.

You also will want to check out the facility, to see if it satisfies your standards of cleanliness, courtesy, safety, environmental quality, and of course, price.

I had a client who previously was placed by a caring adult child in a facility that looked attractive, but wound up being a disaster, at which point the caregiver came to me for advice.

You must shop around for the right nursing home and speak to people there in depth. Unfortunately, most people are not educated on what to look for, what questions to ask, and how to interpret the answers.

There are other serious considerations you should be aware of: Recently, a "20/20" investigative television report revealed that a shockingly high percentage of nursing homes employees have criminal records. And as many as 75% of nursing homes fail to meet federal standards.

Legislation is now being discussed which will deny such homes government benefits, but don't leave it up to the wiles of government to do all the research and first-hand investigations for you.

Before you sign on the dotted line with a nursing home (i.e.: placement), consider consulting with a geriatric care manager. Get an accurate professional assessment of your elderly family member and the facility, to make sure you haven't missed anything, and that nothing has fallen through the cracks.

What if I have a disagreement with the nursing home?

If you have a problem with any aspect of your relative's care, it is your job as a care manager to deal with it. The situation should be handled in the following order:

Talk to the individuals involved
Before making a "federal case" out of a situation, speak to the individual who seems to be causing the trouble. Let's say a particular staff member had an argument with your 85-year-old mother. Ask them what really took place.

Try to moderate a "peace conference" between your mother and the staff person. Often, by tackling disputes when they are still small, you prevent them from inflating into major wars.

Go to the top
If a private conversation doesn't do the trick, or if you should suspect any serious incompetence, then go to the top. Your first stop will be the Director of Nurses, whose job it is to deal with the innumerable ordeals of patient care.

You may also want to go to the Administrator, or even to the private or corporate owner. They will want to know if you are not satisfied with the care your loved-one is receiving at the facility. In most cases, what you want will be acted upon, or at the very least, you'll receive an explanation why it cannot be done.

Call in a professional care manager

Before taking more drastic action, have a geriatric care manager run interference for you by mediating the situation. We can usually put out the fire and restore order, especially if there is mutual respect between the administrator and the care manager.

Call the long-term care ombudsman

As of this writing, each state still has an ombudsman program which investigates and resolves complaints made by, or on behalf of residents in long-term care facilities. In many states, they are remarkably effective.

An **ombudsman** is a specially trained mediator who may legally enter a facility at any time, as advocate on behalf of a resident in need of assistance. The phone number of your ombudsman must be posted on the nursing home bulletin board. If you can't find it, ask.

Tragically, there is a strong misguided attempt by the government to cut funding of the successful ombudsman program. Hopefully, it will survive in some useful, not token, form.

Report the home

If the problem is grave, such as unhealthy living conditions, abuse, or neglect of patients, report the home to state authorities. This should get the state licensing authority and/or state health department involved.

Remove your EFM from the home

Ronald Reagan coined a good phrase: "voting with your feet." After trying all the above routes to get good quality care, if you are still dissatisfied with the care your loved-one is receiving, then vote with your feet: move them to another home. Consult a professional, if necessary, to find a facility which will treat your EFM in the manner you want, and they deserve.

For more information on dealing with problems in nursing homes, contact the National Citizens' Coalition for Nursing Home Reform. Its goals are to improve the long-term care system, and the quality of life for nursing home residents.

There are a lot of other things you will need to know when you act as your own care manager, which will be unique to your own particular circumstances. You may want to consult a professional geriatric care manager if you are in a quandary, or whenever a crisis arises.

TWO VERY DIFFERENT CASE HISTORIES

We've been discussing your involvement in helping an elderly family member. Whether you start from scratch on your own without professional guidance, have a one-time consultation with a geriatric care manager, or choose to contract for continued professional assistance, is up to you.

This decision should be based on a careful evaluation of your time requirements, money availability, individual personality and ability to handle stress, quality of relationship with the EFM, as well as other factors particular to your family situation. Here are stories of two adult daughters, and how they cared for their mothers...

Gladys

Gladys was a bright and alert woman in her nineties. Before immigrating to America, she had a tough life in England, losing five of her six children to early deaths.

Gladys' lovely daughter-in-law, Monica, promised her husband on his death bed that she would look after his mother. Finally, Gladys really needed her help. Monica, now age 73, considered hiring a care manager, but she was dedicated to her mother-in-law and decided to try to do the job herself.

Monica's decision to become a caregiver was not made because of an acute illness or a sudden reduction in Gladys' capabilities. Instead, as is often the case, Gladys slowly declined physically, due to frequent falls and increasingly severe arthritis in her hips and knees. She began to need more and more assistance with performing the tasks of daily living.

Gladys, who survived the London Blitz, was affectionately referred to by her family as a "tough old bird." She had always been fiercely independent and had no intention of moving. So Monica tried to go along with her wishes, letting Gladys stay in her own home.

Like many children who live a distance from their parents, Monica, in Los Angeles, was three hours drive from Gladys, in Santa Barbara. She felt concerned, because the distance prevented her from seeing Gladys on a frequent basis.

After Monica and her son Jim spoke to me about the situation, the family got together and decided upon the following management plan:

• For the time being, Gladys would continue to reside in her nice mobile home.

• Neighbors were quietly recruited to act as Monica's eyes and ears. Since Gladys usually kept any bad news about her condition to herself, a network of "reporters" was established. The neighbors agreed to call Monica if they perceived that Gladys was having any hardship.

• Gladys was persuaded to accept community services which were available to the elderly. Although she agreed reluctantly, soon she found her life much easier. Among the benefits she received were home-delivered meals, an emergency alert response system, a free shopping service run by local volunteers, a companion program operated by a church, and round-trip transportation to her doctor at no cost.

• Gladys agreed to sign a release allowing the doctor to discuss her medical condition with Monica and Jim. She signed a Durable Power of Attorney for Health Care, naming Jim as her health care decision-maker, in the event she couldn't make the decisions herself.

I congratulated Monica and Jim for doing such an excellent job with their management plan.

The plan worked for over two years. During that time, Gladys had one severe medical bout: a bad bacterial infection in her arm which threatened to spread throughout her system and possibly even kill her. Desperately ill, Gladys was hospitalized.

Her doctor and the children decided that it would be best for Gladys to move out of her home and live near Monica. However, Gladys had not been made part of the decision-making process. And since it was her life, she constituted a majority of one.

Gladys loved her community, the weather, her friends, and her fond memories. She was not about to leave. She announced: "I've lived on my own for 70 years and I'm not about to change that now."

To prove her point, she rallied and soon was back to her former state of relatively good health.

After Gladys' hospitalization, the only change in the management plan was that Monica and Jim tried to visit Gladys more often. Instead of going to see her together, they now went separately, thereby doubling the visits she received.

They extracted solemn promises from Gladys that she would call "collect" on a regular basis, and wouldn't withhold information about her health from them. This kind of pact, between an elderly relative and those who are managing their care, is vital for the success of a self-managed care program.

Well, Gladys kept the promises, but she refused to call collect.

As time passed, Gladys slowly grew more frail and really needed around-the-clock care. Monica and Jim couldn't convince her of this fact. They had no legal recourse to force the issue, because Gladys remained mentally sharp as a tack.

Then, Gladys took one fall too many. She finally agreed to sell her mobile home and move near Monica.

Before the sale was finalized, Gladys collapsed and ended up in the hospital again, where she developed a high fever. Even though the mobile home had not yet been sold, the children agreed that a good board and care, or nursing home, must be immediately found for Gladys.

Jim requested my assistance to find placement for his grandmother in the Los Angeles area. But Gladys, absolutely intent on retaining control over her life, decided she didn't want to leave Santa Barbara, period!

So, I referred Jim and Monica to my colleague Suzanne, who advised them about good board and care homes in Santa Barbara. (The doctor determined that Gladys did not need a skilled nursing facility.)

As it happened, the family got lucky. A fine licensed home, which was unusually affordable, had an opening. Jim and Monica took a trip to Santa Barbara and toured the place. It proved to be clean and homey, with sociable, alert residents. With Gladys' consent, they signed her up.

Gladys moved-in as soon as soon the hospital released her. She was thrilled with the move and got along famously with the others. Things went well: the meals were delicious, and the staff gently prevented Gladys from overdoing physical activities.

Although she would rather have had a private room, Gladys got satisfaction from assisting her roommate, who was in the early stages of Alzheimer's disease.

Small board and care homes frequently are willing and able to deal with some serious medical problems, which otherwise would require placement in a nursing home. This solution worked for about a year, until Gladys developed incontinence of both bowels and bladder.

The board and care owners were crazy about her, but they reluctantly had to tell Monica and Jim the bad news: Gladys was fast approaching the borderline when her physical abilities would not meet the home's minimum standards.

It was clear that Gladys was going to need a nursing home. Monica, now 75, didn't have the physical ability to care for Gladys. Grandson Jim, who was married with his own family to care for, was unable to take her into their home.

Gladys, still intellectually unimpaired, continued to insist upon remaining in Santa Barbara. She sold her trailer and had about $20,000 in the bank.

I told Monica that some nursing homes find ways to refuse to accept people on Medicaid, even though it is illegal to do so (they always claim to be "full")... However, once a patient has been admitted, pays for their care, and later runs out of money, the home cannot kick them out and must accept Medicaid as full payment.

Since Gladys had the money, and her health was quickly deteriorating, this seemed like the best time to get her into the right nursing home. She would be able to pay for at least nine months of care, before needing to apply for Medicaid.

So Jim asked Suzanne to recommend good nursing homes in the Santa Barbara area. Then they took Gladys on an outing to look for the best one.

Several women whom Gladys used to know lived in one particularly impressive nursing home. When they met each other, it was like a reunion of long-lost friends. Gladys decided that would be her new home, and she was admitted the same day.

Gladys lived in the nursing home for about a year, receiving frequent visits from Jim and Monica. The staff loved her, especially after Gladys appointed herself the official "shoulder-to-cry-on" for the other residents.

Jim emotionally recalls one of the nursing home patients who called him over to her bedside. She was a quadriplegic, dying of leukemia. The old woman told Jim how much she appreciated his grandmother, who had made such a tremendous difference in her life. Gladys had reached out to become her friend, often visiting her room to bring juice and chat.

Eventually, Gladys' health gave out. She found it hard to eat and lost a lot of weight. Gladys decided that she didn't want to receive medical intervention, and that request was honored. She signed a legal **"Do Not Resuscitate" (DNR)** order, directing doctors not to revive her should she begin to die.

Gladys knew her time had come. She was prepared for it and felt at peace. Gladys ended her life with a sense of integrity, as opposed to depression and despair.

Jim vividly recalls one of his last visits to his grandmother, a few days before she died. He asked Gladys if she would like to see her friend, Mary. Gladys nodded. Jim wheeled Mary to her bed. Gladys was not talking at the time, but words were unnecessary. The two old women grasped each other's hands and looked intently into each other's eyes for more than ten minutes.

"They were saying good-bye," Jim told me, his voice choking with emotion. "It was one of the most beautiful things I have ever seen."

Gladys died at the age of 94, gently and peacefully. Her life had been difficult, but her final years had been a time of meaning and dignity, thanks in large part to the involvement and caring of her loving family care managers.

Gladys' case is an excellent example of what sensitive families can do for their elderly loved-ones. Many caregivers become overwhelmed, burned-out, or even ill, as they try to handle everything by themselves.

Instead, with a little advice from a geriatric care manager and other specialists in elderly care, dedicated people like Monica are able to create a multi-disciplinary team to benefit their loved one. They learn how to best use family support and community resources to achieve truly excellent results.

Linda

Linda is one of my favorite clients. She's a strong, gutsy woman, who is doing an excellent job as a career-woman, wife, mother, and most recently, care manager for both of her parents... under the most trying circumstances.

Linda's parents, Ezra and Ruth, were farmers in Kansas, like their parents before them. When corporate giants took over from family farmers, the bank repossessed their property and they retired to a small town in California.

Before their gerontological crisis hit, Linda's parents, Ezra and Ruth, had reversed roles in relation to the usual cultural norm. More often, it is the woman who cares for the man in our culture, especially as a couple grows older, since men have the tendency to grow sick and/or die earlier than women. However, it was Ezra who wound up taking care of Ruth for many years, because of his wife's chronic illnesses.

But one day, that pattern of family interaction was destroyed ...Ezra, 85, was walking home from a nearby market, when he fell down and broke his hip. As often occurs with older people who suffer such traumatic injuries, the fall was the beginning of a long slide downhill towards incapacity and, ultimately, death.

Following the physical trauma of his injury, Ezra began an unexpected and frightening descent into irrationality while in the hospital. He forgot who his family was. He had no concept of his surroundings. He didn't know what was happening to him.

The suddenness of this cataclysmic change in her father, who had always been rational and independent, was extremely tough for Linda to cope with emotionally.

Now, she had to step-in and act as care manager for her father. Her mother wasn't up to it. Her brother was living in the area, but as all too frequently happens, he left almost the entire burden to his sister. At this point, Linda came to my office on her lunch hour one day, seeking practical guidance and emotional support.

The first task for Linda was to look for a quality nursing home. She scoured the community, checking-out my recommendations. She took off two days from work to tour facilities and interview administrators.

Linda acted as an informed, assertive consumer in the convalescent home marketplace. When the time came for Ezra to leave the hospital, there was already a bed waiting for him at a good facility.

Then a fascinating change took effect. Within a few days of Ezra's admission to the nursing home, he snapped out of his confused state. Suddenly, he remembered his wife and family, and wanted to go home.

For an elderly person, a stay in an acute hospital frequently can be the catalyst into a state of confusion. This confusion may disappear after leaving the hospital and returning to familiar surroundings. Often, the medications given during hospitalization are the cause of these disturbing temporary symptoms.

After a month in the skilled nursing facility, where he received physical therapy and rehabilitation services, Ezra returned home. That's when a second interesting phenomenon occurred: Ezra and Ruth reversed their roles again.

Prior to Ezra's fall, Ruth was the weak, ill one. Now she surprised everyone (including herself) by becoming a capable caregiver for Ezra. She was off the couch - cooking, feeding her husband, helping him shower and dress. Even her hypochondria temporarily disappeared. Meanwhile, Ezra became increasingly fragile and dependent.

For several months, 82-year-old Ruth, "miraculously" freed from her own ailments, cared for and nurtured her husband. But the enormous effort soon began to take its toll on her, reaching a point where she no longer had the physical strength to "do" for Ezra.

Linda was again faced with a crisis. She came to see me to discuss the various options, and also to express her feelings of guilt. She was overwhelmed by the competing demands on her time.

Linda was trying to cope with her challenging job, a husband who had just re-entered school, three children to care for, and two aging parents who constantly needed her.

She investigated several different home care agencies, looking for the right person to assist her mother and father. Finally, she found a capable nurse's aide, whom her parents liked and hired. Linda's concern and intervention stabilized the situation for the moment. Life went on as well as could be expected.

Unfortunately, Ezra continued his decline. He developed an eye disease which destroyed most of his vision. To make matters worse, old conflicts between Linda and her mother, which had never been resolved, were reactivated now that they were having so much daily contact.

Linda joined my support group for caregivers of aging parents. She was able to resolve her feelings of anger, love, responsibility, and guilt toward Ruth.

The time came when Linda's parents no longer could afford in-home custodial care. Again she was faced with finding a nursing home for her father. Her parents were eligible for Medicaid, which would cover the costs. Because of her previous experience investigating nursing homes, Linda was able to quickly choose an appropriate one, and Ezra was admitted.

Linda came for therapy regularly. She found herself crying all the time, because Ruth blamed her for Ezra's subsequent deterioration in the nursing home. The physicians assured Linda and her mother that Ezra was getting the care he needed: the health care team was doing everything that could be done.

After Ezra's death, Linda remained in therapy to work through the grief over the loss of her father, and the conflict with her mother. She continues to manage the care of Ruth, who lives independently with the assistance of part-time in-home help.

Linda is empowered to remain in control. She has the satisfaction of knowing that she gave her father the best care possible, without destroying her own life to do it. And Linda continues to do the same for her mother, nearly ten years later.

CHAPTER 9

Potpourri:
Emotional and Financial Costs

Several other areas bear discussion in a book about managing the care of the elderly. This chapter deals with the impact of eldercare on other family members...who pays the emotional and financial tabs...and what society needs to do to make life easier for seniors and their families.

THE RIPPLE EFFECT

Let's begin by discussing what I call "the ripple effect." I'm sure you have all witnessed what occurs when a stone is thrown into a pond: there's a splash, then ripples flow from the point of impact until they hit the shore.

Family gerontological crises have a similar effect. The specific trouble that the elderly relative experiences can be compared to a stone that hits the water. Immediately, there's a dramatic "splash," then the fabric of the water is violently ripped apart. As the stone sinks, water closes in around it. Soon, the spot where the stone entered is calm, as if nothing had happened.

Likewise, when an acute gerontological problem hits, a family is thrown into dramatic chaos and action. Soon afterward, the new reality is absorbed into the fabric of family life, just as the stone is made a part of the existence of the pond.

However, that is not the end of the story. In the pond, the ripples that are created may cause unexpected consequences. Perhaps an insect is swept into the water, or a spider's web is soaked. Or, perhaps water is forced onto shore, germinating a seed which ultimately becomes a tree.

Likewise, in family life, just because the immediate

gerontological crisis has passed, it does not mean that all the consequences are settled. The ripples that flow from dealing with the needs of an elderly family member may create completely unforeseen circumstances, which can be far worse than the splash of the original "stone."

Horrendous dangers can lurk in the ripple effect, dangers that can physically destroy lives and tear families apart...

Health

When a significant problem strikes an older person, often the caregiver also becomes ill. The key enemy usually is stress. The profound stress created when a loved-one is physically or mentally ill, and needs to be cared for on a continuing basis, can be so severe as to be life-threatening.

It can lead to exacerbation of a caregiver's chronic illness that already exists, or it can trigger new illnesses such as high blood pressure, heart attack, stroke, cancer, ulcers, and alcoholism. Thus, it is vital that a family caregiver make a point of monitoring their own health, as well as that of their elderly family member.

Emotional well-being

Not only can the stress of caregiving result in physical diseases, it can also be the cause of emotional turmoil and relationship disasters. Marriages may be under such stress they can shatter; children might act-out or quit school; former coping mechanisms no longer operate...

I have seen two attempted suicides by teenagers who were distraught over the chaos and changes in family-ties, brought about by their parents caring for the grandparents.

I have seen formerly loving couples torn-apart over caregiving issues.

I have seen caregivers descend into drug abuse and alcohol abuse.

I have also seen elder-abuse by caregivers pushed over the edge of acceptable behavior by the stress in their lives. Ordinarily, these people would never reach this point. When pushed to the brink, the caregiver may have a knee-jerk reaction, similar to an overwhelmed parent spanking a child. In both cases, it would be wise to learn alternative ways to cope with stressful behavior.

Thus, if you find your life, or a family member's life deteriorating under the burden of caring for elderly relatives, please seek guidance as soon as possible:

- Hire a professional care manager to take the burden off your shoulders.
- Access community services such as day-care and in-home help.
- Place your loved one in an alternative living facility.
- Seek family counseling or short-term psychotherapy.

Or to put it another way, do what you can do, but be willing to acknowledge when you have reached the breaking point.

Financial distress

The United States is the only industrialized Western nation, with the exception of South Africa, that does not have some form of guaranteed access to health care for all of its citizens. This shocking fact places incredible financial stress on families.

Aging children caring for aging parents find it an incredible strain on their pocketbooks, as they attempt to provide quality health care for their ill loved-ones. When funds from the patient or family are not sufficient, there's just not much that can be done except to place grandma in a nursing home on Medicaid.

One way of getting needed cash is through what is known as a **reverse mortgage**, which is currently being heavily promoted. The positive and negative viewpoints on this approach are hotly debated. To get information on both points of view, contact the National Center for Home Equity Conversion and the AARP (*see Appendix G and Glosssary*).

Victoria

A good example of the ripple effect can be seen in the story of Victoria, a single-mother and Hollywood writer for films and television. Her neurologist referred her to me because Victoria's father (affectionately known as "Pops") was suffering from Alzheimer's disease, and her mother from Parkinson's disease.

Pops was a prominent dentist before he retired, and had also served as mayor of his small Midwestern town. His wife, Eva, had been suffering from Parkinson's disease for a long time, but Pops had always been able to care for her.

Then his own memory loss and poor judgment made it necessary to obtain care for both of them.

Victoria made arrangements for her parents to move into her apartment complex in California. Since she worked at home, Victoria was able to see them at a moment's notice. And Pops could still function independently, taking care of Eva's needs.

As the months passed, Pops grew less able to care for himself and his wife, so Victoria had to take on more of the responsibilities.

Eva remained mentally acute, but she expressed anger and depression because she could no longer handle all the activities of daily living. Victoria tried her best in every way she could, yet her mother raged at her. It was devastating.

Watching her parents deteriorate was more than Victoria could emotionally bear. To make matters worse, Victoria was spending so much time on care-giving that her career had to be put on hold.

When Victoria came to the realization that she could no longer handle matters alone, she retained me as care manager. I coordinated in-home help and other services that substantially eased the demands on her time.

However, the assistance in caregiving that Victoria received didn't reduce her emotional commitment to her parents. That's where the ripple effect occurred...

Victoria's 11-year-old adopted son, Keith, had always been well-balanced and friendly. But he suddenly changed.

The first indication that her son felt distressed came when

Victoria received a call from his school. Keith had been caught riding his bike, with alcohol hidden in a water bottle.

Victoria was told, to her horror, that Keith had become anti-social and his school work had taken a marked dip in quality. She called me in a panic, her response out of proportion to the problem: "Do I need to send my son to military school?"

"No, but he does need some attention," I said. "Bring him with you for sessions twice a week."

As a licensed family therapist, I was able to offer assistance. Calming her, I pointed-out that Keith's behavior only started recently. We could probably deal with the problem successfully, if we got right to it.

Keith is a lovable boy: handsome, affable, and smart as a whip. His unexpected behavior was a cry for attention and help. Victoria, a wonderful mother, certainly never meant to neglect her son, but with her aging parents in such need of her time and assistance, something had to give.

Victoria and Keith came to therapy for many months. Every session, he sat there petting my dog. For the first time, he heard the details about his adoption, and they openly discussed Victoria's divorce. Two hours a week of undivided attention worked wonders for the boy.

Not only did Keith's relationship with his mother improve, but he was finally able to express anger and dismay over his parents' divorce, as well as working through many of his anxieties about being adopted.

Postscript: Keith is doing very well at a new school. Grandma Eva died, which is a terrible loss. Pops is now in a nursing home that specializes in caring for Alzheimer's patients. And Victoria is finally back at work, writing. In fact, she wrote a best seller!

Victoria's story is a reminder that during a gerontological crisis, not only the patient, but family dynamics have to be dealt with. This often requires the complementary work of a licensed mental health care professional.

WHO PAYS THE FINANCIAL TAB?

One of the most disturbing aspects of elderly care in this country is the cost. It takes a great deal of money to provide an aging dependent with a decent quality of life. As a result, despite a lifetime of successful productivity, family responsibility, and good citizenship, an old person may not receive the quality of care they deserve.

Hiring in-home help privately can cost $8+/hour. Hiring help through an agency costs about $16/hour, usually with a 4-hour daily minimum. A live-in companion for 24-hour custodial care costs $90-150/day.

In-home help costs more than a small board and care facility, where shared rooms usually go for $1200-1500/month, and private rooms are $1800 and up.

A retirement hotel may charge $750-1600/month for a semi-private room, and $1350-2400 for a private room. Adding assisted living services costs one-hundred to several hundred dollars in additional fees.

Nursing homes, for those not eligible for Medicaid, can cost in excess of $5,000 per month.

Most countries recognize their moral obligations to seniors, and provide government benefits to defray most of the cost of gerontological care. For example, Canada's national health system provides in-home or nursing home care at little cost to their citizens.

Unfortunately, in the United States, most of the burden of paying for long-term care falls on the elderly themselves, or their families. Sometimes expenses are so high that a family is rendered virtually penniless if their EFM lives into their 80's or 90's, even if they start with a lot of money.

Medicare

Perhaps it goes a little too far to say that the cost of caring for the elderly is a national disgrace. We do have Medicare, which covers about 36 million citizens, but now the federal government is determined to chip away (or gouge away) at the system, trying to move as many elderly as possible into **Medicare-managed HMOs**, or other managed care and private health plans. Who knows what major changes will take place in the near future?

However, at best, Medicare only alleviates the financial blow. It does not eliminate it. Fundamentally, Medicare is geared to cover acute illness and intermittent skilled care, not chronic illness and long-term care.

Medicare accounts for about 45% of health care spending for the elderly. Medicare "Part A" is an earned benefit for most elderly, requiring no premium upon eligibility. Medicare "Part B" is voluntary and currently costs almost $50/month. Most seniors and disabled people elect to take "Part B."

Let's take a look at what Medicare covers, so the areas not covered will come into sharper focus. This information is accurate as of the writing of this book. Check to see what changes may have taken place since publication.

"Part A"

Medicare comes in two parts. The first, known as "Part A", is a hospitalization plan. There is no cost to eligible recipients, who must be age 65 and qualify to receive Social Security. (Certain people under age 65 with medical disabilities may also qualify for Medicare.) Even if your EFM doesn't qualify for Social Security, they can still buy into Medicare, at a substantial expense.

When faced with escalating medical bills for your elderly family member, it is good to know clearly what Medicare will cover. "Part A" covers the following costs:

1. In-patient hospital care:

You are entitled to receive limited medically necessary hospitalization. Since Medicare rules are unbendable and can be confusing, many patients make errors and lose out. So please read this carefully...

A **benefit period** begins on the first day you receive inpatient services at a hospital, and ends after you have been out of the hospital (or skilled nursing home) for 60 consecutive days, or when you remain in a skilled nursing care facility but do not receive care there for 60 consecutive days.

From day 1 through day 60, you (or your Medigap insurance) pay a $736 deductible for the benefit period.

From day 61 through day 90, your co-payment is $184/day.

From day 91 through day 150, your co-payment is $368/day.

At that point in each benefit period, you're on your own, unless you use your 60 lifetime days of reserve care. If you have used up this one lifetime exclusion, you must then pay $368 per day.

From day 151 on, Medicare covers nothing and you pay all costs.

2. In-patient psychiatric care:

Medicare only pays a total of 190 days lifetime maximum for such care. Many elderly patients have mental disorders, so this limitation proves very troublesome.

3. In-patient skilled nursing care:

You are entitled to receive 100 days of care following a hospitalization, during each benefit period. The care must be *post-hospital,* since the purpose of the skilled care must be recovery from an illness or injury. If the nursing care is for *continuing care,* no benefits apply.

The first 20 days are free, with no deductible. Your copayment is $92/day, from day 21 through day 100. After that, you're on your own again, to the tune of $4,000-$5,000 or more per month.

4. Home health care:

If you need skilled nursing or rehabilitation care in your home for the treatment of illness or injury, Medicare will pay for certain services, providing all the following conditions are met:

• The required care includes intermittent skilled nursing care, physical therapy, or speech therapy.

- You are confined to your home.
- You are under the care of a physician who determines you need home care, and sets up a home health plan.
- The home health agency providing the services is a **participating agency,** i.e. one approved by Medicare.

There is no deductible, no limits on the number of covered days, no required prior hospitalization, and no cost to you for covered services. You must partially pay for durable medical equipment, such as a hospital bed, for which you pick-up 20% of the tab.

5. Hospice care:

A hospice is a public agency or private organization that is primarily engaged in providing pain relief, symptom management, and supportive services to terminally ill people.

Hospice care does not seek to extend life or cure the terminal medical condition, rather it provides **palliative care** (relief of symptoms). But usually a family member must live with the patient, or full-time custodial care must be provided, in order to qualify for hospice care.

The services covered under hospice care include:
- in-home nursing services
- doctors' bills
- medications, including outpatient drugs for pain relief (an exception to Medicare's refusal to pay for prescription drugs), with a $5 co-payment for each prescription
- medical social services
- short-term in-patient care, including respite relief
- counseling.

Hospice services are usually provided in-home. They can also be provided by nursing homes, if the care is only palliative, not **curative.** In some areas, board and care homes can give hospice services, if they have proper licensing. You are entitled to hospice care for an indefinite time, so long as your doctor certifies need. Contact the National Hospice Organization (*see Appendix G*).

If you think you require any of the above services, be sure to speak with the treating doctor. This is especially applicable to in-home health care and hospice treatment, since some doctors have a tendency to forget about these valuable benefits. "Part A" hospitalization operates on what is known as the **DRG (diagnosis related group)** system.

If someone is diagnosed with a disease or injury which requires hospitalization, Medicare may not pay for the *actual* time the patient might need to be in the hospital. Instead, Medicare pays for the number of days that an *average* patient, with the same diagnosis, is hospitalized. In reality, of course, patients heal at different rates. Some patients require longer than average hospital stays, and someone has to pay the additional bill.

Just like HMOs, the DRG payment system puts a great deal of pressure on the hospital to discharge a Medicare patient as soon as is medically possible, since a shorter stay increases profits, while a longer-than-average stay results in a loss.

Hospitals routinely begin to plan for the patient's discharge from the day of admission. This is known as **discharge planning**. Your EFM's private physician has less to say than in the past about this important decision.

As a result of such financial pressure, many doctors and families complain that patients are being sent home sooner and sicker, with almost no follow-up education to accelerate their recovery. And not enough time is taken to teach the patient's *family* how to take care of their ailing loved-one.

Discharge planning sometimes leads to a tragic case of "follow the bouncing ball:" The patient is bounced from the hospital too soon, receiving intermittent in-home help for a recovery that ideally requires hospitalization...then, back to the hospital with a complication or relapse...then, on to a skilled nursing facility...then, back to the hospital again...

This kind of "modern yo-yo treatment" is medically and psychologically stressful at a time when the weakened patient most needs peaceful, secure, caring recuperation.

Subacute care may be a good alternative for many patients who do not require the full extent of hospitalization (*see Glossary*).

With so much at stake, I urge you to understand your rights under the system, to ensure that your elderly family member receives adequate hospital care. There are also appeals procedures that you should learn about, *before* you need them. Contact your local Social Security Administration office for the latest rules on Medicare.

"Part B"

"Part B" of Medicare is the federal equivalent of *major medical* health insurance. It generally pays 80% of physician and outpatient services, after the $100 annual deductible.

Coverage includes: physician services and surgery; outpatient services at a hospital, rehabilitation facility or rural health clinic; treatment for mental health (only pays 50% of approved amount); radiation, speech, and physical therapies; home dialysis equipment and supplies; X-rays, laboratory and other diagnostic tests; mammography screening and pap smears; pathology and radiology services; and ambulances.

"Part B" is not free. It is paid through monthly premiums, usually deducted from recipients' Social Security checks.

Unfortunately, there are many items necessary to maintain good health which are not covered by "Part B". Non-covered services include: most outpatient prescription drugs, routine physical examinations, most preventive care (some preventive care is covered, such as mammograms and flu shots), non-surgical dental services, most routine foot care, eyeglasses, hearing aids, and most long-term care in nursing facilities, in the community, or at home.

Currently, "Part B" does pay 100% of their *approved amount* for clinical lab services.

However, Medicare only pays 80% of the approved amount for medical expenses and outpatient hospital treatment. That means your ill parent or relative will owe 20% of the total bill, plus the $100 deductible, if it hasn't been met during the benefits period. It may not seem like much, but even 20% of a huge medical bill can be financially devastating.

One of the principles you need to understand with regard to "Part B" is that the fees of physicians are different. In essence, there are two kinds of doctors: those who *accept Medi-care assignments,* and those who don't.

If your EFM's doctor does not accept the assignment, you'll have pay the entire bill yourself. And the costs are often far higher than what Medicare would have paid.

A doctor who does accept the assignment is paid directly from Medicare, accepting whatever Medicare determines is *"reasonable payment"* for the service rendered.

Medicare will reimburse the doctor for 80% of this reasonable cost, less the deductible. Unless your EFM has Medigap insurance, you will still have to pay the additional 20%, *plus* any difference between what the doctor actually charges and what Medicare agrees to pay.

Note: Deductibles will undoubtedly increase in coming years, so you must plan ahead.

Medigap Insurance

As you can see, there are a lot of health care services that Medicare does not cover. There's a health insurance policy that addresses this concern, called a **Medicare supplement**, (popularly known as **Medigap insurance**).

Medigap insurance is designed to take-over when Medicare stops. It will cover the 20% reasonable cost of service that isn't paid by Medicare "Part B".

At this time, a good Medigap insurance policy will pay for most of your EFM's health care costs not otherwise covered by Medicare, estimated to be approximately 50% of the total cost of care.

Currently, there are ten standard policies permitted by the government to be sold as Medigap policies (called Plans A-J), although not all companies offer all plans. "Plan A," the cheapest, has the least coverage. "Plan J," the most costly, also covers the most.

The state insurance department will send information on the Medigap policies available in your state, describing the differences between them. Compare the costs of these policies against their respective benefits before your EFM purchases one. (Note: It is still prohibited to sell a person more than one Medigap policy.)

To learn more about Medigap insurance, contact your local chapter of AARP (American Association of Retired Persons, *see Appendix G*).

For low-income seniors who have Medicare, but cannot afford a Medigap policy, there is Medicaid, as well as two other assistance programs: **Special Low-Income Medicare Beneficiaries**, and **Qualified Medicare Beneficiary (QMB)**. To find out about these low-income programs, contact Medicare.

Managed Health Care Plans

Medicare pays for a significant portion of total health care costs. However, many people cannot afford to pay, or do not choose to pay the remaining costs (usually 20% of the bill). Medigap insurance is one way to avoid the 20%. But more and more, people are choosing managed care plans, such as HMOs, POSs, PPOs, and IPAs, as alternatives to Medicare.

If your elderly family member chooses an HMO, for instance, in most cases their Medicare will have to be forfeited to the plan, which covers more of the costs than traditional private *"fee-for-service"* health care. When Medicare pays the HMO, a patient is only entitled to the care offered by that particular HMO, and will no longer receive their previous Medicare benefits.

Rather than making money by *providing care*, managed care plans make money by *controlling costs*.

Managed care plans pay for all covered health care and hospitalizations, including prescriptions (subject to a small co-payment). This can save a lot of money, but patients often must give up their freedom of choice.

With many plans, your EFM can *only* use the doctors and hospitals authorized by the managed care plan. The patient's favorite doctors may be excluded, and even a frail older person may have to go to a hospital a distance away. Not all plans cover every state or every country, so if a patient requires medical attention outside the plan's territory, there may only be limited benefits. Also, there may be a longer wait to get to see a doctor.

Under Medicare, patients are free to go to any specialist, such as a cardiologist, urologist, or neurologist. Members of many managed care plans cannot see specialists unless *specifically authorized* and referred by their **primary-care physicians**, who usually serve as the health plans' "**gatekeepers**," keeping the cost of treatment as low as possible.

It is difficult, for instance, to get a referral to a psychiatrist or geropsychiatrist. They are specialists in prescribing the right *psychotropic drugs* for depression and dementia, and would normally do follow-ups to monitor proper dosage, efficiency, and side-effects. Instead, most managed care plans give their primary care physicians the responsibility of prescribing such medications.

Some managed care plans are also considering the feasibility of letting non-physicians handle some of the medical procedures with diabetic patients, rather than endocrinologists. General practitioners are replacing dermatologists, and other medical specialties, like opthamology and radiology, are in danger of being phased out.

In some cases, your EFM may have to go outside their plan and pay to see a private specialist, if they can afford one.

Due to critical publicity, some plans are modifying or eliminating the role of gatekeeper. Congress may or may not set medical standards in the future, depending on how strong public response to the issue is.

Before choosing an HMO or other managed care option, be sure you and your EFM understand the benefits and detriments of such care. Some plans offer enticing options, such as paying for medications. But it is important to understand that if the patient violates the plan's intricate rules, the entire cost of health care may be left on their shoulders.

Also, if your EFM already has a Medigap policy, before switching from Medicare to a managed care plan, be aware that if they later decide to switch back to Medicare, it is very possible that they will *not* be able to get their Medigap policy again. The aging patient may very well have new medical prob-lems, termed **pre-existing conditions**, which they didn't have at age 65 when the Medigap policy was first taken out.

Some patients have found managed care to be effective, while others have not. Find a managed care plan that suits the particular immediate and projected future needs of your loved one. Investigate the company's record of patient satis-faction...and choose with great caution. Managed care may cost less in actual dollars, but you must be an informed con-sumer about what each plan will do, and what it won't do for your EFM. You cannot afford to be naive.

Geriatric care managers can work with managed health care plans to find the best cost-effective services for elderly family members. The goal of both managed care plans and the fami-lies of EFMs, is, if possible, to keep older patients out of expen-sive, often unpleasant acute care facilities, such as hospitals and nursing homes.

HMOs and other managed health care plans, with all their strengths and weaknesses, are here to stay. We've discovered an exotic new animal, and like explorers, we all are respon-sible for becoming educated.

Nursing Home Insurance

According to elder financial planning expert **Barry S. Siegel**, CLU, ChFC, long-term care in a nursing home ranges between $30,000 - $60,000 per year, depending on what part of the coun-try you live in.

That's a lot of money. Even a few years of nursing home care can deplete all of the assets of most middle-class families, and many well-to-do families. Even a six-figure savings ac-count doesn't last long at those prices, especially since so many seniors are living longer than ever before. As discussed in Chap-ter 5, Medicaid will not pay for care until most assets have been depleted.

This is a primary consideration. The AARP estimates that 60% of all families have faced the need to place a family mem-ber in a nursing home for long-term care.

The California Department of Insurance is a little more optimistic, expecting that about 40% of all persons age 65 or older will require some nursing home care in their lives. (About half of these will not need long-term care.)

There is a relatively new form of insurance you can purchase to pay for nursing home care, called **long-term care insurance** (also known as **nursing home insurance**).

Generally, these are indemnity-type policies, which pay a specific amount per day, for each covered day spent in a nursing home. The policies usually come in two-year, four-year, or six-year benefit periods, and will often pay a substantial cost of such care.

When shopping for nursing home insurance, it is imperative to study the *exclusions* in the contract. These are terms which allow the insurance company to get off the hook from paying benefits that you expect them to cover.

Beware of policies that limit benefits for *custodial care*. Also beware of any *pre-existing condition* exclusions. (Earlier policies excluded Alzheimer's disease, required that the nursing home admission *follow* a hospital stay, and had an *elimination period*, during which time you paid premiums but would not be entitled to benefits.)

One of the most important things is to investigate the strength of an insurance company, before you take out a policy... Your library has reference guides rating insurance companies. Go with an established company. Make sure it's financially sound, so it will still be around when you need the insurance.

Depending on your age, try to get a policy that is *guaranteed renewable for life*, meaning that as long as you pay premiums, your coverage cannot be canceled. Generally, the earlier you take out such a policy, the better off you are, because you won't have pre-existing conditions and rates will be lower.

Nursing home policies are expensive. Only you can decide if they are worth the cost. On the other hand, they can save a lot of money.

In states which have **long-term care partnership insurance** (*see Chapter 5 and Glossary*), such policies can also help with asset protection when planning for Medicaid. Some long-term care partnership policies also cover residential care facilities, and community-based services such as adult day care.

Because the terms of the policies are complicated, the choices so serious, and the consequences of buying the wrong policy so devastating, it is vital that you discuss this with an expert who specializes in this field.

Only consult with those relatively few insurance agents and certified financial planners who have specialized knowledge about elder-care and long-term care. Be sure to get a second opinion. It is often wise to have a group discussion with a financial gerontologist or financial planner, your long-term care insurance agent, elder law attorney, and accountant.

Medicaid and SSI

Long-term care will be paid for by Medicaid (Medi-Cal in California) under certain conditions. A combination of Medicare and Medicaid must be accepted by nursing homes by law, except if they are private and do not receive government funds.

SSI is an additional sum of money given monthly to elderly people who qualify, but it doesn't begin to cover nursing home costs. To get SSI, you must be considered to be "very poor." This is determined by your income. If your Social Security is low enough to meet the means test, you will be entitled to SSI.

Medicare, which you get automatically at age 65, is a completely different program than Medicaid. It is determined by age, not means.

Medicare and SSI allow people who are not in nursing homes to receive certain entitlements, such as in-home *supportive services* and some medications, because the government does not classify them as being on Medicaid. (There are regional differences: check out your state's regulations about this.)

If an elderly family member needs a nursing home and is *already* on Medicare and SSI, they will most likely also be eligible for long-term care Medicaid, which will cover the costs. If your EFM is ready to go into a nursing home, fill out a long-term care Medicaid application.

WHERE ELSE TO TURN

It's not easy getting old, either for the persons whose bodies are aging or for their families. But there is some good news. There are many fine support organizations (*see Appendix G*). Here are just a few of them:

Alzheimer's Association

The Alzheimer's Association deserves special mention because of the prevalence of dementia in society, and because of the depth of care the victims require.

The Association publishes a great deal of useful information, providing emotional support and assistance for the families of dementia patients. They can give you suggestions for legal and financial-planning, the symptoms and course of the disease, and can put you in touch with support groups whose members are stuck in the same quicksand you may be in.

Alzheimer's Disease Education and Referral Center

ADEAR is a service of the National Institute on Aging. They provide extensive information about Alzheimer's and other problems of the elderly, and have "800" numbers on every important topic. ADEAR will do topical searches on long-term caregiving, rural caregiving, special ethnic, racial, and religious considerations, respite care, dementia, confusion, wandering, chemical restraints, international forums, and other resources. Their Combined Health Information Database (CHID) contains material from many other agencies and organizations.

American Association of Retired Persons (AARP)

AARP is still the largest, most widely-known and most influential seniors organization, despite attacks by some Congressional critics. In its over thirty years of existence, AARP has grown to become one of the powerful lobbying groups in Washington. The organization has the following stated goals:

- enhancing the quality of life for older persons
- promoting their independence, dignity and sense of purpose
- taking the lead in determining the role of older people in society
- stimulating the private sector to support and pursue benevolent activities in the field of aging.

You can join if you are age 50 or older. Membership also includes a subscription to their excellent magazine, *Modern Maturity*, as well as discounts on prescription drugs and many other services.

Family Caregivers Alliance

This wonderful organization can help you cope if someone you love suffers a serious memory loss. It assists families and caregivers, offering all kinds of resources for people with brain damage - whether caused by head trauma, stroke, Parkinson's disease, dementia, or other chronic disabling brain disorders.

National Academy of Elder Law Attorneys (NAELA)

NAELA was founded in 1988 as a professional association of lawyers dedicated to improving the quality of legal services for the elderly and their families. Elder law attorneys specialize in serving the complex, unique needs of the aged and their caregiving families.

National Association of Professional Geriatric Care Managers (GCM)

A note about the organization to which I belong and have served as a member of the Board of Directors... GCM is the national voice of my profession.

GCM was formed over a decade ago to fill the fragmentation and gaps in continuity of care for our aging population. Members meet regularly to discuss experiences, social policy, research, and new approaches in the field. There was a vital need to establish a national network of private geriatric care managers who would be available to families for consultations, assessments, referrals, care-coordination and monitoring.

If you and your needy elderly family member live far apart, GCM will refer you to a member who lives near your parent or loved one. You can collaborate with the local geriatric care manager for long-distance caregiving. GCM has members throughout the United States who can provide specific information or comprehensive care - i.e., "balloons or the whole party" - whatever is needed.

GCM has established a "Standards of Practice" (*see Appendix E*) and a "Pledge of Ethics" for members, and offers other essential protections for the public. You should become acquainted with GCM if you are going to work with a care manager.

National Council of Senior Citizens (NCSC)

NCSC serves as an advocate and benefactor for senior citizens and their families. It offers several advantageous programs, such as the Nursing Home Information Service.

NCSC publishes a number of informative pamphlets to assist seniors and their families. It also provides money-saving possibilities in the areas of insurance, health plans, and travel discounts.

Older Women's League (OWL)

OWL is one of my favorite organizations. I worked with the dedicated founders, Tish Sommers and Laurie Shields, and founded a local chapter in its early years. Unlike many other organizations which offer advice to seniors, OWL concentrates on advocacy for the special needs of mid-life and older women. Its stated purposes are:

- providing mutual support for its members
- helping women achieve economic and social equity
- improving the image and status of older women.

These goals may seem obvious and entirely reasonable, but they are pressing concerns, especially when you consider the following (according to OWL):

- over 70% of people over the age of 65 are women
- fewer than 1 in 5 woman over 65 receives pension income
- 85% of all surviving spouses over the age of 65 are women
- 80% of the elderly who live alone are women.

OWL works through local chapters assisting members with these and other complex issues, so they can better plan for the winter of their lives.

CHAPTER 10

Let's Play "Twenty Questions"

Daily in my practice, and whenever I'm a speaker at lectures and symposiums, or a guest on radio or television shows, I'm asked a wide variety of questions about issues concerning care management. For every person who asks a question, there are millions of others who have the same question, who are in the same situation.

This chapter answers some of the most frequently asked questions...

1. <u>I'm feeling overwhelmed and guilty...</u>
    <u>What should I do?</u>
    Recently, I received this letter...
    "As a son, it's painful to see my parents decline in front of my eyes and not be able to help them as much as I want to. I'm trying to assist them to make the necessary changes in their lives, which they don't want to make.
    "I'm going through 'tough love' with both my rebellious teenagers. Now, I have to do the same thing with my aging parents. I have to act like a strict school principal, instead of their loving son. It's emotionally exhausting.
    "I'm under tremendous pressure... The repairs on my house aren't getting done, my job is in jeopardy, my wife is angry at me. The bills are piling up, and my blood pressure is sky-high. The stress of constantly flying to Chicago to help my aging parents through one more crisis has forced me to the breaking point. I'm sad, overwhelmed, and don't know how to cope."

    This brave letter desperately seeks help in finding answers to one of life's tragic realities. I hear such pleas all the time. The great myth of our time is that we should be able to "do it all," like previous generations seemed to have done.

It is true that some of our grandparents and great-grand-parents were cared for at home by their families, but there was usually a close extended family available to pitch-in with the care, which made the burden far easier.

The truth is that their life expectancy was much less than our parents have today, so all the problems of aging were diminished. In 1900, the average life expectancy was only 47 years!

In contrast, the elderly today have a good chance of living 15 years or more from the time they begin to need your assistance. More than 3.7 million Americans are expected to be over age 85 by the year 2000, and 70-million "baby boomers" will be over age 55 by the year 2010, including many of you reading this book.

Being a member of "the sandwiched generation" is like being a slice of bologna, expected to give taste and meaning to two slices of "bread"...your children on one side, and your parents on the other side.

You may very well be exhausted and overwhelmed by the challenges of running two households...yours, and that of your elderly parent(s). Although you deserve a Purple Heart for being "Superson" or "Superdaughter," instead, you feel guilt when you've run out of energy to handle both enormous tasks.

The average woman spends 17 years raising children, and 18 helping aging parents.* Adult children who are handling this burden are modern-day pioneers. There are no road maps to point the way.

You would be well-advised to retain the services of a professional care manager to assess your entire family situation. Within a short period of time, the care manager should be able to answer the following questions:

1. Is your parent still able to live independently in their own home?

2. Would placement in a retirement hotel, assisted living center, board and care home, or nursing home, be a better alternative?

---

*From: "The Daughter Track," by **Jeanne Gordon**, et al, *Newsweek*, 7/16/90.

3. Would bringing your parent home to live with you be a viable option, considering the space you have in your home, the level of their dependency, the impact on other family members, and the availability of outside services?

4. Is in-home help available and affordable?

5. What type of future financial arrangements should be made through lawyers, financial planners, accountants?

Convene a family meeting to see who would be willing to assist you with whatever decision is ultimately selected. Too often, one person in a family tries to do it all alone, rather than asking the spouse, significant other, siblings, aunts, uncles, and other family members who could also contribute to the older person's care.

Remember, the more you are able to delegate some of the caregiving responsibilities to other family members and even close friends, the more you will be able to adequately care for both your aging parent and your own family. One person can't do it all alone: a team effort is a must.

If you still feel racked with guilt and compelled to take the entire burden of your parent's care on your own shoulders, you might need some form of psychotherapy or family counseling.

The care you provide should be motivated by love, not guilt. All of you will thrive if love is the primary impetus to your care-giving. Guilt only leads to resentment, bitterness, and repressed anger, which can destroy family cohesiveness and even cause elder-abuse.

2. When should I start planning to care for my parents?

It's never too early to plan for future geriatric care. Even if you are blessed with healthy parents, you'll be better prepared for the future if you learn about the issues today, which you may face tomorrow.

Take the time and effort, using the depth and breadth of information available to you. Join the AARP and read Modern Maturity magazine.

Be sure to contact the National Council On Aging. They'll send you addresses of local agencies on aging, pamphlets on caregiving, and a list of support groups in your state. You probably will want to read some of the many books on the subject (*see Bibliography*).

One client who started preparing for her mother's old age before the time of need was Liz...

Liz

Liz was unusual, because most caregivers wait until their elderly family member has a crisis to begin preparing a plan of action. As her mother, Rae, was approaching the senior years, Liz read many books and articles on the subject of care. Liz even consulted a geriatric care manager, who put together a team of gerontological professionals she could turn to.

While her husband Doug worked at the office, Liz worked hard as a traditional housewife, raising their large family, She even started a small business at home, to help pay the kids' huge college tuition bills. Staying afloat financially kept Liz and Doug extraordinarily busy.

Trouble hit Rae in the form of severe hypochondria. So Liz moved her mother from Denver into a retirement hotel in Los Angeles. Rae began to call Liz at all hours, day and night, complaining of terrible physical symptoms.

For months, Liz responded by making sure Rae got thorough check-ups by trusted physicians. Again and again, the doctors said they couldn't find anything wrong with Rae. There was nothing they could do.

Finally, Liz had to admit that her mother's complaints were not caused by her physical condition. I referred Rae to a good geropsychiatrist, who diagnosed her condition as a form of depression.

Depression in the elderly often manifests itself in one or more physical symptoms. Rae underwent treatment for depression, and Liz's family entered into brief family therapy, which improved their communication. As a result, Rae's hypochondria has abated and she is doing well.

Had Liz, the primary caregiver, not prepared ahead of time for the crisis, she might have suffered severely debilitating stress, and Rae could have ended up prematurely or unnecessarily as a nursing home statistic.

At first, Liz tried to do everything herself. Families often try to do the best they can alone, for as long as they can, before they finally seek outside help.

Only about 2% of my clients come in ahead of time. In the initial consultation, they are given pertinent information, a useful bibliography, a list of good doctors, and referrals to other geriatric specialists.

Families with the courage of foresight are prepared to take immediate action, with the minimum amount of stress possible, when an inevitable crisis hits their elderly loved-one.

3. **I have mixed feelings about helping my parent...**
    How can I sort out love and responsibility?

People who consult with a geriatric care manager often come in with a lot of mixed feelings and hidden agendas. This is reality. A significant percentage of adult children, spouses, grandchildren, nieces and nephews, consult with geriatric care managers because they feel a *responsibility*, yet do not feel real love. This is completely understandable and even healthy, depending on the unique circumstances behind each relationship. Remember: you don't have to be, or pretend to be, a "saint" when you consult with a GCM. We understand... Believe me, we understand. We have parents, too.

Many caregiving clients have truly loving relationships with their elderly family members. Some clients accept responsibility for EFMs, because they're the only relatives around who will do it. Other clients do not have such positive relationships or fond memories, yet they still act responsibly to help the EFMs. In explanation of their generosity of the spirit, they have said, "I don't do it for Mom/Dad, I do it for me."

This is admirable, but the stress of caregiving can easily rekindle unhappy childhood feelings, leading to anger, as well as a crushing sense of being trapped and emotionally manipulated.

For example, Mr. Woodbury, a concerned friend, referred Phil to me. Phil was valiantly trying to take care of his father by himself, even though they were never close. The bitterness Phil felt toward the 95-year-old man was pushing him to the edge of verbal and physical abuse, and he was wracked with guilt.

After assuring the overwhelmed and overwrought son that there was absolutely no reason for him to feel guilty, because he was doing the very best he could do alone in an intolerable situation, Phil wound up hiring professional help for his father. This definitely averted a family crisis and allowed their normal cordial, but distant relationship to resume.

Time does not necessarily heal all wounds. Supportive counseling could be helpful to get you through the caregiving experience in one piece.

If life has dealt you an unjust hand and your parent is far less than ideal, a geriatric care manager can stand with you...and between you. Using a GCM as an intermediary and negotiator can be very useful when a previously abusive mother or father has become even more impossible to deal with, because of declining mental and physical health.

It's very sad, but all parents are not automatically lovable or loved, just because they've grown old. Unlike in Hollywood "G-rated" family films, they may not even be nice people. And there are also a lot of caregiving spouses who are angry at their needy spouses, and have been for years, perhaps for their entire marriages. A couple's 50th anniversary celebration can be an Ode to Joy, or a dirge, depending on the family.

On the other hand, the very act of caregiving has often changed old feelings of resentment. One thankful client told me, with tears in his eyes: "Before I started being my father's caregiver, I dreaded the idea and actually got physically sick to my stomach thinking about the never-ending sacrifice I would have to make for a person I didn't really know or even like. Now, for the first time, I have good feelings about taking care of Dad. We were always emotionally distant, but we're closer now, and I love it... We both do!"

The clearer you are about your honest motives for helping an elderly family member, the better the chance that the experience will be rewarding, or at least, not as traumatic. Don't become a caregiver for the sole reason of being loved. Face it: if your previous long-time relationship with a parent or spouse has not been emotionally fulfilling until now, the likelihood is that you will never get the love you want and deserve, no matter how much you do to help them.

If you choose to be a caregiver, please do not add the unwarranted burden of guilt to your already heavy responsibility, otherwise, "your cup may runneth over."

4.   How can I help my parent cope with widowhood?

Most surviving spouses who come in to see me are widows, because wives are usually younger than their husbands and women generally live longer, but I've been seeing more and more bereaved men in recent years.

Whether the survivor is female or male, when a spouse dies, grief is the natural, healthy reaction. However, many family members become alarmed at the long-term grieving. They make the mistake of trying to talk the surviving parent into leaving their own home and moving into a retirement hotel.

In fact, most widows and widowers want to, and need to stay in their old familiar surroundings. Such wishes should certainly be honored.

An adult child can be of great benefit to a mourning parent. In the early weeks of grief, a child should just "be there" for Mom or Dad. Make a point of visiting and calling often. Be there...just to talk, share memories and tears. Discuss the loss with your parent's friends. Make sure there is a support network to see them thorough the bereavement.

You might also urge your parent to get involved in **bereavement counseling** or **grief counseling**. Such counseling assists the spouse to work through issues, such as unresolved conflicts that may have existed between the couple, and the fear of living alone. In my experience, grief counseling almost always works to smooth out the bumps during this most painful time of life. Look for social and support groups for widows and widowers. AARP has a wonderful program called the **Widowed Persons Service**.

A major concern for many families is knowing when "normal" grieving turns unhealthy or pathological. That's not as easy to determine as it may seem. Grief is a common experience, expressed in unique ways. The way in which one person expresses this primary emotion may not be the same as another.

That being said, normal grieving usually lasts between one and two years before it declines, allowing for resumption of normal life. It is commonly expressed by crying, feelings of exhaustion and emptiness, a tightening of the throat or even a sensation of choking. There also may be a preoccupation with the dearly departed, and memories of more joyful times. Anger at the spouse for dying is common. Unfortunately, so is guilt over feeling such anger, and even guilt for remaining alive.

Grieving turns unhealthy in any of several ways. For example, grief may be completely suppressed. The person you expect to be crying and suffering, acts as if nothing has happened. This can "build a dam" against feelings, which eventually flood into rage, mental illness, or even suicide. Other signs of unhealthy grieving include symptoms of depression, anorexia, and dementia.

If grief becomes a habitual state, consult a geropsychiatrist or other licensed mental health professional.

5.   <u>Should I encourage my EFM to talk about the past?</u>
In my view, allowing the elderly to freely reminisce about their lives is *critically* important for them to live out their old age with quality and fulfillment.

In fact, several recent books cite the benefits of reminiscence. It stimulates seniors who are cognitively alert, and those whose long-term memory is still intact, despite loss of short-term memory due to dementia.

The tendency for an older person to review their life is

often misinterpreted by family members and caregivers as an indication of recent memory loss, and thus, a symptom of senility.

Actually, these reminiscences are part of the normal life-review process. They should be encouraged by health care professionals and family members. Remembering and retrospection are part of your EFM's need to put their life in order, as preparation for its end.

In late life, memory is particularly vivid. A person can often recall past events with sudden, remarkable clarity. This may occur with the full realization of their mortality...the knowledge that their sojourn on earth has a definite limit. Engaging in an assessment of their life, if done properly, can lead to a sense of satisfaction and positive feelings of having finished a job well-done.

Sometimes, older people decide that their lives were a total waste of time. This tragic, misguided conclusion can lead to severe depression.

A sensitive psychotherapist can enable your EFM to achieve useful breakthroughs with **life-review therapy.** Positive results often include acceptance of mortal life, a sense of serenity, pride in accomplishments and coping strategies which were effectively used earlier in life. This may lead to applying winning past strategies to solve current problems.

Successful life-review therapy also gives an EFM the opportunity to make plans for the time they have left, in order to leave emotional and material legacies. Often a senior will record or videotape their life-review, leaving it as a wonderful gift to family members and future generations.

6.   What can be done about insomnia?

Insomnia is one of the most common complaints of older people, who usually mention this sleep pattern: they have trouble falling asleep...sleep poorly...awaken...then can't fall back to sleep.

Another complaint is exhaustion, even when they do manage to fall asleep. Often, an elderly person will say, "I just don't sleep like I used to."

While physical pain, mental illness and depression frequently disturb sleep in the elderly, there are also some normal changes in sleeping patterns which occur as we age. Doctors at the University of Arizona College of Medicine recently studied these changes. They found that an average 25-year-old woman spends 6-1/2 to 8 hours in bed at night, while an average 75-year-old woman spends up to 10 hours in bed.

However, the younger woman sleeps 90% of the time, while the older woman only sleeps 65% of the time. In addition, the 25-year-old usually falls asleep in less than 30 minutes, while it often takes more than an hour for the elderly woman to do so.

Finally, while the younger woman awakens three times per night and passes through fewer than 50 sleep stages, the older one awakens up to 20 times a night and goes through as many as 100 stages of sleep.

So, we can see that major sleep changes appear to be a normal part of aging, albeit an extremely distressing one to many older people. However, we still should try to give our relatives methods for relief. Some of the steps suggested by health care professionals, which may help the elderly sleep better at night, include:

1. Help your EFM understand that changes in sleeping habits are a fact of aging. Realizing that nothing is wrong often alleviates fear, promoting better sleep patterns.
2. Find out what their normal bedtime rituals have been in the past. If they have changed much, work to reestablish them.
3. Try making changes in the physical environment, such as opening a window, adding an electric blanket, or putting a board under the mattress. Use a radio or tape recorder with soft music to assist sleep. Allow a beloved pet to sleep nearby, or if that's not possible, try a stuffed animal in bed. Some people find that chamomile tea, or warm milk and honey, can be soothing. The right fragrance and color scheme in the bedroom may also be helpful.

4. Help establish a program of regular exercise, consistent with the physical capabilities of the senior. However, exercise should not be done right before bedtime.

5. Try comforting touch... Gently stroke your loved-ones head and hands. Give them a relaxing hot bath before retiring.

6. Use supportive counseling to ease their depression over losses.

7. Do not serve heavy meals at night.

8. Promote a regular bedtime hour.

9. If your EFM lives in a retirement hotel or nursing home, encourage them to find a friend who also stays awake at night, so there will be someone to talk to if they can't fall asleep.

10. Encourage appropriate romantic intimacy and sexual activity if your EFM feels comfortable with it...and overcome your own possible discomfort.

11. When your elderly relative can't sleep, encourage them to get out of bed, if they are safely able to do so. That way, the bed will be associated with sleep, rather than with frustration, thus promoting better sleeping patterns.

12. Your EFM can call the many free "800" numbers to receive catalogues and information, to talk with a soothing, usually polite voice.

13. Keep a radio on all night, softly playing "easy listening," classical music, or talk shows.

14. Try to avoid sleeping medications unless medically indicated. Many of our parents were raised with the idea that there is a pill to cure every plight. Unfortunately, using drugs for normal insomnia are not worth the risk. There may be possible side-effects or adverse interactions with other drugs, even including some cases of suicidal and/or violent impulses.

Another potential problem with sleeping medications is that a groggy patient who goes to the bathroom at night can easily fall and break a hip. In addition, such medications may cause a patient to become dependent upon them.

7.   Is it okay for my EFM to have a sex life?

Even at this stage of knowledge about human sexuality, many people are still ambivalent or unwilling to consider such an idea. Sexuality is one of the most important aspects of life that families and health care professionals overlook in the elderly. Maybe, it's our Puritanical heritage, or the naive belief that at their ages, "Mom would never want sex, and Dad, if he does, would be considered a 'dirty old man.'"... Such an attitude on the part of society is very sad.

Whatever the cause, elder-sexuality is an undervalued issue in the care of our older loved-ones. Exploring sexuality is a meaningful way to affirm life and make it more worth living. It fosters a sense of belonging and self-esteem in the elderly, and quite simply, puts gusto back into life.

Studies show that a healthy interest in sex does not disappear as we grow older. In "*Love, Sex and Aging*," a study sponsored by Consumers Union, Edward Brecher reported that in the 70 years and older age bracket, 75% of men and 59% of women express a moderate or strong interest in matters sexual.

Even among men 80 years and older, fully 50% reported that they are still sexually active. Since there are more older women than men, it's no surprise that 43% of unmarried women expressed their sexuality through self-stimulation.

This is not to say that there are no physical limitations to deal with as we grow older. However, most of these limitations are psychological, rather than physical, which leaves great hope for a cure and a renewed sex life.

Some sexual changes take place as a normal part of the aging process, much the same as wrinkles and gray hair. As men age, they may find that it takes longer to achieve arousal or a full erection. The good news, for men and women alike, is that once obtained, older men can often maintain their erections for a longer time than their younger brethren.

As women age, they face changes in hormones, a thinning of the vaginal wall, and lack of lubrication. Of course, there are many lubricants on the market which can assist couples in facilitating intercourse.

Of somewhat more concern, is the fact that some women experience painful uterine contractions during sex. They may also have a slowed response to sexual stimulation and a shorter orgasmic phase. Thus, the lyrics, "I want a man with a slow hand, I want a lover with an easy touch," takes on an enhanced meaning. It is true that medications and illnesses can inhibit sexual function. However, I strongly believe that each one of us has the right to live a full, complete sex life. It is disrespectful to our older people to prevent them from expressing their sexuality.

One of the happy results of the more open expression of senior sexuality, is that we are seeing a great many courtships, and an increased number of weddings among the elderly. Viva romance!

8. How do I find a good geriatrician?

As I've stressed throughout this book, it is essential that seniors be treated by well-trained doctors who have been schooled in the field of elder-medicine. These doctors are already board certified, either in internal medicine or family medicine. Geriatric medicine specialists must pass a rigorous examination for certification.

But how to find the right geriatrician? It's not as hard as it may seem...

• **Ask a geriatric care manager in your community.**
One of the most important functions of a care manager is to refer clients to the best health care and other professionals who serve senior citizens.

• **Ask a medical doctor.**
Physicians generally know other well-qualified doctors in the community, and know which doctors to avoid. If you have a relationship with a general practitioner or a specialist, ask them to give you the name of a good geriatrician. If your EFM is in an HMO or other managed care plan, be sure to ask the administration which of their doctors specialize in caring for the elderly.

- **Ask a friend.**

Some of the best referrals come from friends and acquaintances who may be going through, or have gone through, circumstances similar to yours. If you know people who have elderly family members, ask them which doctors are treating their loved-ones, and whether they are satisfied.

- **Ask a local hospital.**

Many hospitals have referral services, part of their marketing strategy to get new business. They only refer you to doctors who are affiliated with the hospital. However, the referral service may refer you to an excellent physician, especially if the hospital makes a point of serving senior citizens.

- **Ask your local medical society or medical school.**

These are good sources for referrals to doctors who specialize in geriatric medicine. You might also try the Board of Internal Medicine and the Board of Family Practitioners.

9.   **What are HMOs, POSs, PPOs, and IPAs?**

Managed health care is here.* Today, one in five elderly citizens is enrolled in a managed health care plan, such as a **Health Maintenance Organization (HMO), Point of Service Plan (POS), Preferred Provider Organization (PPO),** or an **Independent Practice Association (IPA).**

With this reality comes complex new problems, undreamed of only a decade ago. One important role of geriatric care man-

_____

*About 10% of those enrolled in Medicare have already joined HMOs (25% in California, a state which is at the vanguard of every movement, good and bad). Both Republicans and Democrats in Congress want to shift as many elderly citizens as possible into managed care plans, to save the Federal government money.

The government currently spends approximately $4900 per person on Medicare. The 10% who are most ill cost up to $28,000 per person. Although a great deal of pressure and salesmanship is being used, the shift to managed health care is currently voluntary, but at some point it may become mandatory.

agers is to guide you through the fragmented managed health care maze, acting as your strong advocate and ombudsman, serving your elderly family member as a "surrogate adult child," and helping you to fill gaps and coordinate care.

If your elderly family member is considering joining a managed care plan, here are some things to consider...

When a patient goes to a free clinic, or enrolls in certain managed care plans, they may be assigned or will have to choose doctors from their roster.

If the EFM is lucky, their current private doctor will be on the managed care plan's roster, but even so, the relationship between aging patient and doctor may change. It may take much longer to get an appointment, and even longer to be referred to a specialist, if the referral is approved.

Your EFM may "fall through the cracks" with a new managed care doctor who doesn't know their history or personality.* The doctor may not have the time to carefully follow-up on treatment, or monitor their medical needs.

HMO doctors, for instance, are often required to serve as "gatekeepers," forcing them to divide their loyalty between their patients and their employer. Some HMOs severely limit doctors' fees, referrals to specialists, and testing. There is evidence that reaction against these new medical concepts may result in some regulatory action by Congress to protect the quality of care and make the system more patient-friendly.

Managed care plans sometimes pay doctors a *flat fee* per patient per month (e.g.: $27.91), whether or not the patient receives medical care. Health care plans contract with doctors or

---

*Unless you're an innovative 90-year-old, like Ted, who gleefully told me: "I had to change primary health care doctors," so I said, 'Doctor, this being my first visit with you, it's only fitting and proper that I tell you my previous family doctor knew me by name. How can I help you remember me, with all the patients you have?... How about if I were to tell you that as a young man, in the early part of the Century (remember, I don't look so young), I helped a fellow by the name of Howard Carter discover King Tut's tomb, and it was quite exciting.' The doctor laughed and said, 'I will remember you.' And now every time I visit, he asks me, 'Done any cave exploring lately?' "

medical groups on a *capitated basis*. Capitation is a specific fee paid to handle patients, over a certain length of time (usually a month), no matter what their individual medical problems are. Any additional, unexpected medical costs come out of *doctors'* profits.

Shorter hospital stays are becoming the norm. Doctors may be given bonuses for keeping the length of time patients are hospitalized below the managed care plan's accepted number of hospital days, eliminating "unnecessary" bed-days. Outpatient care replaces hospital care. Some hospitals are discharging patients to subacute care.

Such major changes in their traditional medical practices have increased patient-loads. It's understandable why some doctors involved in managed care plans would rather be relaxing with their families. After all, doctors are human too.

Managed care plans, created to solve the frightening costs of medical treatment which were escalating out of control, have created a whole new set of problems. This new reality must be dealt with fearlessly. A geriatric care manager can be of great help to relieve your anxiety and give you a firmer sense of security about future medical necessities.

Send for "Checklist for Comparing Health Care Plans," a useful free brochure from the National Patient Empowerment Council (*see Appendix G*).

10. Will Medicare pay for nursing home care?

Medicare will pay for the first 20 days in a nursing home, only if a patient enters the nursing home immediately after being in an acute care hospital for 3 days. After that, from day 21 through day 100, the patient must pay $92/day, before Medicare pays the difference. After day 100 of each benefit period, Medicare does not pay for further nursing home care.

Always check to see what the most current laws are, since they may be revised.

11. Will Medicaid pay for nursing home care?

Medicaid (Medi-Cal in California) pays most of the cost for unmarried patients over age 65 or disabled, who have under $2000 in non-exempt assets. Medicaid will pay for married patients, after allowing the spouses to keep about $76,000 of their non-exempt assets.

12. Should your EFM sell their house to qualify for Medicaid?

Most elder law attorneys and financial advisors believe it is not a good thing to do. The exempt house would be converted to cash, which probably would make the patient ineligible for Medicaid.

13. Can Medicaid put a lien on the house of a patient or their spouse?

Generally, Medicaid does not go after the house of a surviving spouse or patient who is a permanent nursing home resident. To find out the details, check the laws of your EFM's state.

14. What is Parkinson's disease?

Parkinson's is a neurological disease caused by a degeneration of the nerve cells within the brain. It usually affects the elderly. According to the American Medical Association, one person in 200 is affected by Parkinson's, with men more likely to develop the condition than women.

Symptoms of the disease may include: tremors, stiffness and weakness, resulting in a shuffling gait, trembling hands, rigid posture, and slow movements.

While both Parkinson's disease and Alzheimer's disease are linked to irreversible dementia, their causes and some of their symptoms differ.

Parkinson's may *result* in dementia; Alzheimer's is progressive dementia from its beginning. With Parkinson's, the *motor system* is affected, but the mind is usually unaffected for awhile, or not at all. With classic Alzheimer's, the opposite is usually true: the mind is destroyed first, then the body.

At present, Parkinson's disease is incurable. However, unlike Alzheimer's, some forms and symptoms can be alleviated by prescription medication, exercise, special aids in the home, and emotional support from family members and professionals.

Jim Spar, MD, from UCLA's Neuropsychiatric Institute (NPI), has taught me a lot about Parkinson's Disease. There are now Parkinson's medications which are extremely helpful for a long time, such as L-dopa, but the window for medicating can get smaller and smaller. Unfortunately, as the disease progresses symptoms tend to become more and more resistant to treatment. Sadly and ironically, drugs that control symptoms such as hallucinations, may often increase the stiffness and rigidity brought on by Parkinson's; while drugs that help the rigidity, may often increase the number and intensity of psychotic episodes.

There are also exciting experimental treatments for Parkinson's that show great promise. Be sure to consult with a neurologist regarding the newest treatment options.

Unfortunately, such interventions do not prevent the disease from progressing. In later stages of the disease, many sufferers exhibit characteristics of depression and dementia.

Caregiving is a particularly relevant issue, because the disease usually reduces the victim's independence over an extended period of time. If a member of your family is diagnosed with Parkinson's, it is essential to begin planning for their future care sooner, rather than later. For more information, contact the Parkinson's Disease Foundation, and join a Parkinson's support group.

15. How do I handle problems caused by dementia?

Being aware of common triggers for problem behavior can be a big help. There are a number of **triggers** which can affect your EFM, especially a person with dementia:

- Time of day ("Sundowner's Syndrome").
- Complex, demanding tasks (e.g.: bathing).
- Presence or absence of a caregiver (or certain other people).
- An environment with too much stimulation (e.g.: mall, party).

- A sudden overload of new information or instructions.
- Reminders of their loss of memory and functioning.
- Response/attention to the EFM who exhibits problem behavior.

16. How do I handle problems caused by dementia?

According to what stage of dementia your EFM is in, these suggestions, or modifications of them, may be very useful:

1. Try to determine the real cause of the behavior - frustration, change in the environment (e.g.: furniture was moved), change in daily routine, physical discomfort which isn't obvious, lack of communication with the caregiver.

2. Be consistent and stick to an established routine, which reassures a confused elderly person, even if it becomes boring to you.

3. Build on past habits. Don't expect an EFM with dementia to learn new ones, and don't get angry when they can't. Remember, you're dealing with a human computer without memory.

4. Provide simple, clear explanations of what is happening now, and what will happen in the *near* future, even if it is obvious to you.

5. Adopt a firm, positive, and supportive approach.

6. Let your EFM do what they can (and only what they can) without pushing, judging, intimidating, embarrassing, blaming, or shaming them.

7. Diversion with an activity can be useful, such as taking a short walk or listening to music they like.

8. Reassurance with a touch of the hand can go a long way in calming a person and communicating what words cannot.

9. Look at their body language. Respond to your EFM's feelings, as well as their words, or lack of words... Listen to the "melody" behind their "song." Pay attention to the real feelings behind what they say.

10. Logic doesn't always work, nor should it.

11. If outbursts are frequent and intolerable, medication

may be required, after consulting a physician who is experience with the elderly.

12. Allow yourself "free time" to get away on a regular basis, so you don't become burned out, ineffective, contributing to the problems.

13. Seek and accept help from friends and professionals.

Helpful hints (applicable depending on the severity of the dementia)...

1. Clearly print a list of the major items in each drawer and closet, and tape the list on the outside at eye level for your EFM.

2. Familiarize a friend or family member with your home, so they can give your EFM assistance if you aren't there.

3. If your EFM misplaces things, keep their glasses on a neck chain, and put their house keys on a holder which buzzes when they clap their hands.

4. Leave several scratch pads with pencils tied on strings around the house, so your EFM can make notes of things to remember.

5. Put an easily read list of important telephone numbers next to each phone, listed in the order of numbers used most often.

6. Write simplified instructions for taking medications in large print, posting it near where the pills are kept, and attached to each vial.

7. Make a list of each thing your EFM must do before leaving the house, number them, break down each task into its components, and keep instructions simple.

8. Put a card in your EFM's wallet or purse, giving clear directions to get back home, and to places they regularly go.

9. Write instructions to strangers/police on how to help your EFM and how to contact you, in case they wander and get lost. Put copies in the pockets of each of your EFM's shirts, dresses, or pants. Utilize the "Safe Return Program" of the Alzheimer's Association (*see Appendix G for address*).

10. Present new information slowly, clearly, and in small pieces.

11. Simplify your schedule and that of your EFM, so you only do things that really have to be done.

17. What if my EFM won't cooperate with the care they need?

One of the most heartbreaking dilemmas a family can face is the "Mom or Dad refuses to get help" scenario... For example, your loved-one may refuse to eat properly or to take necessary medication. He/she might smell bad because they won't bathe or take care of personal hygiene, endangering their health, welfare, and well-being. Or the elderly family member, who is obviously in desperate need, rejects all assistance and won't move near their adult children.

If you run into such a problem, here are steps you can take to handle the situation:

• **Try it the easy way:**
Bring in people whom your recalcitrant EFM has always trusted: a sibling, a child, an old friend, or a member of the clergy. Try to break through the impasse with old-fashioned persuasion. Stubbornness and fear can be dissolved through persistent, loving, personal intervention on the part of family or friends.

• **Contact a lawyer:**
If the older person still refuses help, unfortunately you'll have to contact an attorney to find out the state laws concerning such matters. In all likelihood, you will be advised to seriously consider getting a conservatorship. This gives you control of your EFM's financial affairs on their behalf and/or control of their personal decisions.

•**Contact an emergency team:**
Roughly 50% of a geriatric care manager's work is crisis-oriented. If you do not have a geriatric care manager, and the matter is an emergency, you may have no choice but to call adult protective services. They may contact a psychiatric emergency team (PET).

The PET will determine whether there's a reasonable chance your elderly relative is a danger to himself/herself or to others. If so, they will consider the senior gravely disabled and take them to a hospital for a 72-hour observation.

During this initial period, psychiatrists, doctors and other experts evaluate the condition of the patient to determine their long-term needs. Then, they will make a recommendation to the court if longer-term involuntary commitment is necessary.

The laws of each state vary regarding involuntary commitment, so if you find yourself in this tragic circumstance, be sure to ask the geriatric care manager, social worker, lawyer, or other professional in your case, what will take place, step-by-step.

18. What is a Conservatorship?

The most common form of conservatorship (sometimes called a guardianship) is of a loved one's estate.

When you are named as **Conservator of an Estate**, you are given the legal right to control the business and financial affairs of that person (known as the *conservatee*). The conservator pays bills, makes decisions about investments, files taxes, and otherwise controls all aspects of the conservatee's estate.

This power is not unlimited. Because of the potential for abuse or fraud, the conservator is supervised by the court and must account for income and expenditures of the estate. A bond should be posted to protect the assets of the estate, in the event that the conservator commits malfeasance.

Since this can be a lot of work, the conservator is paid by the estate for services rendered. The amount of compensation is usually set by court order.

If the elderly dependent person is physically, emotionally or mentally unable to control their life, a **Conservatorship of the Person** can be established.

This conservator has the power to make basic life decisions, such as where the conservatee will live, what medical treatment is administered, and the like.

When a court appoints a Conservator of the Person, they are also usually appointed Conservator of the Estate. If there isn't much money involved, such as when a monthly Social Security check is the only asset, Conservatorship of the Estate may not be necessary.

Conservatorships can be *voluntary or involuntary.* If the elderly person and the conservator agree, there will be few complications - just file an application and attend a brief court hearing, and you're all set.

However, if the proposed conservatee objects, they are entitled to a court hearing. The proposed conservator has to prove that the conservatorship is necessary.

19. Is there any way to avoid Conservatorship?

Many families prefer not to go the conservatorship route, because it can be expensive (a lawyer is usually required) and time-consuming (the conservator has to account for their actions to the court). Many want the benefits of a conservatorship without the burdens.

In fact, there are other ways to go:

• **Power of Attorney**

One valuable tool is the Power of Attorney. This legal power allows an appointed person (called an "Attorney-in-Fact") to act on behalf of the elderly person.

General Power of Attorney lapses if the elderly person becomes incompetent. *Durable* Power of Attorney, however, remains effective, even if the elderly person becomes incompetent.

Two forms of Durable Power of Attorney are: **Durable Power of Attorney for Assets** and **Durable Power of Attorney for Health Care.** Durable Power of Attorney can take effect immediately, or it can lay dormant until the person is rendered incompetent by illness or injury. Often, it has to be renewed periodically. Check your state law.

Durable Power of Attorney remains in effect indefinitely, or until the expiration of the state's time rules, unless expressly provided otherwise. However, if a competent person decides to "take the power back," they are absolutely free to do so at any time by writing a letter rescinding the Durable Power of

Attorney.

Unlike a Conservatorship, a Durable Power of Attorney does not require court oversight. On the plus side, this means no lawyers and no accounting to the court. On the minus side, there are more chances for fraud and abuse, thus it is fundamental that the person chosen to exercise the Durable Power of Attorney be trustworthy.

It is of great importance to fully understand the ins and outs of the Power of Attorney laws as they exist in your state.* You should discuss the matter with an elder law attorney, who can also prepare the necessary documents.

According to elder law attorney **Daniel G. Fish**, of Freedman and Fish, New York City, "The greatest challenge is to maintain independence in the face of disability. The Power of Attorney can insure that a person's wishes regarding financial and medical decisions are respected."

• Joint Tenancy

Another avenue many seniors take is to put a child's name on their property, so they become Joint Tenants. This makes the child an equal owner of the property. Thus, if and when something hits the senior, be it death or disability, the Joint Tenant continues to control the property.

Joint Tenancy has several benefits: it is quick, easy, and may not need the services of an attorney. However, many attorneys recommend against taking this route, because giving-up sole title to property also means giving-up sole control. Additionally, if parents and adult children ever get into a dispute over the property, a painful lawsuit can result.

20. Who will make my EFM's health care decisions?

There is much controversy in the news these days about "death with dignity," and the right to "pull the plug" on medical technology when death is inevitable and/or life has lost its meaning. This is a highly-charged issue involving emotions,

---

*You also might want to read "The Power of Attorney Book," Nolo Press (see Bibliography).

personal ethics, and morality. It also presents legal issues.*

Everyone should have the right to refuse unwanted medical treatment, including life-saving medical treatment. But what if one is unconscious or otherwise unable to decide for themselves? What then? Increasingly, many people are making provisions for such a contingency by signing a legal document known as **an advance medical directive**.

This directive allows a person to give instructions, prior to need, as to how she/he is to be medically treated, should a severe health condition prevent them from making decisions...for example if there's been an accident and they are unconscious.

The three primary advance medical directives are: Durable Power of Attorney for Health Care, a Living Will, and a "Do Not Resuscitate" Order:

- **Durable Power of Attorney for Health Care**

Many believe that Durable Power of Attorney for Health Care (also known as a Health Care Proxy) is the best of the advance medical directives. This document legally allows a person to select an "agent" (proxy) to make decisions about their health care, in the event they are unable to do so themselves. This proxy "steps into the shoes of the patient."

The beauty of the Durable Power of Attorney for Health Care is that it most closely approximates the powers a patient has when competent, allowing them informed consent or informed refusal of medical care.

The Agent or Proxy is authorized to ask questions, get sec-

---

*Many people have questions about the legality of assisted suicide and euthanasia. Currently, assisted suicide (patient kills self with advice from doctor or third person) and euthanasia (mercy killing by doctor or third person) are illegal in the United States. In the Netherlands, it is accepted, though not technically legal. In Northern Australia, laws against such suicide are not in force.

In 1994, voters in Oregon passed the first law authorizing doctors to write lethal prescriptions for terminally ill patients to use in order to commit suicide, but a federal court over-turned it. Since there is a strong movement for such laws, the legal situation is currently in flux.

ond opinions, authorize treatment, or refuse treatment. These decisions are based on instructions in the Power of Attorney, and on private discussions that the maker has with the Agent or Proxy about their philosophy of care.

The patient decides whether to accept medical treatment to prolong life, or whether to reject medical treatment if terminally ill or likely to be disabled.

If feasible, have the whole family come in to sign together. If your aging loved-one is hesitant or afraid of signing such a document, you may honestly say that it is a way for them to maintain control, by keeping the control over their long-term health care in the hands of someone they trust. If the elderly family member doesn't select someone to have Power of Attorney while they're still able to, in the future a stranger may wind up with control over their life.

The Durable Power of Attorney for Health Care gives seniors dignity and self-respect by allowing them to control their own destinies, even after they become incompetent.

- **Living Will**

This advanced directive instructs a doctor not to provide medical treatment if the signer becomes incapacitated and is likely to die or wind-up severely disabled.

The differences between the Living Will and Durable Power of Attorney for Health Care are as follows: In most states, a Living Will is only effective if the signer is *terminal* and unable to make their own decisions, while a Durable Power of Attorney does not require that death be imminent, only that the person who signed be unable to make decisions.

Another difference is that with the Living Will, a doctor decides whether the document is in effect, and then, carries out its instructions. With Durable Power of Attorney, it is the Health Care Agent or Proxy chosen by the elderly family member, who makes the decisions.

The Living Will has been touted as an empowering document that prevents unwanted end-of-life treatment. It has also been criticized for giving decision-making power to a doctor, rather than to a trusted agent or proxy,

The Living Will makes a decision before the exact nature of a medical trauma is known. There have been cases of Living Wills being misapplied.

Many lawyers advise having *both* a Living Will and Durable Power of Attorney for Health Care, since they operate under different circumstances and have different purposes.

- **"Do Not Resuscitate" Order (DNR)**

Terminally ill people may wish to sign a DNR to prevent themselves from being resuscitated should they suffer a cardiac arrest or respiratory failure.

DNRs bind medical personnel at hospitals and nursing homes, as well as paramedics responding to an emergency call. (Not all states include paramedic resuscitation.)

For more information on the benefits of advance medical directives, contact your local chapter of AARP, your local Area Agency on Aging, and Choice In Dying.

For information about the potential dangers of a "Living Will," contact the International Anti-Euthanasia Task Force. (*See Appendix G.*)

21. <u>Should I promise Mom and Dad that I'll never put them in a nursing home?</u>

If there is one thing that is extremely dangerous and harmful, it is to promise someone, or ask someone to promise you, anything of this sort. I have seen more adult children and spouses who initially made this promise, later overwhelmed by guilt and anxiety, because they had no choice but to renege on their good intentions.

You never know what is going to happen in the future. Please don't burden yourself by making such a promise to your elderly loved-one, or by soliciting such a promise from your adult children. It is unfair. The most that can be promised is that any decision will be made from the heart, out of love. That's the best anyone can do.

CHAPTER 11

Going For The Gold

You still sense the life in everything
and see the life in yourself.
Potential, that means strength,
the ability to find what still gives joy.
Even at the beginning of this 94th year
you teach us,
by your long life,
that each day is unique and worth living,
not just for you,
but for all of us.

- from "At 94," by Elsa M.S. Garcia,
in tribute to her mother.*

The time has come to take a small side-trip to discuss the underlying foundation of all that I do. On the surface, it might appear that the purpose of my work is for people to live longer. And that's true, as far as it goes. But I hope my work goes far beyond mere "survival."

The goal really is to go to bat for my patients, so that they (and their families) can live the best lives possible, despite their difficult situations. Sometimes it isn't easy, but believe it or not, it is often elderly men and women who wind-up leading the most rewarding lives of all.**

---

*Copyright © by Elsa M. S. Garcia. All rights reserved. Reprinted by permission

Much of the inspiration for my work, and many of the ideas expressed in this chapter, are the product of efforts and work by **Priscilla Ebersole and **Patricia Hess**, authors of "*Toward Healthy Aging*" (see Bibliography).

In this culture, which places such a heavy emphasis on youth, many do not believe that the elderly can lead enjoyable, productive lives. Old age is conceived solely as a time of losses: the loss of loved-ones and old friends; the loss of physical prowess; the loss of sexuality; the loss of health; and eventually, the loss of life.

Much of this can be true. Those who make it into their 70s, 80s and 90s do lose spouses, siblings and dearly-beloved friends. Many find themselves with significant physical impairments. And, as we all know, one of the two sure things in life is the process known as dying, which takes on a new and more imminent reality as we get older.

Is it any wonder, then, that many of our elders suffer depression and a loss of *joie de vivre*? But it doesn't have to be that way.

<u>Normal aging is not an illness</u>. We often treat the elderly with condescension, talking down to them as if they are naive children, instead of people who have experienced more of life than we have, who have wisdom and insights to offer us.

In most other world cultures, younger people look up to older people and prize their wisdom. In our culture, however, we often do not take either children or the elderly seriously. Not only does this unnatural attitude hurt them deeply, it also deprives us personally and impoverishes our culture.

Despite the multitude of losses that accompany the "golden years," millions of older Americans enjoy an exceptionally high quality of life. That doesn't mean they can run ten-kilometer races, although some of them do run marathons. Nor does not it mean that life is necessarily a bed of roses. But then, when is life ever?... Remember, roses have thorns.

What it does mean is that old people can often live lives of significance and fulfillment*...even if they suffer from illnesses or physical disabilities... even if they are what is called "alone in the world."

As stated above, a key part of my work is to contribute my knowledge and experience, so that the elderly reach their highest potentials at any given stage during their aging process. This can be of enormous benefit. After all, a quality life is a life worth living.

It is also of great use and value to the families who enjoy seeing their loved-ones living in "happy" circumstances. Watching an old person respond positively to my intervention gives me great personal satisfaction.

THE DEFINITION OF "QUALITY LIVING"

What do I mean when I refer to the "joys of quality living?" Well, I'm going to have to get a little technical here. After all, my colleagues and I spent years studying that exact concept. But bear with me. This isn't a textbook and there won't be a test. And, I promise my best to keep most of the "mumbo" out of the "jumbo"....

In the 1960s and 1970s, several notable scholars and researchers tackled the subject which I have defined as "quality of life." One of them, **Abraham Maslow**, a renowned humanistic psychologist, developed his Theory of Motivation and Development. He used a pyramid to diagram his thesis. The most basic needs a person must meet for life are at the bottom levels of the pyramid, while the needs which make life rich and fulfilling are at the top.

The pyramid represents an important tool...it is a framework I use for assessing and evaluating which needs of patients are being met, and which need to be realized. The pyramid can also be of significant value for the reader, when evaluating their family's circumstances (*see Chapter 8*).

According to Maslow, the goal for each of us, no matter

---

*For example, my own father, the **Honorable Raymond Reisler**, was a respected State Supreme Court Judge in New York well into his eighties.

Mary B. Moorhead, an Elder Care Specialist in the Berkeley area, writes about renowned painter Willem de Kooning, who painted some of his best work in his late 70's and early 80's, after a decade of depression and during the early phases of brain impairment, which was probably Alzheimer's. Art historians have even introduced the idea of *altersstil* ('late style'), a term used about artists who painted into their 80's and 90's.

what stage of life we are living in, is to "climb the pyramid." We should move upward, from meeting our biological needs (at the bottom), towards achieving **self-actualization** (at the apex).

Let's discuss each stage and relate it to the needs of older people...

Biological integrity

I'll start by stating the obvious: none of us can achieve self-actualization if we aren't alive. And at its most basic, achieving biological integrity means that you are alive and kicking. Anyone on this planet who is not six feet under has, at least, achieved the first stage of the pyramid. Congratulations!

**MASLOW'S DEVELOPMENTAL TASKS OF LATE LIFE
IN HIERARCHIC ORDER**

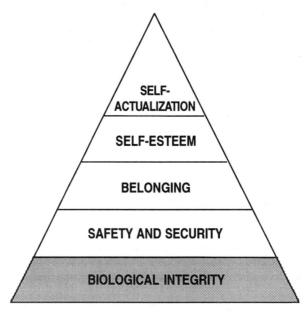

But biological integrity means more than just physically being alive. After all, even plankton are alive. No, as humans, we want much more than that.

Unlike plankton, we are not content to drift with the current. We need to control our environment to ensure our continued existence.

Most of us do this, to one extent or another, by providing ourselves with shelter, food, medical care, and adequate clothing, enabling us to move up the pyramid toward a meaningful life.

However, providing for even the basic biological needs may not come as easy for older people. Illness and the physical effects of aging keep many from exploring the higher aspects of human living.

In order to move up in Maslow's Hierarchy, many older persons need assistance, to a greater or lesser degree, with some elements of providing for their biological integrity. In order to achieve this biological integrity, older people need to attend to the following:

1. Seek adequate health maintenance services.

Just as an older car needs more maintenance to keep it on the highways, so too, an older body needs more medical attention. This is especially true because many seniors suffer from chronic conditions that need continuing medical scrutiny. A good gerontological internist or family care specialist physician is indispensable to the care of an old person.

There is a special certification that geriatric medicine specialist physicians can obtain from either the Board of Internal Medicine or the Board of Family Care Practitioners. If your doctor has such a certification, it is a good indication of their expertise and desire to engage in the treatment of the elderly.

2. Adapt to physical limitations.

One of the hardest things for many older people to do is to admit that they aren't spring chickens anymore. That is not to say, of course, that exercise and physical activity must be eliminated. In fact, just the opposite is true. Beware of using old age as an excuse to become a couch potato.

But if biological integrity is to be maintained, adjustments in physical activity must be made. Frequently, oldsters have no choice in the matter, as the spirit may be willing, but the body is weak.

The key, then, is to "make lemonade out of lemons"...roll with the punches, and take care to treat the body's physical plant with the respect that its advanced years dictate. Accepting limitations gracefully, and creatively adapting to them, vastly increases the chances for a rich and meaningful life.

One of the most common adaptations which must be made is accommodating the phenomenon known as "slowing." A prevalent misconception among the elderly (and their families), is that many think they can no longer perform the varied tasks of living.

This simply isn't true. Older people can and do engage in many activities, ranging from love-making to learning exciting new ideas and concepts. It's just that their pace is slower and more carefully executed. Adapting to this slower life style, both physically and emotionally, goes a long way toward preventing accidents, illness and stress.

3. Transcend the body.

At some point, the force of gravity and the passage of time must be acknowledged. The mirror tells us the honest truth: wrinkles can no longer be denied, hearing aids are a necessity, teeth are in a glass at bedtime.

Thus, in order to feel fulfilled, older persons must stop thinking in terms of the "body" and start thinking in terms of the "self." They must also learn to rise above their physical limitations of age and get on with the business of living, whatever that may mean to each individual.

Also, matters of the spirit often take on greater significance during the senior years. For many, religion and spirituality prove to be the essential key to a rewarding and contented old age.

Safety and security

Physical needs are not the only problems which must be faced. Moving toward a meaningful life means we must also focus on preserving our safety and security.

A safe, secure life is one lived without anxiety. This means a stable, protective environment to call home...whether it is the senior's own home, the caregiver's home, a residential hotel, a board and care, or even a nursing home. There must be a sense of physical, financial, and legal security.

MASLOW'S DEVELOPMENTAL TASKS OF LATE LIFE IN HIERARCHIC ORDER

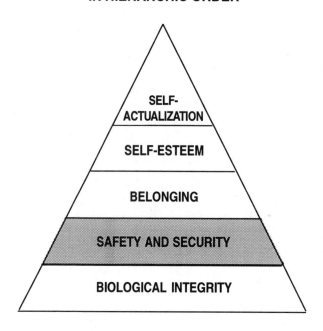

On the emotional level, one building block of quality living has to do with an older person learning to cope with the losses of old age, and the natural by-product of such major losses, depression.

As with many aspects of quality aging, life must be adjusted to meet the new realities. Thus, savvy seniors and their caregiving families will work on the following matters, in order to keep the safety and security aspects of their lives in good working order:

1. Budget income and energy to meet urgent future needs.

As we advance in years, we must recognize when the time has come to plan ahead. For some, this may be a small adjustment, such as moving out of the fast lane into the slow lane on the "highway" of life. For others, it will mean getting off the highway altogether, and onto a user-friendlier surface road, where life moves at a more leisurely pace (such as moving to a senior community).

Some may have to get off of the roads altogether, and stay on the sidewalk where it is safe and relatively risk-free.

Metaphors aside, older people have to learn to judge what they can and cannot do. For example, during peak income-producing years, it may be just fine to take one's savings and invest in a risky capital venture. While no one likes to lose, there will still be time to make the money back if the worst comes to pass.

However, in the senior years, unless an older person is one of the truly wealthy, such risks are more than a bump in the road. They threaten the very quality of life. Money lost will probably never be regained, and many, if not most, seniors need to use their accumulated estates to live on.

Budgeting income and energy is really a way of prioritizing. As we approach our later years, we simply have less of both to squander.

It is essential to use our limited resources (and all resources are limited) for things which are really necessary to fashion a senior life substantially free of anxiety and worry over the basics. Such a plan goes a long way toward bringing the "gold" into the "golden years."

2. Find a living situation which maximizes independence.

People who are old are no different than those of us who do not yet qualify for senior discounts: they want to live rich, fulfilling lives. A major building-block toward this goal is independence.

Of course, it is not always possible for aging people to live as the independent entities they once were. Declining health, a loss of mental acuity, and other impediments, frequently put a stop to their ability to live freely without assistance.

Many people are under the mistaken assumption that seniors must either live completely independent, or almost totally dependent in a nursing home. Nothing could be further from the truth.

Today, there is a tremendous diversity of life-styles available to seniors. Retirement communities offer an active life of fun and recreation in a secure setting, while retirement hotels offer increased assistance, with a more hands-on approach.

Board and care facilities allow as much independence as possible, yet give the utmost in personal care, including meals, personal hygiene, safety needs, and ensuring that medication is properly taken. Finally, convalescent hospitals provide for all custodial and medical needs of older people, within a skilled nursing facility.

The dignity and self-respect of your EFM are enhanced when they live as independently as their welfare allows. When a senior feels in control, living in a safe and secure environment which provides for their needs, many of the stumbling blocks to a satisfying old age will have been consigned to the junkyard, where they belong.

3. Learn to tolerate losses.

We have discussed the fact that old age is a time of losses. However, it can also be a time of gains. There is *always* potential for growth. Thus, while their health and vigor may decline, their spouses and old friends may pass away, many courageous elderly people are able to overcome their deep heartaches and get on with the business of living.

In this regard, my former neighbor, Mr. Abrams, comes to mind. He is a 98-year-old blind widower who still lives in his own house in New York. His vision and hearing may be diminished...but talk about enjoying life!

Mr. Abrams truly relishes his meals. He takes an active interest in those he loves, for instance, recently flying *alone* to California to be with us for an important family celebration. And he goes out of his way to help others.

A few years ago, I was severely incapacitated by a neuro-

muscular disease which left me somewhat enfeebled and using a cane. I visited my former home and met Mr. Abrams. He
insisted that we "hook up"...I literally became his eyes and he
became my sense of balance, assisting me in walking around
town. Meanwhile, my 80-year-old father poked fun at us for
being too slow!

Meeting such people is inspirational. They are positive role
models, showing us the potentials of old age, how our own
lives can be later on.

Many seniors turn to new activities and make new friends,
in order to get past the sometimes oppressive realities of old
age. This may mean enrolling at a senior center, where recreational activities, new experiences, and interaction with others
in similar circumstances, take the edge off the loneliness that
many old people feel.

Some seniors even find romance. Others may turn to
church activities or volunteerism. Whatever may turn on a
particular elderly person, once they "get on with getting on,"
will move up the pyramid to the level of "belonging."

Widowhood is an unquestionably real and tragic part of
life. Getting past this emotional blow is tough. But the only
thing to do is grieve, overcome the loss by accepting the cards
that life has dealt, and move on. As Art Linkletter says, "old
age is not for sissies."

4. Accept help when needed.

When it comes to matters of safety and security, financial
and legal planning are essential aids to maintain personal control over one's life. The fact is that matters of this kind are
much too complicated these days.

For example, a good **certified financial planner**, especially
one who specializes in working with seniors, will be of great
service.

If a retired couple has a decent nest egg, a financial planner
can suggest ways to maximize the income, while reducing the
risks of investment. A certified financial planner can also recommend appropriate insurance, such as long-term care policies, to assist in time of need.

In addition to an experienced financial advisor, sooner or later, most seniors and their families will need the counsel of an attorney who specializes in **elder law**.

Elder law is a relative new field which deals with the legal complexities and entanglements faced by seniors as they age. Elder law attorneys can help their clients in the following ways...

- **Estate planning**

Careful drafting of wills and trusts deals with the technicalities of gift-giving. Estate taxes are reduced or eliminated, probate costs limited, and passage of the senior's estate is provided for should they die. Taking care of such matters goes a long way toward bringing peace of mind. It gives an elderly person the freedom to look forward rather than backward.

- **Personal planning**

In addition to preparing for the end, an elder law attorney can also assist in planning for the time that is left. If an advanced medical directive is created, a patient will be able to direct their own health care decisions, even if incapacitated.

If the senior does not want the responsibility for health or financial decisions, a lawyer can prepare powers of attorney or conservatorships, whereby these powers can be delegated to trusted loved-ones or business associates.

Even if the older person does not recognize the need for assistance (e.g., when Ma refuses to adequately house and feed herself), the family can request an elder-law attorney to file for conservatorship, in order to protect the patient.

Conservatorship can only take place if the court finds a legal necessity for such action. A judge is the ultimate protector of the aged who are mentally incapacitated.

- **Financial planning**

An elder law attorney can also assist in times of tragedy, to soften its impact on the family. For example, if a spouse is stricken with Alzheimer's disease, the reality is that the victim will slowly but steadily deteriorate. Eventually, they will end up in a nursing home under constant physical care.

Medicare normally doesn't cover the cost of a nursing home, adult day-care, or in-home help. The immense financial expense that long-term care will cost the family can virtually bankrupt most households. So you must plan ahead for long-term care.

Steps must be taken to preserve assets. The government is attempting to make such financial protection more complicated.

This is where an elder law attorney can provide vital assistance. Through careful advance planning, often working with a certified financial planner, the attorney can conserve assets and prepare for receiving government benefits that will be needed in the future.

Note: Good financial planning is essential before benefits are needed, to prevent spousal impoverishment, which is all too common. If you wait until a crisis happens, it may be too late.

- **Preserving rights**

An elder law attorney will also be able to work through the courts to preserve senior rights (or refer you to a litigation lawyer who can). Whether the problem is denied Social Security benefits, or the loss of a job due to age discrimination, seniors can rely upon elder law attorneys to fight for their rights.

Belonging

With "belonging," we now get to the higher levels of the human experience, as illustrated in Maslow's Hierarchy. Belonging refers to the ability to love. A person who has such ability gathers a network of friends and loved ones around them, forming the healthy foundation for a loving environment in which to live life.

In the younger years, this comes more easily. We have significant romantic relationships which usually culminate in bonding, marriage, and the start of a new family. Friends flow to us through work, family, social and recreational activities, which are a natural part of an active life.

MASLOW'S DEVELOPMENTAL TASKS OF LATE LIFE
IN HIERARCHIC ORDER

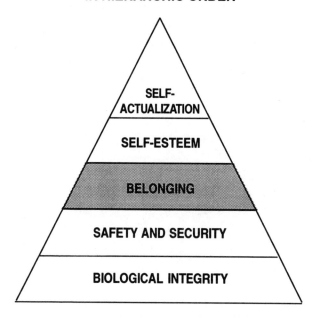

SELF-
ACTUALIZATION

SELF-ESTEEM

BELONGING

SAFETY AND SECURITY

BIOLOGICAL INTEGRITY

However, once we reach the 70s, 80s and 90s, life may not be so plush...

Spouses may be ill, dead, or especially these days, divorced. Children, who provide such a wellspring for feelings of belonging, have long-since left the nest and frequently live far-away. More than likely, they may be so busy with their own lives that they can spend little quality time with parents.

Old friends may be dead, too ill to socialize, or lack mobility. Drivers' licenses have been voluntarily given up or taken away. Public transportation is sporadic, expensive, and/or dangerous, since little thought is given by city planners to the special needs of the elderly. Walkers or wheelchairs make it too strenuous to get together often.

Life-long friends may have finally moved to be close to their families... far-away from the center of an elderly person's once-active social life. Neighbors are now strangers who have no connection to the ever-lonelier senior's life. Instead of the hoped for richness of old age, they may feel utterly abandoned.

Under such circumstances, it is up to the elderly who experience such threats to their sense of belonging to, as the old song goes, "pick themselves up, dust themselves off, and start all over again."

In short, an old person in search of a meaningful life may have to recreate their universe. Here are some vital things for them to do which will help...

1. Develop new, less intense relationships.

The ability to love, and to recreate a sense of belonging with new friends, is one of the most meaningful tasks facing people in the last stage of life. While these relationships may not be as intense as those in the past, they can still be totally rewarding. A major impediment to forging new relationships is that older people don't know where to look. But opportunities abound.

A *pet*, for example, is a marvelous giver and receiver of love, providing much-needed companionship. Dogs and cats are well-known for their ability to comfort people at unexpectedly deep levels. Petting an animal can be very soothing for your EFM. Neutered and innoculated pets are available at low or no cost through animal shelters and rescue organizations. Don't forget to get an I.D. for your EFM's pet, so it can be returned if it strays.

Even if health rules or living environments prohibit owning active animals, birds or fish can alleviate loneliness and give a sense of being needed. Caring for anything alive, including plants, is an extension of caring for themselves.

There are dangers to watch out for, such as an elderly person tripping over a sleeping or fast-moving pet. A pet is good if your EFM can see well enough, with reasonably normal gait, balance, physical agility, and sufficient energy. The EFM must also have enough money to feed the pet. The sad fact is that all too often, seniors must give away beloved pets because they cannot afford them, or are physically unable to care for them.

Relating to their human peers is certainly very fulfilling for the elderly, too. Membership in a senior center can bring with it a harvest of new friends, along with activities to enjoy together.

The elderly often thrive when they have contact with younger people. For most, grandchildren and great-grandchildren inspire delightful experiences. Even when grandchildren are not around, there are still abundant opportunities for meaningful interaction between the generations, such as volunteer work, church and service club activities.

For example, my client Esther (whose husband is my patient) volunteers with a disabled youngster once a week. She swears that the joyful satisfaction this work gives her, is more of a boost to her energy and morale than the strongest vitamin pill.

2. Serve as historian for younger people.

One of the most substantial contributions old people can make to a society is to share the wisdom of their years. When one contributes to the good of the whole, they experience a consummate sense of having value to others.

Now, it is said, we are a society that does not value such wisdom. It's true that we may not reward old persons with the respect that we once did, and which many societies of the world still do. But there are still innumerable possibilities to share the lessons of a lifetime.

In truth, opportunities to communicate about their long lives to willing and enthusiastic listeners abound for the senior who is willing to do a little looking.

3. Accept one's share of responsibility for the past.

Even the happiest life brings with it disappointments, missed opportunities, and mistakes. Who of us can say that if we had to do it all over again, we would have done nothing differently?

These "glitches" have value, although we may not see it at the time. Wisdom is achieved, in part, by learning from one's mistakes. And many dark clouds have silver linings. If we look back objectively, we'll be able to see that a lot of the best times in our lives have arisen, like a phoenix, from the worst.

The real tragedy doesn't come from disappointments or

failures in life, but from becoming embittered by them...blaming others for things that went wrong in ourselves...allowing the past to take the joy out of the present. Such negativity blocks the ability to change and improve life, and stops all future potential.

Seniors can prevent this personal tragedy from harming the rest of their lives, by honestly examining their lives and the circumstances in which they were lived. In this way, seniors may finally accept responsibility for what occurred, instead of blaming others or themselves for realities of life which were not under their control.

By taking one's rightful share of responsibility for the past, forgiveness can take place. With forgiveness comes resolution of old conflicts, and the re-establishment of the ties that bind.

I've seen the quality of clients' lives improved tremendously by reconciliation with siblings, or by forgiveness of parents/ spouses who may have died. And with the loss of bitterness, the bile of a grudge held close to the heart, comes the warmth of inclusion and love. This is what all humans need in order for life to be worth living.

Many people wrongfully interpret the tendency of older people to reminisce as an indication of senility, or being "over the hill." In most cases, nothing can be further from the truth.

Remembering the past is absolutely natural and healthy, as life draws toward its close. It allows an older person to put things into perspective and gain a sense of worth.

I strongly urge older people to engage in reminiscence and life review therapy.

4. Accept the death of a spouse.

When people die, there isn't anything we can do to bring them back. This may seem obvious, but the truth is, many old people stop moving forward when a beloved husband or wife passes away. It's as if life stops for them and they become mired in the past, waiting for the time when their bodies will cease to function.

However, the simple truth is that a meaningful life cannot be lived in the past. It can only be lived in the present, as each moment makes its inevitable way toward the future.

By refusing to accept that a spouse is no longer here, far too many seniors miss out on the sweetness that life still has to offer them. So it is every widow's and widower's task, painful as it is, to grieve, bury the dead, and move forward by interacting with the living. This is the way to achieve quality of life.

I know this is not as easy as it sounds. Fortunately, there are many options available, such as grief counseling and survivor groups, to assist a widowed senior in getting on with the job of living.*

5. Plan for death.

Finally, part of developing a sense of belonging in later life is to plan for one's own death. Morbid as this may sound, it is surprising how satisfying it can be.

In doing this, there are two areas which should be addressed:

• Identify a legacy and plan of dispersal... Each of us has the right to direct what will be done with our money, our property, and our physical remains, after our demise. We can significantly increase our sense of belonging to a family and to a community. The most effective way is by establishing our legacy, and planning for its dispersal according to our own specific desires.

• Implement the plan... This is done with a will, gift-giving, and instructions to physicians and attorneys. Once completed, seniors can go about life. They will have the secure knowledge that, even after they die, their presence will continue to be felt and their influence experienced by those who remain behind.

---

*For greater depth, I recommend the following books: *"On Death and Dying"* and *"Death, the Final Stage of Growth,"* both by Elizabeth Kubler-Ross (see Bibliography).

Self-esteem

Once we have secured a loving place among our family, friends and society, the next step toward a quality life is finding love within ourselves.

We have to get closer to who we really are. This is not our public image or our family role. Nor is it dependent on what we do for a living. It is much deeper than that. "Just me" is when everything else is stripped away.

MASLOW'S DEVELOPMENTAL TASKS OF LATE LIFE IN HIERARCHIC ORDER

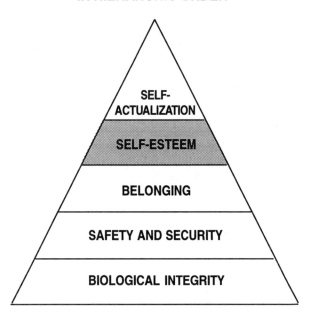

Sadly, loving oneself and achieving an innate sense of self, is profoundly more difficult than achieving a sense of belonging. After all, we're our own worst critics. To put it bluntly, it's not always easy to look into the mirror of our souls and like what we see.

Many younger people define themselves through material things - the kind of jobs they have, the type of cars they drive, their looks, and how attractive their lovers are.

Older people usually have to find a new approach. The material possessions of the world no longer carry the same weight in their lives, and may, in fact, be less obtainable. Their job is to find a new way to measure self-worth, coming to the realization that, "I don't have to be perfect. I just have to be me."

Here's how:

1. Cultivate the masculine and the feminine.

Generally speaking (and many books have been written on this topic), each of us possesses some aspect of the "masculine" (animus/ying), and the "feminine" (anima/yang).

The masculine refers to the logical, the protective, the active. The feminine refers to the loving and the nurturing qualities of the personality. Each of us has both the ying and the yang in some measure... We must, in order to be well-balanced.

For example, Harry had a fulfilling career as a city administrator. He managed a great many employees and administered a huge budget.

In later years, this hard-driving "masculine" personality suffered a severe heart attack. After his recovery, Harry retired and decided to explore the nurturing side of himself.

So he volunteered at a local hospital, working closely with patients. Harry loved this so much more than his previous occupation, even though he worked "for free." His days became richer and more rewarding than ever before.

Harry was actually given an award by the President for senior volunteerism. He flew to Washington and accepted the award in person.

Likewise, another type of personality, who has always been dependent and caring, may find it desirable or necessary to learn how to be more assertive.

Many widows have lived the traditional roles of housewife and mother. After the loss of their spouses, they develop the means to be in control of their own lives, which they would have thought impossible only ten years before.

The bottom line, then, is for each senior to develop his/her range of potential and humanhood, in order to become a more balanced person.

2. Separate identity from work role.

Retiring can be the hardest thing many people ever do, especially for those who attach a strong sense of self to their income earning activities.

Similarly, when the "chicks" leave home, the "empty nest" can bring a wrenching sense of loss, especially for people (usually women) whose "working" role has been primarily as homemaker and parent.

A tremendous vacuum in self-identity often occurs when the pillars of self-worth in younger years (working and/or parenting) are removed or substantially reduced. Many feel a dizzying sense of purposelessness.

"What's it all about?" is a question most seniors ask themselves as they enter the last stages of their lives. Failing to find a substitute sense of self to replace that which has been discarded or, as I prefer, outgrown, can lead to severe depression, loss of health, and even premature death.

3. Develop latent talents and interests.

Saying that one must separate their sense of identity from work, and successfully doing it, are two different things. It isn't going to happen by just sitting around and waiting for lightning to strike. As with other things worth achieving, it must be pursued and worked on.

Most of us have interests and talents which we have been forced to put on the back-burner during our younger years, in order to develop careers, raise families, and pursue the activities of an energetic life.

A good example of this is a patient of mine, who had always loved animals. After he retired, his beloved dog died. This led him to make a donation to a university for the training of future veterinarians.

Well, one thing led to another, and pretty soon this delightful older man became involved with the Delta Society, an organization which effects relationships with pets, convinces hospitals to allow pets in, etc.

Now, this former big-time show business type finds himself traveling around the country, giving talks on the importance of pets and the love they bring to people. Happily, he is more fulfilled by this selfless endeavor than he ever was in his "career mode."

4. Leave a legacy.

There are many kinds of legacies. People don't have to change the world, like Freud, Darwin, or Einstein, in order to leave a rich, lasting legacy. For some fortunate people, their children are their legacies. Legacies are also gifts to children, grandchildren, and the people who love you, because you will continue to reside in their memories and hearts. Help your elderly family member leave a legacy, and support their choices. Here are some meaningful possibilities to suggest to your EFM:

- Record an oral history, or write an autobiography
- Share memories
- Teach the skills learned throughout a lifetime
- Create works of art or music
- Write poems and essays about growing old
- Donate organs of the body to save lives and give hope
- Set up an endowment, scholarship or grant
- Pass on each prized possession to the right individual
- Give tangible assets to those who really need them
- Share their philosophy of life.

5. Achieve inner-peace and self-acceptance.

The key to developing self-esteem is self-acceptance and inner-peace is self-acceptance, firm in the knowledge that, "I like myself... I have value... My life is worth living."

Once achieved, there's a whole new meaning in that old advertising slogan, "You're not getting older, you're getting better."

Self-actualization

We are now at the highest state: a manner of being that implies serenity, joy, wisdom. Not that there aren't complications, for as we all know, into every life a little rain must fall. But there is an acceptance, an ability to deal with what is, and keep on going.

Little things no longer seem as consequential. It is much easier to simply get into life and what it has to offer. The self-actualized person lives from an inner-conviction, more absorbed in ideas and ideals than people and things. Eastern mystics call it "oneness with the universe." It's the highest sense of Self.

MASLOW'S DEVELOPMENTAL TASKS OF LATE LIFE IN HIERARCHIC ORDER

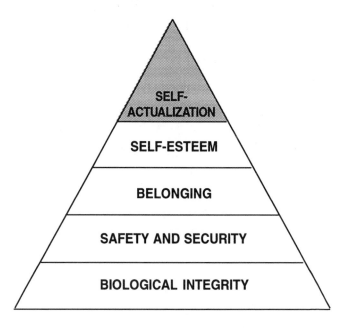

There are several traits which are common to people who live quality lives...

They are time-competent, that is, they live fully in the present, instead of fretting about the past or worrying about the future.

They are inner-directed, so their primary source for direction comes from within, rather than from others.

Their flexibility allows them to react appropriately and make the most of the moment, rather than allowing a rigid adherence to pre-conceptions keep them from realizing all that life has to offer.

They have a positive outlook about life and other people, realizing that the ups and downs of life are part of the greater scheme of things, which ultimately works toward the betterment of mankind.

They are capable of true intimacy, finding great joy in developing warm relationships, unencumbered by expectations of how others "should" react or behave toward them.

Interestingly, most self-actualized people are elderly. How is this achieved? How are people who may be infirm, suffering the loss of a mate or even their own children, able to overcome adversity and truly live? That's hard to say, but according to Maslow, they will:

• **Continue to develop curiosity**
People who are self-actualized continue to grow and search for new horizons. What these new horizons are, will, of course, differ from person to person.
The classic trademark of self-actualization is a person who is not living in the past, who does not feel self-pity over lost glories or missed opportunities. The senior who is self-actualized looks forward and asks, "What's next?" They squeeze all the remaining juices out of life.
Thus, one person may become a political activist who attends city council meetings to keep the rascals in line. Another

may be found at the center of their peers in a nursing home, comforting the ill and working to make life in the institution worthwhile.

A third may be bar-mitzvahed at age 75, or finally get a college degree. A fourth, like a beautiful 88-year-old I know, may arrange for authors to appear in weekly lectures at the city library.

In short, these people are living one day at a time, giving their all to productive and rewarding experiences.

- **Transcend ego**

Transcending ego is one of the most demanding things any of us can accomplish. It requires leaving behind the self-centered concepts of "me," "mine," and "I want."

Instead, there is a strong desire to be of service, to bring peace and wholeness to one's situation. Such selflessness is indeed a rare quality, but for those who are able to achieve it, the abundant rewards are the gifts of peace, tranquility, harmony and joy.

- **Share wisdom**

Older persons who are self-actualized become magnets for those who want to learn the secrets of a life well-led. Their need to serve compels these "human gifts-to-the-world" to share their knowledge with others, making the world a better place. They have so much to teach about how to live and die uniquely.

And if people don't want to listen? Since they've transcended their egos, self-actualized individuals refuse to allow their feelings and sensibilities to be hurt or shut-off.

The point of this discussion has been to illustrate issues I work with, assisting patients and their families as they deal with the ups and downs of life in the golden years...as they strive to enjoy quality lives. Now, let's see how all of this works in real life...

Nomie

The most self-actualized older person I know is my good friend and nonagenarian (ages 90-99), affectionately known by those of us who love her, as Nomie.

I first met Nomie when she baby-sat my children. Over the years, we became extraordinarily close...so close that she became their surrogate grandmother, rather than their baby-sitter.

Her life certainly hasn't been a bed of roses. When she was a 30-year-old teacher, she suffered a devastating stroke which put her into a coma. Unconscious for months, Nomie lost weight until she weighed only 58 pounds.

Nomie awoke that Easter Sunday, crying, because she thought she was at her own funeral. (Her husband was a minister, and her room was across from his church.)

It took years for Nomie to recover from the effects of the stroke. She had to re-learn how to talk, read and walk, like an infant. Such a daunting, depressing burden would have defeated most people, especially since this occurred in the 1930's, long before medical science had the capabilities to treat stroke victims.

"I'm French-stubborn," she says today, explaining how she was able to overcome such terrible trauma, "and when you're stubborn, you don't just lie down and give-up."

This stubbornness (courage) continues to serve Nomie today, although she has suffered the losses of old age: her beloved husband died, and she lost her only grandchild in a tragic accident.

Nomie lives in a very small run-down house, at poverty level. She requires a four-pronged cane to walk, has trouble sleeping, and suffers much back pain, due to degenerative arthritis of the spine. To add an irritating insult to injury, Nomie must also cope with *tinnitus* (constant ringing in the ears).

Despite all these painful obstacles, Nomie LIVES...boy does she ever! She is the epitome of what Maslow was discussing when he created his hierarchy. Briefly, allow me to illustrate, using the pyramid:

**MASLOW'S DEVELOPMENTAL TASKS OF LATE LIFE
IN HIERARCHIC ORDER**

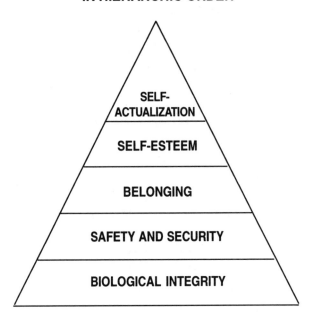

Biological integrity...

Nomie, despite her "French-stubbornness," has had to make compromises to old age. For example, she's been forced to give-up driving. When she kept falling, the time came for her to get a cane. Talking her into getting a cane was about as easy as getting the Palestinians to talk to the Israelis. But she has made the transition and has learned to live with this indignity.

Nomie has learned to slow down and think about every physical action, in order to keep from falling. Finally, she has accepted the fact that she needs assistance, and now receives home-delivered meals and housekeeping services. Luckily, Nomie has the support of an excellent doctor, who is knowledgeable in caring for the elderly.

Whenever she gets discouraged about her physical disabilities, Nomie says to herself: "You damn fool, you're alive! When you were thirty, they thought you wouldn't live. Now, snap out of it!"

As a result of Nomie's attitude, she has successfully come to grips with all the biological necessities of life.

Safety and security...

Nomie also has this priority under control. She lives next to her daughter, which provides a secure feeling that someone is there in case of need. A whole network of friends check-in on her from time-to-time. Although poor, Nomie is able to budget her money successfully, taking care of her own diet and other needs.

Thus, Nomie lives an independent life, while at the same time having back-up support in the event of need.

Belonging...

In the area of belonging, Nomie really shines. An active church member, she participates in as many activities as possible. She particularly enjoys working with church youth, all of whom enjoy her company and love her.

Nomie has accepted the death of her husband, from whom she was inseparable. To fill the gap, she's created many new, less intense relationships. I'm happy to say that this includes my family. Nomie is beloved by her friends, family, and many of my gerontology students whom she has been happy to meet over the years.

Self-esteem...

Meeting Nomie, you know that she loves herself. It shows in the open way she relates to others, her spontaneity, her continued zest for living. Nomie accepts herself the way she is. While she cannot physically do the same things she used to, she can still enjoy life.

Her primary passion is reading. Nomie devours books, reading about 10 every two weeks. She also enjoys watching educational television and attending lectures.

Nomie doesn't depend on others to make her happy. If you call, terrific! If you don't, well that's okay too...so no guilt trips.

Self-actualization...

Nomie truly lives by her inner convictions. She attends the church of her choice because it challenges her and offers ideas to ponder. In fact, Nomie lives for ideas and the joy of thinking things through. She lives a life of integrity, honest about who she is and what she believes.

When it comes to her own death, Nomie describes how she wept bitterly over its nearness. But she quickly got over the feeling and doesn't think much about the matter anymore, preferring instead to live each moment that she has left to its fullest.

Nomie is there for anyone who needs her, day or night, willing to listen or share her years of wisdom. She is able to accept whatever fate brings with a sense of dignity, self-respect, and resilience.

"I've seen so many people make their lives miserable, because they won't accept 'what is.' So they moan and they whine, and then no one wants to be with them. That's not my way, not ever."

I guess we could say that Nomie has it all.

Not everyone can become self-actualized, of course. But most of us can develop self-esteem and a sense of belonging. That's part of what I attempt to do: helping people live as well as they can, based on the extremely formidable challenges which they face and must overcome.

The same holds true for their families. In many ways they receive as much, or more, benefit from my services as do those whom I serve directly. And isn't that as it should be?

"Go for the gusto," I say, "and may the path always rise to meet your feet!"

Epilogue

It's best to close this revised Second Edition with a short revisit to my good friend Nomie. Now into her 90's, Nomie continues to perfectly express a quality-filled, highly-evolved life. She epitomizes the kind of life we should all hope to lead as we enter our final years.

After the last chapter was written for the first edition, Nomie suffered a severe gerontological crisis. One day, while carrying a pot of freshly brewed coffee to the table, she slipped and fell. The scalding-hot coffee spilled on her, severely burning her arms, face, and parts of her upper body.

Nomie tried to tough it out at first, but soon fell gravely ill. I insisted that she agree to be hospitalized, and her life was saved by exceedingly good medical care.

But Nomie grew uncharacteristically despondent. This was more than sadness and was quite atypical of her. Her depression grew so severe that I feared she was experiencing mental illness and called a geropsychiatrist.

Diagnosed with clinical depression, Nomie received anti-depressant medication, which worked to the extent that she could leave the hospital. However, she wasn't well enough to live independently back home. Nomie seemed to have lost that incredible drive and zeal for life which had marked her personality before the accident.

Her daughter didn't know what to do. I assisted her in placing Nomie in a small residential care home, where she was cared for with great love and skill. Nomie was doing so poorly that her daughter considered selling her beloved house, so she could afford a quality nursing home if it become necessary.

However, if there is one thing that is true about my wonderful friend, it is this: she may be knocked down, but there is no way she will stop doing her damnedest to get back up. And Nomie did.

A few weeks after her placement, I began to notice that Nomie's old feisty personality was beginning to reassert itself.

She became aware of her surroundings and began to talk about going home.

Within six weeks, I was astounded to see that Nomie was well enough to return to her little home...again proving that a <u>placement is not always permanent</u>.

Once Nomie returned home, she thrived even more. She accepted outside help to assist her with chores, ordered home-delivered meals, and allowed her daughter to assist with finances.

Nomie and her daughter have been able to resolve their old disputes and are getting along better than ever. She agreed to give-up driving, and to accept friendly calls from a local volunteer group that provides transportation.

Nomie remains active in her church. She continues to keep busy by voraciously reading the books delivered by a library service. This amazing young-at-heart old lady now looks forward to her 95th year.

When I grow into my nineties, I want to be like Nomie. She is a treasured friend and an inspiration. Her spirit typifies what growing old should and can be all about.

APPENDIX A

"Is Anybody Listening?"

In closing, I would like to reprint the following poignant letter, from the landmark book: "Medical Care in the Nursing Home," by **Joseph G. Ouslander, MD, Dan Osterweil, MD,** and **John Morley, MD:**

"I am an 84-year old woman, and the only crime I have committed is that I have an illness which is called "chronic." I have severe arthritis, and about five years ago I broke my hip. While I was recuperating in the hospital, I realized that I would need extra help at home. But there was no one... So I wound up at a convalescent hospital in the middle of Los Angeles.

"All kinds of people are thrown together here. I sit and watch, day after day. As I look around this room, I see the pathetic ones (maybe the lucky ones - who knows?) who have lost their minds, and the poor souls who should be out, but nobody comes to get them, and the sick ones who are in pain. We are all locked up together...

"For the last few years I have been reading about the changes in Medicare regulations. All I can see from these improvements is that nurses spend more time writing. For, after all, how do you regulate caring? Most of the nurses' aides who work here are from other countries. Even those who can speak English don't have much in common with us. So they hurry to get their work done as quickly as possible. There are a few caring people who work here, but there are so many of us who are needy for that kind of honest attention.

"A doctor comes to see me once a month. He spends approximately three to five minutes with me, then a few more minutes writing in the chart or joking with the nurses. (My own doctor doesn't come to convalescent hospitals, so I had to take this one.)...

"I noticed that most of the physicians who come here don't even pay attention to things like whether their patients' fingernails are trimmed, or whether their bodies are foul-smelling. Last week, when the doctor came to see me, I hadn't had a bath in 10 days because the nurse's aide took too long on her coffee break. So she wrote in the chart that she gave me a shower - anyway, who would check or care? I didn't say anything, because I would be labeled as a complainer, or losing my memory, and that would be worse...

"I remember how I used to bake pies and cakes and cookies for friends and neighbors and their children. In the five years I have been here, I have had no choice - no choice of when I want to eat or what I want to eat...

"As I write this, I keep wishing I was exaggerating...

"I am writing because many of you may live to be old like me, and by then it will be too late. You, too, will be stuck here and wonder why nothing is being done, and you, too, will wonder if there is any justice in life. Right now, I pray every night that I may die in my sleep and get this nightmare of what someone has called life over with, if it means living in this prison day after day."

- Abstracted from an anonymous letter published in the *Los Angeles Times*, September 23, 1979

APPENDIX B

The Tragic Progress of Dementia

Loss of short-term memory and impairment of judgment

This is not to be confused with the normal loss of memory that takes place during the aging process, known as **age-associated memory impairment** or **benign senescence**. Logic and reasoning deteriorate, so everyday situations become stressful problems that cannot be easily solved.

You can make life much easier for your loved-one by patiently listening and really hearing what they are trying to communicate, giving them clear non-judgmental advice, and leaving notes with simple point-by-point instructions.

Beginning dementia

Confusion may lead to unpleasant personality changes, such as self-absorption, mild panic, repetition, and withdrawal, because the patient knows something is wrong with them. Even more attention must be paid to the old person. Your verbal and written instructions must be simple and clear, as the person understands things much more literally.

Significant dementia

There is a noticeable loss of the ability to use words and put together correct sentences, a condition known as **aphasia**. At first they can recognize and correct their errors, but this skill gradually diminishes and disappears.

The patient loses the sense of direction and gets lost. They react slower and cannot process all the competing sensory information. This may lead to inappropriate or even aggressive reactions.

The ability to time and accomplish bodily functions deteriorates (a condition known as **incontinence**). Scheduled toilet times, or even diapers may be necessary.

Continue giving patient, simple instructions using visual clues, and slowly show your loved-one how to do things.

Severe dementia

By this time, the ability to understand language and instructions has greatly deteriorated. Incontinence is complete. The patient can be constantly agitated, and afraid of new things, people, and imagined threats. You must take their hands and slowly lead them through activities, using great patience, calmness, and sensitivity.

The final stages

Your loved-one may no longer respond to things around them. They may even become verbally or physically aggressive, attacking others and themselves. There is good evidence that gentle talk, soft music, a calm environment, and caring touch are of great benefit.

This will be one of the most exhausting, painful periods in your life, but if you handle it with as much humane care as possible, you and your beloved family member will feel a sense of dignity and love.

APPENDIX C

Definition of Assisted Living and Philosophy of Care

An assisted living residence has a special combination of housing, supportive services, personalized assistance and health care designed to respond to the individual needs of those who need help with activities of daily living and instrumental activities of daily living.

Supportive services are available, 24 hours a day, to meet scheduled and unscheduled needs, in a way that promotes maximum dignity and independence for each resident and involves the resident's family, neighbors and friends.

Assisted living facilities should:

- offer cost-effective quality care personalized for the individual's needs
- foster independence for each resident
- treat each resident with dignity and respect
- promote the individuality of each resident
- allow each resident choice of care and lifestyle
- protect each resident's right to privacy
- nurture the spirit of each resident
- involve family and friends, as appropriate, in care planning and implementation,
- provide a safe, residential environment
- make the assisted living residence a valuable community asset.

- Philosophy of care from the policy position of the Assisted Living Facilities Association of America

APPENDIX D

Employers and Elder-Care in the Workplace

An increasing number of caregivers are working adults. About 45% of caregivers under age 65 are employed outside the home. As life spans continue to lengthen, more and more elderly parents will require care from their families. The conflicting demands of our time and energy from family, job, and caregiving can be overwhelming.

Well-known eldercare researcher, **Andrew Scharlach,*** estimates that each caregiver-employee costs employers an average of $2500/year in time-off and turnover.

In a study for Metropolitan Life Insurance Company, Sally Coberly of the Washington Business Group on Health, and Gail Hunt of the consulting firm Gibson-Hunt Associates, Washington, D.C., provide an assessment of eldercare costs.

Their study of workers at one 87,000-employee industrial manufacturer focuses specifically on employee-caregivers who provide their elderly loved-ones with "personal care," such as helping with the basic needs like eating, bathing, and dressing.

Using conservative assumptions, the researchers conclude that <u>each caregiver-employee costs the company $3,142/year</u> in absences, work interruptions, added supervisor workload, medical and employee assistance costs, and replacing those who quit.

A national survey by the Families and Work Institute predicts that caregiver-employees will reach 18% of the total workforce in 1998. Women, usually the primary caregivers,

---

*Andrew Scharlach, PhD, is the Eugene and Rose Kleiner Professor of Aging at University of California, Berkeley, and senior research associate at Andrus Gerontology Center, University of Southern California.

comprise 46% of the workforce. The direct and indirect costs to employers of caregiver-employees will be over $17-billion dollars.

Caregiving can become an enormous added burden to employees' lives. For example, an elderly family member suffers a stroke and moves in to live with an employee, who then must spend many hours trying to arrange services for this person. Time-off from the job must be taken to transport the patient to medical appointments.

The caregiver-employee may come to work in the morning exhausted, after being awakened several times at night to help the patient to the bathroom. The employer, however, does not know about the problem, and may become increasingly exasperated by the employee's inability to concentrate on work.

The leading edge of the Baby Boomer generation is now moving into their 50's, the peak age for elder caregiving. By 2050, the ratio of parents who need support, to employees in their caregiving years, will more than triple, encompassing everyone from the CEO to the mailroom clerk.

Employers increasingly recognize that this trend will grow. Some have tried to provide Adult Day Care and Inter-generational Day Care, but it is costly. Other employers offer seminars on elder-care and information about community resources.

Forward-thinking companies often pay for a one-time assessment by private geriatric care managers of their key employees' aging parents or loved ones. Among the giants, General Motors is considering the idea. Such an assessment identifies individual problems and offers practical solutions.

This approach offers the best possible resolution for the employee, the elderly patient, and the employer. Professional GCMs are experts in doing an assessment which identifies for both caregiver and employer the problems...and brainstorming to propose the most cost-effective plan to manage the elderly person's care.

A solid care management plan can take a great responsibility off the shoulders of an employee, allowing him/her to have more relaxation time at home, and more energy to commit at work.

APPENDIX E

Standards of Practice of the National Association of Professional Geriatric Care Managers

1. While the "primary client" usually is the older person whose care needs have instigated the referral to a professional geriatric care manager, all others affected by her/his care needs should be considered part of the "client system."

2. To the greatest extent possible, the professional geriatric care manager should foster self-determination on the part of the older person.

3. The professional geriatric care manager should respect the older person's and, when applicable, the family's right to privacy by protecting all information which is given in confidence and all information of a confidential nature. It should be made clear to the client the limits of confidentiality as appropriate.

4. The professional geriatric care manager should define her/his role clearly to other professionals.

5. The professional geriatric care manager should strive to provide quality care using a flexible care plan developed in conjunction with the older person and other persons involved in her/his care.

6. The professional geriatric care manager should act in a manner that insures her/his own integrity as well as the integrity of the client system.

7. All fees for professional geriatric care management services are to be stated in written form and discussed with the person accepting responsibility for payment prior to the initiation of the service.

8. Advertising and marketing of services should be con-

ducted within all guidelines and laws governing the advertising of professional management services as they relate to the provision of professional geriatric care management.

9. The professional geriatric care manager who accepts a fiduciary responsibility should act only within her/his knowledge and capabilities and should avoid any activities which might comprise a conflict of interest.

10. The professional geriatric care manager should be familiar with laws relating to employment practices and should not knowingly participate in practices that are inconsistent with these laws.

11. The professional geriatric care manager should provide full disclosure regarding business, professional or personal relationships she/he has with each recommended business, agency or institution.

12. The professional geriatric care manager should participate in continuing education programs and be a member of her/his respective professional organization in order to enhance professional growth and to provide the highest quality care management.

13. The GCM should not exploit professional relationships with clients and families for personal gain.

APPENDIX F

Additional Acknowledgments

I am a "people person," and have built my practice based upon personal relationships.

Since this book, as well as my practice, is my legacy, I wish to mention some of the wonderful professionals and friends who have contributed to my career and my life. The list is quite long, so I ask the reader's indulgence as I pay tribute. If ever you have a chance to work with any of these individuals, you can't go wrong...

The type of work I do necessitates the need for excellent communication with specialists in the health care field. I've had to call up many at home and at odd hours on critical cases. Their professional commitment and dedication are certainly greatly appreciated by my clients and the many elderly people I serve, whose lives are often in our hands.

Among the MDs, who have supported my work, and been of invaluable assistance, are...

Psychiatrists: James E. Spar, Jeffrey L. Cummings, Dave Trader, Bob Kahn Rose, Steve Read, Gary Small, Dan Plotkin, Mike Frankel, Jack Dender, Steve Abrams, Keith Markley, Barry Friedman, Oscar Pakier, Irwin Rubin, Roland Jacobs, Walter E. Brackelmanns, Steve Soldinger, Herbert Ruderman, Stephen Klevens, George McAuley, Malcolm Valentine, Romeo Isidro, Scott Cherkasky, Cliff Feldman, and James Weishaus, MD.

Neurologists: Neal R. Cutler, Art Kowell, Lorne Label, Meryl Platzer, Ron Ziman, John Dietz, Ron Baum, Paul Rosenthal, and Steve Novum.

Geriatricians: Dan Osterweil, Joe Ouslander, Jim Davis, Bob Wang, John Hoh, and Kate Brustoff.

Internists: Burt Leibross, Nick DiDomenico, Al Kornbluth, Sheila Beirne, Gil Saliba, Peter Katona, Bob Goodman, Richard Minter, Lou Fishman, Mark Bamberger, Randy Pearlstein, Eu-

gene Fishman, Glenn Randall, Harry G. Cohen, Richard L.
Wulfsberg, and Mark Romoff, Frank Weil, Gary Profett, Larry
May, Howard Bliman, David Kayne, Edwin Shulkin, Armen
Dumas, and Sridhar Ramachandran.
Cardiologists: Julius Woythaler and "Venk" Venkatesh.
Urologists: Don Motzkin and Malcolm Cosgrove.
Endocrinologists: Helen Adelberg and Ken Honbo.

My work could not be complete without the committed help
of other specialists, including...
Psychotherapists: Erna Osterweil, Florence Miller, Gelene
Weiner, Linda Metzger, Francine Snyder, Judy Turner, Marjorie
Roberts, Donald Kern, Gina Clewley, Tanya Moradians, Amy
Gross, Harriet Soares, Max Fuhrmann, Marilyn Ruman, Karin
Marin, Diane Gough, Valerie Susman, Tom Glennon, Sylvia
Weishaus, Ph.D., Joy Brewer and Sandy Plone.

Neuropsychologists: Paula Fuld, Judy Zarit, Bob Tomaszew-
ski, and Rochelle Medici.

As a geriatric care manager, the lawyer/gero team is essen-
tial to preserve the rights of patients and their families. Par-
ticular thanks go to the following JDs: Marc Hankin, Barbara
Bergstein, Ruth Phelps, Stu Zimring, Leah V. Granof, Steve
Friedman, Howard Schnee, Joel Simon, Glenn Alperstein, Ralph
Palmieri, and Marshal Oldman, Linda Paquette, Alice Bennet
Juanita Miller, Bruce Givner, Katherine Ballsun, Bruce
Dizenfeld, Patricia Boldra, George Whitaker, Jay Fuller, Duane
Conover, Sibylle Grebe, Irene Silverman, Robert McGowen,
Mitch Karasov, Bruce Tammi, Michael Gilfix, Peter J. Strauss,
and Daniel G. Fish.

Financial Planners: Barry S. Siegel, Robert Knudsen, and
Bob Detterman.

Geriatric care managers, across the country with vision:
Rona Bartelstone, Leonie Nowitz, Sarah Cohen, Paula Hurn,
Evelyne Hutkin, Mary LaNier, Lenise Dolen, Eleanor Rubin,

Peter Belson, Deborah Newquist, Robert O'Toole, Suzanne Fritts McNeely, Roberta Weissglass, Sheila Bergman, Rose Kleiner, Susan Goldsmith, Cathy Cress, Monica White, Nancy Alexander, Steven Barlam, Elizabeth Bodie Gross, Mary Miner, Ann O'Neil, Pam Erickson, Pat Percival, Paula Tchirkow, Lois Brandriet, Dianne Boazman, Connie Rosenberg, Anne Rosenthal, Erica Karp, Judith Tobenkin, Miriam Berman, Catherine Thompson, Jacquelyn Efram, Elana Peters, Emily Stuhlberg, Joyce Engel, Rebecca Rengo, Connie Deschamps, Anetta Kraus, Mary Morrhead, Bev Shannon, Marcie Parker, Miriam Aronson, Irma Hausdorff, Maria Estrada, Pat Bowden, Sherry Johanson, Pam Goodman, Marilyn Carlander, Joyce Marvan-Hyam, and Alan McBroom. I'd like to mention many other excellent GCMs, but my publisher has a weight limit for this book!

Facility owners and executives: Jacob Friedman, Stephen Reissman, Sanford Deutsch, Emil Fish, Bernie Rosenson, Emanuel Newman, Steve Galper, Stella Henry, Ted Greenberg, and Ira Alpert.

Facility Administrators: Cathy Mason, Michael Torgan, Tim Coury, Anne Harbison, Bernice Holmes, Anne McCormick, Barb Lipka, Inga Jakobovich, Diane Parker, Jan Frank, and Tess Mohr.

Educators: Robert Butler, MD, Lissy Jarvik, MD, James Birren, Ph.D., Vern Bengtson, Ph.D., Neal Cutler, Ph.D., Ed Cox, Ph.D., Rita Wik, Ph.D., Norma Jones, RN, and Sandy Lampert, MA.

Adult Day Care Professionals: Lynn Engelbert, Marilyn Fried, Bill Martin, Eileen Haller, Betty Field, Alice Manion, and Roberta Morgen.

Special thanks to my friends who have made a difference: Rabbi and Mrs. Joe Weiss, Nancy Carter, Ellen and Marshall B. Cole, Kathrine and John Ayer, Erela and Ben Farber, Eric and Harriet Leibovitch, Alan and Gay Weinstein, Don and Evelyn

Motzkin, Elaine and Al Pasternack, Julie and Jim Norton, Melanie and Michael Smith, Mary Norcross, Kathy Hyatt, Georgia Davis, Martha Nields, Fran Schneider, Celeste Bocian, Barbara Miras, Marilyn Fried, Helen Moriarity, Harriet Wolfson Flehinger, and Betty Roark.

Other friends include my college cohorts Margo Bates and Chris Schneider, author Noriko Kaldma, poetess Nita Yore Kelsey, Silva Andonian, Conley Falk, Marjorie Diamond, Susan Latta, Jan Andrew, Barry S. Siegel, Eileen Fletcher, Daga Peterson, Terry Voges, Barbara Bergstein, Mark Hankin, Jenny Feuerstein, Ellen Tischler, Karen White, Pat Jackson, Darlene Weiner.

Also, Carla Schlessinger, Rona Bartelstone, Leonie Nowitz, Evelyn Hutkin, Florence Miller, Ilene Gold, Sue Ackerman, Flip Cornwell, Sue and Al Ruh, Jack and Annie Dender, Linda Metzger, Maria Robles, Agnes Lacsamana, Micha Shtrol, Angela Anastasi, Cathy Mason, Dave Trader, Vera Tweed, Sharon Wolfe, Cookie Lewis, Fran Schwartz, Joyce Flint, Leslie Downie, Viki Mason, and Donna Malouf.

My gratitude to Lita Weissman and Cynthia Leggitt from Barnes & Noble.

Last but not least, much appreciation goes to my typist Cheryl Sager who always has more work than is possible to do—and still gets the job done.

APPENDIX G

Resources, Referrals, and Assistance

ADMINISTRATION ON AGING
Dept. of Health and Human Services, 330 Independence Ave., Washington, DC 20201, 202/619-0724.

ALZHEIMER'S ASSOCIATION
(Publishes many informative brochures. Has listing of all large-scale clinical Alzheimer drug trials which are recruiting patients.) 919 N. Michigan Ave., #1000, Chicago, IL 60611-1676, 800/272-3900, 800/621-0379, 312/335-5729. (Internet: http://www.alz.org)

ALZHEIMER'S DISEASE EDUCATION AND REFERRAL CENTER (ADEAR)
(Publishes "Home Safety for the Alzheimer's Patient" and many other informative brochures. Provides education and support.) PO Box 8250, Silver Spring, MD, 20907-8250, 800/438-4380.(Internet: adear@alzheimers.org)

ALZHEIMER'S DISEASE RESEARCH CENTER
225 Dickinson St., San Diego, CA 92103-1990, 619/543-5306.

AMERICAN ACADEMY OF ORTHOPAEDIC SURGEONS
(Publishes free brochure: "Live It Safe: Preventing Hip Fractures.") PO Box 1998, Des Plaines, IL 60017.

AMERICAN ASSOCIATION FOR CONTINUITY OF CARE
(Non-profit organization of multi-disciplinary health care professionals promoting continuity of care. Publishes: "Access" Magazine.) 638 Prospect Ave., Hartford, CT 06105-4250, 203/586-7525.

AMERICAN ASSOCIATION OF HOMES AND SERVICES FOR THE AGING
(Represents 4800 non-profit organizations dedicated to providing quality health care, housing and services to the elderly. Publishes: "Currents Newsletter," and "The Future of Continuing Care Retirement Communities.") 901 "E" St., NW, #500, Washington, DC 20004-2037, 800/508-9442.

AMERICAN ASSOCIATION FOR MARITAL AND FAMILY THERAPY
(If the stress of caregiving is breaking up your family, ask for a referral to a counselor near you.) 800/374-2638.

AMERICAN ASSOCIATION OF RETIRED PERSONS (AARP)
(Largest organization for seniors. Source of information and help, such as their Widowed Persons Service. Publishes "Modern Maturity" magazine, and product reports on hearing aids, PERS systems, wheelchairs, life insurance, living trusts and wills, funerals.) 601 "E" St., NW, Washington, DC 20049, 800/424-3410, 202/434-2277.

AMERICAN BOARD OF MEDICAL SPECIALISTS
(Find out if a doctor is Board-Certified.) 800/776-2378.

AMERICAN CANCER SOCIETY
1599 Clifton Rd., NE, Atlanta, GA 30329, 800/227-2345.

AMERICAN COUNCIL ON THE BLIND
1155 - 15th St., NW, Washington, DC 20005, 800/424-8666.

AMERICAN COUNCIL FOR HEADACHE EDUCATION
800/255-2243.

AMERICAN DENTAL ASSOCIATION
211 E. Chicago Ave., Chicago, IL 60611, 312/440-2500.

AMERICAN DIABETES ASSOCIATION
1660 Duke St., Alexandria, VA 22314, 800/232-3472, 800/342-2383.

AMERICAN DIETETIC ASSOCIATION - CONSUMER NUTRITION
800/366-1655.

AMERICAN HEALTH CARE ASSOCIATION
(Publishes: "Professional Development Catalogue," resources for health care.) 1201 "L" St., NW, Washington, DC 20005, 800/321-0343, 202/842-4444.

AMERICAN HEART ASSOCIATION
7272 Greenville Ave., Dallas, TX 75231, 800/242-8721, 214/373-6300.

AMERICAN LIVER FOUNDATION
1425 Pompton Ave., Cedar Grove, NJ 07009, 800/223-0179.

AMERICAN LUNG ASSOCIATION
1740 Broadway, New York, NY 10019-4374, 800/586-4872.

AMERICAN MEDICAL ASSOCIATION (AMA)
800/621-8335.

AMERICAN OPTOMETRIC ASSOCIATION
314/991-4100.

AMERICAN PARALYSIS ASSOCIATION
500 Morris Ave., Springfield, NJ 07081, 800/225-0292.

AMERICAN PARKINSON'S DISEASE ASSOCIATION
(Publishes: "Handbook" and "Be Active: A Suggested Exercise Program.") 1250 Hylan Blvd., #4B, Staten Island, NY 10305, 800/223-2732, 718/981-8001.

AMERICAN PHARMACEUTICAL RESEARCH COMPANIES
(Publishes: "HealthMatters.") 800/862-4110.

AMERICAN SOCIETY ON AGING
833 Market St., #511, San Francisco, CA 94103-1824, 415/974-9600.

AMERICAN SPEECH - LANGUAGE-HEARING ASSOCIATION
10801 Rockville Pike, Rockville, MD 20852, 800/638-8255.

ARTHRITIS FOUNDATION
1314 Spring St., NW, Atlanta, GA 30309, 800/283-7800.

ASSISTED LIVING FACILITIES ASSOCIATION OF AMERICA
(National non-profit trade organization dedicated to enhancing the quality of life in assisted living residences. Provides a forum for consumers and professionals. Publishes: "Assisted Living Today" magazine.) 9411 Lee Highway, #J, Fairfax, VA 22031, 703/691-8100.

ASSOCIATION FOR GERONTOLOGY IN HIGHER EDUCATION
(Promotes intergenerational education.) 1001 Connecticut Ave. NW, #410, Washington, DC 20036, 202/842-1275.

BETTER SLEEP COUNCIL
333 Commerce St., Alexandria, VA 22314, 703/683-8371.

CALIFORNIA DEPARTMENT OF AGING
600 "K" St., Sacramento, CA 95814, 916/322-2887.

CALIFORNIA PARTNERSHIP FOR LONG-TERM CARE
714 "P" St., #616, Sacramento, CA 95814, 800/434-0222.

CENTER FOR THE STUDY OF SERVICES
(Non-profit group. Publishes: "Consumers' Guide to Health Plans," with advice, ratings of 250 HMOs, and consumer satisfaction.) 733 - 15th St. NW, Washington, DC 20005, 800/475-7283.

CENTER FOR UNDERSTANDING AGING
PO Box 246, Southington, CT 06489-0246.

CENTERS FOR DISEASE CONTROL AND PREVENTION - NATIONAL AIDS HOTLINE
800/342-2437 (24 hrs.); 800/344-7432 (in Spanish).

CHILDREN OF AGING PARENTS
1609 Woodbourne Rd., #302A, Levittown, PA 19057-1511, 800/227-7294, 215/945-6900.

CHOICE IN DYING
(Makes copies of the "Living Will" available.) 200 Varick St., New York, NY 10014, 800/989-9455.

COMMISSION ON ACCREDITATION OF HEALTHCARE ORGANIZATIONS
(Issues performance reports on individual hospitals.) 708/916-5800.

COMPASSION IN DYING
Non-profit organization which supports the right of terminally-ill patients to choose to die without suffering and pain, offering guidance and assistance.) PO Box 75295, Seattle, WA 98125-0295, Tel: 206/624-2775, Fax: 206/624-2673.

COMPASSIONATE FRIENDS
(Bereaved parents.) PO Box 3696, Oak Brook, IL 60522, 708/990-0010.

ELDER ABUSE HOTLINE
800/992-1660.

ELDERCARE LOCATOR
(Area Agencies on Aging's national referral service for nursing homes: gives phone numbers of resource agencies, but cannot make recommendations. Also provides information on home care fraud and other complaints.) 1112 - 16th St., NW, #100, Washington, DC 20036, 800/677-1116.

ELDER CRAFTSMEN
(Encourages all elderly people to be creative, productive, and independent. Offers intergenerational programs, training programs, selling handicrafts.) 921 Madison Ave., New York, NY 10021, 212/861-5260.

ELDER GAMES
(Publications and activities designed to stimulate the memories and imaginations of older adults.) 800/637-2604.

ELDERMED AMERICA
(Offers discounts for prescriptions, dental, eyeglasses, travel, etc.) 800/227-3463.

THE ELF TEAM
(Emotional, legal, and financial problems associated with aging. Consultations and referrals for homecare, adult day-care, alternative living arrangements, medical and geriatric professionals.) See: GAP

FAMILY CAREGIVERS ALLIANCE
(Focuses on the caregiver of patients with any type of brain impairment received after age 18. Excellent source of referrals for Alzheimer's, Parkinson's, respite care, counseling, support groups. Publishes "Hiring In-Home Help," and information in Spanish and Chinese.) 425 Bush St., #500, San Francisco, CA 94108, 415/434-3388; 800/445-8106 (in California only).

FAMILY SERVICE AMERICA
(International non-profit association dedicated to strengthening family life through services, education, and advocacy. Assists with elder care problems, parent-child tensions, family violence,

marital difficulties.) 11700 W. Lake Park Dr., Milwaukee, WI 53224, 800/221-2681.

FOOD AND DRUG ADMINISTRATION - CONSUMER AFFAIRS
5600 Fishers Lane, #HFE-88, Rockville, MD 20857, 301/443-3170.

FOOD AND NUTRITION INFORMATION CENTER
U.S. Dept. of Agriculture, National Agricultural Library, 10301 Baltimore Blvd., #304, Beltsville, MD, 407/705-2351.

FOR WIDOWS ONLY
(Support groups and information.) 800/554-9436.

FOSTER GRANDPARENT PROGRAM
(See: NATIONAL SENIOR VOLUNTEER CORPS)

FOUNDATION FOR LONG TERM CARE
194 Washington Ave., Albany, NY 12210, 518/449-7873.

GAP
(GERONTOLOGY ASSOCIATES, ALZHEIMER'S CASE MANAGEMENT ASSOCIATES, PROFESSIONAL NURSING HOME PLACEMENT SERVICES.) Nancy Wexler, MA, MFCT, Director. 800/626-2993, 818/342-3136, 310/475-0810; fax: 818/881-5225.

GENERATIONS UNITED
(Cooperative coalition of 130 nonprofit organizations representing 70 million Americans. Examines intergenerational issues; promotes programs for aging and children's networks to work together for their mutual well-being.) 440 First St., NW, #310, Washington, DC 20001, 202/638-2952.

THE GERONTOLOGICAL SOCIETY OF AMERICA
(Publishes "The Gerontologist," an excellent magazine for professionals.) 1275 "K" St., NW, #350, Washington, DC 20005-4006, 202/842-1150, 202/842-1275. (Internet: majordomo@po.cwru.edu)

GRANDPARENT INFORMATION CENTER
AARP, 601 "E" St., NW, Washington, DC 20049, 202/2434-2296.

GRAY PANTHERS
(Effective, honorable activist group which fights for the rights of the elderly, founded and administered by senior citizens.) 1424 - 16th St., NW, Washington, DC 20036, 202/387-3111.

HEALTH INSURANCE COUNSELING AND ADVOCACY PROGRAM
(Referrals, free community education and counseling on Medicare, supplement policies, HMOs, and long-term health insurance.) California Department of Aging, 800/824-0780, 800/434-0222.

HEREDITARY DISEASE FOUNDATION
(An organization with integrity, spending less than 1% of contributions for salaries, office expenses, and fund-raising...the lowest in the U.S.) 1427 - 7th St., #2, Santa Monica, CA 904401.

HMO HOTLINE
(California only: to report complaints.) 800/400-0815.

INTERNATIONAL ANTI-EUTHANASIA TASK FORCE
PO Box 760, Steubenville, OH 43952.

IMPOTENCE INFORMATION CENTER
PO Box 9, Minneapolis, MN 55440, 800/843-4315.

MEALS ON WHEELS
(Provides nutritious hot meals at minimum cost, nationwide.) 616/531-9909.

MEDI-CAL (California only)
Dept. of Health Services, Sacramento, CA 95814, 800/541-5555.

MEDIC ALERT
(Provides bracelets with medical information and warnings.) Turlock, CA 95381, 800/344-3226.

MEDICAL BUSINESS ASSOCIATES
(Will handle all medical bills and insurance claims for one low monthly fee. Sponsored by United Seniors Health Cooperative.) 800/659-3171.

MEDICAL DIRECTIVE
(Information and forms on Power of Attorney, organ donor, medical choices for the elderly and dying.) PO Box 6100, Holliston, MA 01746-6100, 800/214-4553.

MEDICARE
(Publishes free pamphlets in English and Spanish: "The Medicare 1996 Handbook," "Medicare and Managed Care Plans," "Guide to Health Insurance for People with Medicare.") 800/772-1213, 800/638-6833.

MEDICARE BENEFICIARIES DEFENSE FUND
(National not-for-profit organization providing assistance and information to people with disabilities on Medicare.) 1460 Broadway, 8th Floor, New York, NY 10036, 212/869-3850.

MEDICARE FRAUD AND ABUSE
(To report health-care providers who are abusing the system.) 800/447-8477.

MENTAL HEALTH FACILITY LOCATOR
800/262-4444 (24-hours).

NATIONAL ACADEMY ON AGING
1275 "K" St., NW, #350, Washington, DC 20005, 202/408-3375.

NATIONAL ACADEMY OF ELDER LAW ATTORNEYS (NAELA)
1604 N. Country Club Rd., Tucson, AZ 85716, 520/881-4005.

NATIONAL AIDS TREATMENT HOTLINE
800/822-7422, 800/344-7432 (Spanish), 800/243-7889 (TDD/Deaf Access).

NATIONAL ALLIANCE FOR THE MENTALLY ILL
200 Glebe Rd., #1015, Arlington, VA 22203-3754, 800/950-6264.

NATIONAL ASSOCIATION OF AREA AGENCIES ON AGING
800/677-1116, 202/296-8130.

NATIONAL ASSOCIATION OF THE DEAF
(Has 4000 captioned films and videos for free loan to the hearing impaired.) 1447 E. Main St., Spartanburg, SC 29307, 800/237-6213.

NATIONAL ASSOCIATION FOR HOME CARE
(Largest national trade association working on behalf of home care and hospice. Publishes "Caring" magazine and "Homecare News.") 519 "C" St., NW, Washington, DC 20002, 202/547-7424.

NATIONAL ASSOCIATION OF PROFESSIONAL GERIATRIC CARE MANAGERS (GCM)
1604 N. Country Club Rd., Tucson, AZ 85716, 520/881-8008, fax: 520/325-7925

NATIONAL ASSOCIATION FOR VISUALLY HANDICAPPED
(Large-print library for loan at no charge.) 3201 Balboa St., San Francisco, CA 94121, 415/221-3201.

NATIONAL BONE MARROW BANK
800/627-7692.

NATIONAL CENTER ON ELDER ABUSE
810 First Street, NE, #500, Washington, DC 20002, 202/682-2470.

NATIONAL CENTER FOR HOME EQUITY CONVERSION

(Publishes list of public and private sector reverse mortgage programs, useful as a method to get cash without selling your EFM's home.) 7373 - 147th St., West Apple Valley, MN 55124, 612/953-4474.

NATIONAL CITIZENS' COALITION FOR NURSING HOME REFORM

1424 - 16th St., NW, #202, Washington, DC 20036, 202/332-2275.

NATIONAL CLEARINGHOUSE FOR ALCOHOL AND DRUG INFORMATION

(Information on the diseases/addictions affecting 2.5 million older adults.) PO Box 2345, Rockville, MD 20847-2345, 800/729-6686.

NATIONAL COMMITTEE FOR QUALITY ASSURANCE

(Evaluations of HMOs.) 202/628-5788.

NATIONAL CONSUMERS LEAGUE

(Publishes "Consumer's Guide to Life-Care Communities.") 815 - 15th St., NW, #928-N, Washington, DC 20005.

NATIONAL COUNCIL ON AGING

409 Third St., SW, #200, Washington, DC 20024, 800/424-9046.

NATIONAL COUNCIL OF SENIOR CITIZENS

1331 "F" St., NW, Washington, DC 20004, 202/347-8800.

NATIONAL ELECTRONIC ARCHIVE OF ADVANCE DIRECTIVES

(Registry that stores and instantly sends living wills, medical power of attorneys, and medical instructions to hospitals and doctors.) 11000 Cedar Ave., Cleveland, OH 44106, 800/379-6866.

NATIONAL EYE INSTITUTE

2020 Vision Place, Bethesda, MD 20892-3658.

NATIONAL FOUNDATION FOR DEPRESSIVE ILLNESS
(Major depression strikes about 15% of the population.) 800/ 245-4381.

NATIONAL FRAUD INFORMATION CENTER
(To report telephone scams against the elderly.) 800/876-7060.

NATIONAL HEALTH INFORMATION CENTER
(Publications, referrals, databases, disease prevention.) PO Box 1133, Washington, DC 20013-1133, 800/336-4797 (Spanish-speaking operators available).

NATIONAL HOSPICE ORGANIZATION
1901 N. Moore St., #901, Arlington, VA 22209, 800/658-8898, 713/ 243-5900.

NATIONAL INSTITUTE OF ADULT DAY-CARE
National Council on the Aging, 409 - 3rd St., SW, 2nd Floor, Washington, DC 20024, 202/479-1200.

NATIONAL INSTITUTE ON AGING
(Information and literature in English and Spanish.) P.O. Box 8057, Gaithersburg, MD 20898-8057, 800/438-4380, 222-2225.

NATIONAL INSTITUTE OF ARTHRITIS, MUSCULOSKELETAL, AND SKIN DISEASES INFORMATION CLEARINGHOUSE
(40 million Americans have arthritis, 30 million have osteoporosis or other bone disorders, 60 million see doctors for skin diseases, 8 in 10 have back problems. These diseases cost over $100 billion/year.) National Institute of Health, 1 AMS Circle, Bethesda, MD 20892-3675, 301/495-4484.

NATIONAL INSTITUTE ON DEAFNESS & COMMUNICATION DISORDERS
1 Communication Ave., Bethesda, MD 20892-3456, 800/241-1044.

NATIONAL INSTITUTE OF MENTAL HEALTH
(Information on anxiety disorders, etc.) 5600 Fishers Lane, Room 7C-02, Rockville, MD 20857, 800/64-PANIC (24-hrs.)

NATIONAL INSTITUTE OF NEUROLOGICAL DISORDERS AND STROKE
(Publishes "Parkinson's Disease, Hope Through Research") National Institute of Health, PO Box 5801, Bethesda, MD 20824, 800/352-9424.

NATIONAL KIDNEY FOUNDATION
800/622-9010, 800/747-5527.

NATIONAL KIDNEY AND UROLOGIC DISEASES CLEARINGHOUSE
(Information on incontinence.) 3 Information Way, Bethesda, MD 20892, 800/891-5390, 301/654-4415.

NATIONAL LIBRARY SERVICE - BLIND AND PHYSICALLY HANDICAPPED
(Recorded and Braille books and magazines; cassette players for loan.) Library of Congress, 1291 Taylor St., NW, Washington, DC 20542, 800/424-85567, 202/707-5100.

NATIONAL MULTIPLE SCLEROSIS SOCIETY
733 Third Ave., New York, NY 10017, 800/227-3166.

NATIONAL ORGANIZATION FOR RARE DISORDERS
(Provides low-cost reprints of articles from database on over 1000 diseases and medical conditions. Publishes "Physicians' Guide to Rare Diseases.") PO Box 8923, New Fairfield, CT 068122-8923, 203/746-6518.

NATIONAL OSTEOPOROSIS FOUNDATION
(Works to find solutions to the effects of the disease, which is most often found in older women.) 1150 - 17th St., NW, #500, Washington, DC 20036-4603, 202/223-2226.

NATIONAL PATIENT EMPOWERMENT PROJECT
(Publishes "Checklist for Comparing Health Care Plans") PO Box 668, Pine Brook, NJ 07058, 201/244-0083.

NATIONAL REHABILITATION INFORMATION CENTER
8455 Colesville Rd., #935, Silver Spring, MD 20910-3319, 800/346-2742.

NATIONAL SENIOR VOLUNTEER CORPS
1201 New York Ave., NW, Washington, DC 20525, 800/942-2677.

NATIONAL SHARED HOUSING RESOURCE CENTER
(Information on home sharing for the elderly and infirmed.) 321 E. 25th St., Baltimore, MD 21218, 410/235-4454.

NATIONAL STROKE ASSOCIATION
800/787-6537.

NURSING HOME INFORMATION SERVICE
(See: NATIONAL COUNCIL OF SENIOR CITIZENS)

OFFICE OF MINORITY HEALTH - RESOURCE CENTER
(Will do a customized database search for information on any health topic affecting a minority population.) PO Box 37337, Washington, DC 20013-7337, 800/444-6472.

OLDER WOMEN'S LEAGUE (OWL)
666 - 11th St., NW, #700, Washington, DC 20001, 202/783-6686

PARKINSON'S DISEASE FOUNDATION
710 W, 168 St., New York, NY 10032, 800/457-6676.

PARKINSON'S SUPPORT GROUPS OF AMERICA
11376 Cherry Hill Rd., #204, Beltsville, MD 20705, 301/937-1547.

RESOURCES FOR THE BLIND AND DYSLEXIC
(Lends academic textbooks on cassette and computer disk.) 20 Roszel Rd., Princeton, NJ 08540, 800/221-4792.

SAFE RETURN
(Nationwide community-based safety net sponsored by the Alzheimer's Association. Helps identify, locate and return people with memory loss.) PO Box A-3956, Chicago, IL 60690.

SELF-HELP FOR HARD OF HEARING PEOPLE
7910 Woodmont Ave., #1200, Bethesda, MD 20814, 301/657-2248.

SENIOR COMPANION PROGRAM
(A program of ACTION, the Federal Domestic Volunteer Agency.) Washington, DC 20525.

SENIOR NET
(Non-profit group for older adults who use, or are learning to use computers.) 1 Kearny St., 3rd Floor, San Francisco, CA 94108, 800/747-6848.

SOCIAL SECURITY
800/772-1213.

UNITED NET FOR ORGAN SHARING
800/243-6667.

UNITED SENIORS HEALTH COOPERATIVE
(Up-to-date information on Medicare, Medicaid, Medigap, long-term care insurance, home care, finances, and health problems.) 1331 "H" St., NW, #500, Washington, DC 20005, 800/637-2604, 202/393-6222.

UNITED STATES HEALTH CARE FINANCING INFORMATION
(File complaints about Medicare and Medicaid.) 415/744-3617.

UROLOGIC DISEASES
300 W. Pratt St., #401, Baltimore, MD 21201.

VISITING NURSE ASSOCIATIONS OF AMERICA
(Information on home-care.) 3801 E. Florida Ave., #900, Denver, CO 80210, 800/426-2547.

WELL SPOUSE FOUNDATION
(Sponsors nationwide support groups for spouses of the ill and disabled.) 610 Lexington Ave., #814, New York, NY 10022, 800/838-0879, 212/644-1241.

YOUTH EXCHANGING WITH SENIORS (Y.E.S.)
(Programs for youth who provide assisted-living services to help elderly live independently, focusing on rural America.) Texas Tech University, Box 41161, Lubbock, TX 79409.

CATALOGUES AND PRODUCTS

The following are a few of the better established companies offering excellent products geared especially for the elderly and infirmed. Call to receive their catalogues and information:

ADAPTABILITY
(Catalogue of health care products.) 800/288-9941.

CARING CONCEPTS
(Comfortable, well-made clothing specifically for nursing home residents.) 800/336-2660.

COGNEX®
(A drug which may improve some of the effects of Alzheimer's.) Parke-Davis, 800/600-1600.

COMFORTABLY YOURS
(Catalogue of clothing and comfort aids.) 800/521-0097.

COMPU-MED
(Automated medication dispensers, with 24-hour telephone monitoring.) 800/722-4417.

ENRICHMENTS
(Excellent catalogue of products which make life easier for the elderly.) 800/323-5547.

FRED SAMMONS'
(Grab bars and other safety devices for geriatric patients.) 800/ 323-5547.

GERIATRIC RESOURCES
(Catalogue of sensory stimulation products and AD caregiving resources.) 800/359-0390.

G.K. HALL
(Catalogue of large-print books.) 70 Lincoln St., Boston, MA 02111, 617/423-3990.

HOUSE CALLS
(Catalogue of health-care products.) 800/460-7282.

LUMEX
(Catalogues of devices to assist in the home.) 800/645-5272.

MAKING LIFE MORE LIVABLE
(Products for people with vision problems.) 800/829-0500.

MEDI-SENSE
(Hand-held blood glucose testing system, for patients with diabetes to monitor their own condition.) 800/527-3339.

NANITAX
(Tax preparation services designed for employers of in-home companions and health workers.) 800/626-4829.

NOLO PRESS
(Self-help books on legal matters.) 800/992-6656.

PRODUCTS FOR THE PHYSICALLY CHALLENGED
(Catalogue of home health aids.) 800/321-0595.

SENIOR COM
(On-line computer service providing information and products to the elderly.) 800/206-6989. (World Wide Web at http://www.senior.com)

WANDER WATCH ALERT SYSTEM
(For patients with dementia who wander. Prices start at $1000.) 800/881-8502.

WHEELCHAIR HOUSE
3500 S. Lincoln, Englewood, CO 80110, 818/772-8595, 303/761-3883, 303/482-7116.

Bibliography

The following books, videotapes, and audio cassettes are particularly useful in caring for your elderly family member, as well as for research and education. While there are also many other books easily available in the "Self-Help" or "Aging/Gerontology" sections of a good bookstore, these are worth searching out.

(c) = children's book
* = geared more toward professionals

Aging and the Law, by Peter J. Strauss, JD, Robert Wolf, JD, and Dana Schilling, JD, Commerce Clearing House, 4025 W. Peterson, Chicago, IL 60646, 800/248-3248.

Aging & Mental Health: Positive Psychological and Biomedical Approaches, by Robert N. Butler, MD, and Myrna I. Lewis, ACSW, C.V. Mosby Co., 11830 Westline Industrial Dr., St. Louis, MO 63141, 314/872-8370.

Aging, Money, and Life Satisfaction: Aspects of Financial Gerontology, by Neal E. Cutler, Davis W. Gregg, and M. Powell Lawton, Springer Publishing, 536 Broadway, New York. NY 10012.

Aging Parents, edited by Pauline K. Ragan, University of Southern California Press, Los Angeles, CA, 213/740-2311.

The Ageless Self: Sources of Meaning in Late Life, by S. Kaufman, New American Library, 375 Hudson St., New York, NY, 212/366-2000.

Alzheimer's: A Caregiver's Guide and Sourcebook, by H. Gretzner, available from American Health Assistance Foundation, 15825 Shady Grove Rd., #140, Rockeville, MD. 20850, 800/437-2423; or from, John Wiley & Sons, 1 Wiley Dr., Somerset, NJ 08875, 800/225-5945.

Alzheimer's Disease: A Guide for Families, Lenore S. Powell, EdD, and Katie Courtice, Addison-Wesley Publishing, 1 Jacob Way, Reading, MA, 800/238-9682.

Alzheimer's Disease: The Standard Reference, edited by Barry Reisberg, MD, The Free Press/MacMillan, 866 - 3rd Ave., New York, NY 10022, 212/702-2000.

Alzheimer's and Related Dementias Homes That Help: Advice from Caregivers for Creating a Supportive Home, by Richard V. Olsen, PhD, Ezra Ehrenkrantz, FAIA, and Barbara Hutchings, M.Arch., published by Architecture and Building Science Research Group/School of Architecture, New Jersey Institute of Technology, University Heights, Newark, NJ 07102, 201/596-3097.

Anatomy of an Illness as Perceived by the Patient, by Norman Cousins, W.W. Norton Publishers, 500 Fifth Ave., New York, NY 10110, 212/354-5500.

Answers: The Magazine for Adult Children of Aging Parents, PO Box 9889, Birmingham, AL 35220, 800/750-2199.

Between Home & Nursing Home: The Board and Care Alternative, by Ivy M. Down, MA, and Lorraine Schnurr, PhD, Prometheus Books, 718/927-0858.

Care of Alzheimer's Patients: A Manual for Nursing Home Staff, by Lisa P. Gwyther, ACSW, Alzheimer's Association, 919 N. Michigan Ave., #1000, Chicago, IL 60611, 800/272-3900.

A Career in Caring (videotape), produced by Rose Kleiner, LCSW, for Terra Nova Films, 9848 S. Winchester Ave., Chicago, IL 60643, 312/881-8491. (Training for home-care aides.)

The Caregiving Dilemma: Work in an American Nursing Home, by Nancy Foner, University of California Press, 2120 Berkeley Way, Berkeley, CA, 510/642-4247.

Caregiving Training: Training Materials for Caregivers & Professionals Caring for Brain-Impaired Adults and the Frail Elderly, Alzheimer's Family Center, Area Agency on Aging, Southern Regional Resource Center.

*Careguide for the Confused Resident (videotape and manual), by M.A. Wylde, Health Professions Press, PO Box 10624, Baltimore, MD 21285-0624, 410/337-9585.

Caring for a Loved One with AIDS: The Experience of Families, Lovers, and Friends, by Marie Brown and Gail Powell-Cope, University of Washington Press, PO Box 50096, Seattle, WA 98145.

*Child Care in Long-Term Care Settings, Foundation for Long Term Care, 194 Washington Ave., Albany, NY 12210. (Programs which combine care of frail older adults and healthy young children.)

*Childhood and Society, by Erik Erikson, W.W. Norton Publishers, 500 Fifth Ave., New York, NY 10110, 212/354-5500.

Complaints of a Dutiful Daughter (videotape), produced by Deborah Hoffman, Women Who Make Movies, 462 Broadway #500C, New York, NY 10013, 212/925-0606.

The Complete Elder Care Planner, by Joy Loverde, American Medical Association, 800/621-8335.

The Complete Guide to Barrier-Free Housing: Convenient Living for the Elderly and the Physically Handicapped, Betterway Publications, Crozet, VA.

*Concise Guide to Geriatric Psychiatry, by James E. Spar, MD, and Asenath La Rue, PhD, American Psychiatric Press, 1400 "K" St., NW, Washington, DC 20005.

Consumer Reports: "Nursing Homes," "Financial Aspects," "Alternatives to Nursing Homes." CU Reprints, 101 Truman Ave., Yonkers, NY 10703.

The Core of Geriatric Medicine: A Guide for Students and Practitioners, edited by Leslie S. Libow, MD, and Fredrick T. Sherman, MD, C.V. Mosby Co., 11830 Westline Industrial Dr., St. Louis, MO 63141, 314/872-8370.

Counting on Kindness: The Dilemma of Dependency, by Wendy Lustbader, Free Press/Simon & Shuster, 200 Old Tappan Rd., Old Tappan, NJ 07675, 800/223-2336.

Cutting Loose: An Adult Guide to Coming to Terms with Your Parents, by Howard M. Halpern, PhD, Simon & Schuster, 1230 Ave. of the Americas, New York, NY 10020, 212/ 698-7000.

Death, the Final Stage of Growth, by Elizabeth Kubler-Ross, Prentice-Hall, Highway 9W, Englewood Cliffs, NJ 07632, 201/ 592-2000.

Design for Dementia: Planning Environments for the Elderly and the Confused, by Margaret P. Calkins, M. Arch, National Health Publishing/ Williams & Wilkins, 99 Painters Mill Rd., Owings Mills, MD 21117, 301/363-6400.

Determined Survivors: Community Life among the Urban Elderly, by Janice A. Smithers, Rutgers University Press, 30 College Ave., New Brunswick, NJ 08903.

Don't Forget! Easy Exercises for a Better Memory, by D.C. Lapp, Addison-Wesley Publishing, 1 Jacob Way, Reading, MA, 800/238-9682.

Elder Care and the Work Force: Blueprint for Action, by Andrew E. Scharlach, PhD, Beverly F. Lowe, PhD, and Edward L. Schneider, MD, University of California, Berkeley. Lexington Books/D.C. Heath, 125 Spring St., Lexington, MA 02173, 800/ 235-3565.

Essentials of Clinical Geriatrics, by Robert L. Kane, MD, Joseph G. Ouslander, MD, and Itamar B. Abrass, MD, McGraw-Hill Co., 1221 Ave. of the Americas, New York, NY 10020, 212/512-2000.

Failure Free Activities for the Alzheimer's Patient: A Guidebook for Care Givers, by Carmel Sheridan, order through: Elder Books, PO Box 490, Forest Knolls, CA 94933, 415/488-9002.

*Families Who Care: Assisting African American and Rural Families Dealing With Dementia, edited by C.L. Coogle and R.B. Finley, Virginia Commonwealth University, Virginia Center on Aging, PO Box 980229, Richmond, VA 23298-0229, 804/828-1525.

Final Exit: The Practicalities of Self-Deliverance and Assisted Suicide for the Dying, Derek Humphry, The Hemlock Society, PO Box 11830, Eugene, OR 97440, 503/342-5748.

Free Stuff for Seniors, by Matthew Lesko, Information USA, PO Box "E," Kensington, MD 20895, 301/924-0556.

Freedom In Meditation, Dr. Patricia Carrington, Anchor Press/ Doubleday, 1540 Broadway, New York, NY 10036, 212/3544-6500.

The Gadget Book: Ingenious Devices for Easier Living, Scott Foresman Publishers, 1900 E. Lake Ave., Glenview, IL, 60025, 708/ 729-3000.

*Generating Community: Intergenerational Partnerships Through the Expressive Arts, by S. Perlsetin and J. Bliss, Elders Share the Arts, 57 Willoughby St., Brooklyn, NY 11202.

*Geriatric Psychiatry and Psychopharmacology: A Clinical Approach, by Michael A. Jenike, MD, Mosby-Year Book, 11830 Westline Industrial Dr., St. Louis, MO 63146.

Getting Through: Communicating When Someone You Care For Has Alzheimer's Disease, by Elizabeth Ostuni and Mary Jo Santo Pietro, The Speech Bin, 1766 - 20th Ave., Vero Beach, FL 32960

Gone Without a Trace: An Exceptional True Story, by Marianne Dickerson Caldwell, Elder Books, PO Box 490, Forest Knolls, CA 94933. (Guidance to families who must search for a missing elderly "wanderer.")

(c) Grandma's Bill, by Martin Waddell, Orchard Books.

(c) Grandpa - and Me, by Stephanie S. Tolan, Charles Scribner's Sons, New York, NY, 212/702-2000.

Grandparents/Grandchildren: The Vital Connection, Transaction Publishers, Rutgers University, 30 College Ave., New Brunswick, NJ 08903.

*A Guide to Community: An Intergenerational Friendship Program Between Young People and Nursing Home Residents, Bi-Folkal Productions, 809 Williamson St., Madison, WI 53703.

A *Guide to Helping Elderly Relatives Near and Far* (audio cassette tape), by Pamela Erickson, RN, and Gordon Wolfe, MSW, Eldercare Press, Professional Respite Care, 6000 E. Evans Ave., #I-340, Denver, CO 80222, 303/757-4808.

*Handbook of Geriatric Assessment, by Joseph J. Gallo, MD, William Reichel, MD, and Lillian Andersen, RN, Aspen Publishers, 200 Orchard Ridge Dr., Gaithersburg, MD 20878.

Hard Choices for Loving People, by Hank Dunn, A & A Publishers, PO Box 1098, Herndon, VA 22070, 703/707-0169.

Hasta Que Haya Una Cura: La Diagnosis de la Demencia en la Southwestern Clinic for Alzheimer's and Related Diseases (videotape), produced by the University of Texas Southwestern Medical Center, available from Alzheimer's Disease Education & Referral Center, PO Box 8250, Silver Spring, MD 20907, 800/438-4380. (One family's experience. For caregivers and health service professionals, in Spanish.)

The Hidden Victims of Alzheimer's Disease: Families Under Stress, by Steven H. Zarit, Nancy K. Orr, and Judy M. Zarit, New York University Press, Washington Square, New York, NY 10003.

Hiring Home Caregivers: The Family Guide to In-Home Elder Care, by D. Helen Susik, MA, American Source Books/Impact Publishers, San Luis Obispo, CA, 805/543-5911.

Home Safety Guide for Older People: Check It Out, Fix It Up, Serif Press, 1331 "H" St., NW, Washington, DC, 202-737-4650.

(c) How Does It Feel to be Old? by Norma Farber, E.P. Dutton Co., New York, NY, 212/366-2000.

How to Survive the Loss of a Love, by Melba Colgrove, PhD, Harold H. Bloomfield, MD, and Peter McWilliams, Bantam Books, 1540 Broadway, New York, NY 10036, 212/354-6500.

How We Die: Reflections on Life's Final Chapter, by Sherwin B. Nuland, MD, Vintage Books/Random House, 201 E. 50 St., New York, NY 10022, 212/751-2600.

*I Never Told Anybody: Teaching Poetry Writing in a Nursing Home, by Kenneth Koch, Random House, 201 E. 50 St., New York, NY 10022, 212/751-2600.

In Our Fifties: Voices of Men and Women Reinventing Their Lives, by William H. Bergquist, Elinor Miller Greenberg, and G. Alan Klaum, Jossey-Bass Publishers, 350 Sansome St., San Francisco, CA 94104, 415/433-1767.

*Intergenerational Readings/Resources 1980-1994, Generations Together, University of Pittsburgh, 121 University Place, #300, Pittsburgh, PA 15260.

Just For You: A booklet for people who have recently heard they have Alzheimer's disease, Alzheimer's Society of Canada, 1320 Yonge St.,, #201, Toronto, Ontario M4T 1X2, Canada. ($1.50)

Keeping Active: A Caregiver's Guide to Activities with the Elderly, by Susan Walker, American Source Books, PO Box 280353, Lakewood, CO 80228, 303/980-0580.

Keeping Busy: A Handbook of Activities for Persons With Dementia, by J.R. Dowling, The Johns Hopkins University Press, 701 W. 40th St., Baltimore, MD 21211, 800/537-5487.

Later Life: The Realities of Aging, by Harold Cox, Prentice-Hall, Highway 9W, Englewood Cliffs, NJ 07632, 201/592-2000.

Legacies: Stories of Courage, Humor, and Resilience, of Love, Loss, and Life-Changing Encounters, by New Writers Sixty and Older, edited by Maury Liebovitz and Linda Solomon, USHC Publications, 1331 "H" St., NW, #500, Washington, DC 20005, 202/393-6222.

"The Life Review: An Interpretation of Reminiscence in the Aged," by Robert Butler, published in Psychiatry, 1966.

Life Review Training Manual, Elders Share the Arts, 57 Willoughby St., Brooklyn, NY 11202. (Tools to help elders look back into their memories.)

Living Buddha, Living Christ, by Thich Nhat Hanh, G.P. Putnam's Sons, 200 Madison Ave., New York, NY 10016. (The crossroads of compassion and holiness where the two traditions meet.)

Long Distance Caregiving: A Survival Guide for Far Away Caregivers, by Angela Heath, American Source Books, PO Box 280353, Lakewood, CO 80228, 303/980-0580.

Long-Distance Grandparenting, by Rose Marie Barhydt and Bonnie Potter, Blanfield Publishing, PO Box 130316, Ann Arbor, MI 48113.

The Loss of Self: A Family Resource for the Care of Alzheimer's Disease and Related Disorders, by Donna Cohen, PhD, and Carl Eisdorfer, MD, W.W. Norton Publishers, 500 Fifth Ave., New York, NY 10110, 212/354-5500.

Magic of Humor in Caregiving, by James E. Sherman, Pathway Books, 700 Parkview Terrace, Golden Valley, MN 55416-3439.

The Man Who Mistook His Wife for a Hat, and Other Clinical Tales, by Dr. Oliver Sacks, Summit Books/Simon & Schuster, 1230 Ave. of the Americas, New York, NY 10020, 212/698-7000.

*Managing Health Care for the Elderly, by Cynthia Polick, Marge Parker, Margaret Hottinger and Deborah Chase, United Healthcare Corporation/John Wiley & Sons, 1 Wiley Dr., Somerset, NJ 08875, 800/225-5945. 212/850-6238.

The Measure of My Days, by Florida Scott-Maxwell, Penguin Books, 40 W. 23 St., New York, NY 10010, 212/645-3121, 212/366-2000.

*Medical Care in the Nursing Home, by Joseph Ouslander, MD, Dan Osterweil, MD, and John Morley, MD, McGraw Hill, 1221 Ave. of the Americas, New York, NY 10020, 212/512-2000.

Memories of Love: Families Caring (videotape), Alzheimer's Disease Education & Referral Center, PO Box 8250, Silver Spring, MD 20907, 800/438-4380. (African American caregivers share their experiences.)

*The Merck Manual of Geriatrics, edited by William B. Abrams, MD, and Robert Berkow, MD, Merck & Co., 126 E. Lincoln Ave., Rahway, NJ., 908/594-4000.

*Mirrored Lives: Aging Children and Elderly Parents, by Tom Koch, Praeger, New York, NY,

(c) My Grandma Has Black Hair, by Mary Hoffman and Joanna Burroughs, Beaver Books.

My Journey Into Alzheimer's Disease: A Protestant minister's diary of his unexpected journey into Alzheimer's, Tyndale House, PO Box 80, Wheaton, IL 60189, 800/323-9400.

Necessary Losses: The Loves, Illusions, Dependencies and Impossible Expectations That All of Us Have to Give Up in Order to Grow, by Judith Viorst, Ballantine Books/Random House, 201 E. 50 St., New York, NY 10022, 212/751-2600.

New Passages: Mapping Your Life Across Time, by Gail Sheehy, Random House, 201 E. 50 St., New York, NY 10022, 212/751-2600.

Nutrition and the Later Years, by Ruth B. Weg, Ethel Percy Andrus Gerontology Center/University of Southern California Press, Los Angeles, CA, 213/740-2311.

Nursing Administration of Long-Term Care, by Charlotte Eliopoulos, RN, Aspen Systems, 1600 Research Blvd., Rockville, MD 20850.

The Nursing Assistant's Casebook of Elder Care, by George H. Weber and George J. McCall, Auburn House Publishers, 14 Dedham St., Dover, MA 02030-0658.

Nursing Homes: How to Evaluate and Select a Nursing Home, People's Medical Society, 14 E. Minor St., Emmaus, PA 18049, 215/ 967-2136.

On Death and Dying, by Elizabeth Kubler-Ross, MacMillan Publishers, 866 Third Ave., New York, NY 10022, 212/702-2000.

Ourselves, Growing Older: Women Aging with Knowledge and Power, by Paula Brown Doress and Diana Laskin Siegel, Touchstone Books/ Simon & Schuster, 1230 Ave. of the Americas, New York, NY 10020, 212/ 698-7000.

Parent Care, by Gary W. Small, MD (Chief of Geriatric Psychiatry, UCLA), with Lissy Jarvik, MD, PhD, Bantam Books, 1540 Broadway, New York, NY 10036, 212/354-6500.

Parkinson's: A Patient's View, by Sidney Dorros, Seven Locks Press, Washington, DC.

Parkinson's Disease: A Guide to Patient and Family, by Roger Duvoisin, MD, Lippincott-Raven, PO Box 1610, Hagerstown, MD 21741, 800/777-2295.

Peace, Love & Healing, by Bernie S. Siegel, MD, Harper & Row, 10 E. 53 St., New York, NY 10022.

The Perfect Fit: Creative Ideas for a Safe & Livable Home, by Jon Pynoos, PhD, and Evelyn Cohen, MA, Arch., published by AARP, Consumer Affairs Section, Program Coordination and Development Dept., 601 "E" St., NW, Washington, DC 20049, 800/424-3410.

Power of Attorney Book, Nolo Press, 950 Parker St., Berkeley, CA 94710, 800/992-6656.

Principles and Practice of Geriatric Medicine, edited by M.S.J. Pathy, John Wiley & Sons, 1 Wiley Dr., Somerset, NJ 08875, 800/225-5945, 212/850-6238.

Psychosocial Needs of the Aged: A Health Care Perspective, edited by Eugene Seymour, MD, Ethel Percy Andrus Gerontological Center/ University of Southern California Press, Los Angeles, CA, 213/740-2311.

Recovering After a Stroke: A Patient and Family Guide, by the U.S. Dept. of Health and Human Services, available free from Agency for Health Care Policy and Research, 2101 E. Jefferson St., #501, Rockville, MD 20852.

The Relaxation Response: A Simple Meditative Technique, by Herbert Benson, MD, Avon Books/Hearst Corp., 959 - 8th Ave., New York, NY 10019, or William Morrow, 105 Madison Ave., New York, NY 10016.

Reminiscence, by Carmel Sheridan, Elder Books, PO Box 490, Forest Knolls, CA 94933, 415/488-9002.

Reshaping Dementia Care: Practice and Policy in Long-Term Care, edited by Miriam K. Aronson, EdD, Sage Publications, 2455 Teller Rd., Thousand Oaks, CA 91320,

Role Transitions in Later Life, by Linda K. George, PhD, Brooks-Cole Publishing/Wadsworth, 511 Forest Lodge Rd., Pacific Grove, CA 93940, 408/373-0728.

Sensory Awareness: The Rediscovering of Experience, by Charles V.W. Brooks, Viking Press, 625 Madison Ave., New York, NY 10022.

Set Me Free: Towards More Appropriate Use of Physical Restraints, by J.A. Lever and D.W. Hamilton, McMaster University Press, 673 Upper James St., PO Box 60515, Hamilton, Ontario L8W 1Z1, Canada, 905/527-4322.

*Sex Education and Counseling of Special Groups: The Mentally and Physically Disabled, Ill, and Elderly, by Warren R. Johnson, Ed.D., and Winifred Kempton, MSW, Charles C. Thomas Publishers, 2600 S. First St., Springfield, IL 62717.

Sexuality, Intimacy and Alzheimers (videotape), Terra Nova Films, 9848 S. Winchester Ave., Chicago, IL 60643, 312/881-8491.

Share It with the Children: A Preschool Curriculum on Aging, edited by C. Mack and J. Wilson, available from Generations Together, University of Pittsburgh, 121 University Place, #300, Pittsburgh, PA 15260. (Vital education for children about aging, with 45 appropriate activities to share.)

Someone I Love Has Alzheimer's Disease (videotape), produced by Alzheimer's Association of Eastern Massachusetts, Lifecycle Productions, PO Box 183, Newton, MA 02165, 617/964-0047.

*Taber's Cyclopedic Medical Dictionary, edited by Clayton L. Thomas, MD, F.A. Davis Co., 1915 Arch St., Philadelphia, PA 19103.

Taking Care of Aging Family Members: A Practical Guide, by Wendy Lustbader and Nancy Hooyman, Free Press/Simon & Shuster, 200 Old Tappan Rd., Old Tappan, NJ 07675, 800/223-2336. (Deals with cultural diversity, lesbian/gay caregivers, stepfamilies, grandchildren, long-distance caregiving.)

Talking With Your Aging Parents, by Mark A. Edinberg, Shambhala Publications, 300 Massachusetts Ave., Boston, MA, 617/424-0030.

(c) Things I Like About Grandma, by Francine Haskins, Children's Book Press. (An African American girl and her grandmother share memories.)

The 36-Hour Day: A Family Guide to Caring for Persons with Alzheimer's Disease, Related Dementing Illnesses, and Memory Loss in Later Life, by Nancy L. Mace, MA, and Peter V. Rabins, MD, MPH, The Johns Hopkins University Press, 701 W. 40th St., Baltimore, MD 21211, 800/537-5487. (Also available in Spanish.)

*A Time to Grieve: Loss as a Universal Human Experience, by Bertha G. Simos, Family Service Association of America, 44 E. 23rd St., New York, NY 10010.

Time-Out Program Development Manual, Temple University Center for Intergenerational Living, 1601 N. Broad St., #206, Philadelphia, PA 19122. (Training manual for college-age students who provide in-home respite care for caregivers of older adults.)

*To Be Old and Sad - Understanding Depression in the Elderly, by Nathan Billig, MD, Lexington Books/Simon and Schuster, 1230 - 6th Ave., New York, NY 10020, 212/698-7000.

To Heal Again: Towards Serenity and the Resolution of Grief, by Rusty Berkus, Red Rose Press, PO Box 24, Encino, CA 91426.

To Lead a Life (videotape), project of the U.S. Administration on Aging, National Council on Patient Information, and Glaxo, Inc. For free tape, call 800/546-7988. (Teaches the elderly how to take medications safely, and what to ask doctors and pharmacists.)

*Toward Healthy Aging: Human Needs and Nursing Response, by Priscilla Ebersole and Patricia Hess, C.V. Mosby Co., 11830 Westline Industrial Dr., St. Louis, MO 63141, 314/872-8370.

Understanding Alzheimer's Disease: A Specific Guide for Families, Eisenhower Memorial Hospital, Alzheimer's Diagnostic Center, Wright Bldg. #108, 39000 Bob Hope Dr., Rancho Mirage, CA 92270.

Understanding Alzheimer's Disease: What It Is; How to Cope

With It; Future Directions, from the Alzheimer's Disease and Related Disorders Association, Charles Scribner's Sons, New York, NY, 212/702-2000.

The View from 80, by Malcolm Cowley, Viking Press, 120 Woodbine St., Bergenfield, NJ 07621, 800/331-4624.

*Vision and Aging: Issues in Social Work Practice, edited by Nancy Weber, MSW, Haworth Press, 10 Alice St., Binghamton, NY 13904.

(c) **What's Wrong With Daddy?**, by Alida E. Young , Willowisp Press.

When Parents Die: A Guide for Adults, by Edward Myers, Viking Press, 625 Madison Ave., New York, NY 10022.

When Someone You Love is Dying, by Norma S. Upson, Simon & Schuster, 1230 Ave. of the Americas, New York, NY 10020, 212/698-7000.

When Your Parents Grow Old, by Jane Otten and Florence D. Shelley, Thomas Y. Crowell Co., 666 Fifth Ave., New York, NY 10019.

Where Can Mom Live? A Family Guide To Living Arrangements for Elderly Parents, by Virginia F. Carlin and Ruth Mansberg, Lexington Books/Simon and Shuster, 1230 Ave. of the Americas, New York, NY 10020, 212/698-7000.

When Bad Things Happen to Good People, Harold Kushner, Schocken Books.

Women Take Care: The Consequences of Caregiving in Today's Society, by Tish Sommers and Laurie Shields, Triad Publishing, 1110 NW 8th Ave., Gainesville, FL 32601.

Working with the Elderly: Group Process and Techniques, edited by Irene Mortensson Burnside, Duxbury Press, 20 Providence St., Boston, MA 02136, 617/482-8957; or Wadsworth Publishing Co., 10 Davis Drive, Belmont, CA 94002, 415/595-2350.

Wrestling with the Angel: A Memoir of My Triumph Over Illness, by Max Lerner, W.W. Norton & Co., 500 Fifth Ave., New York, NY 10110, 212/354-5500.

You and Your Aging Parent: The Modern Family's Guide to Emotional, Physical, and Financial Problems, by Barbara Silverstone and Helen Kandel Hyman, Pantheon Books/Random House, 201 E. 50th St., New York, NY, 212/751-2600.

Glossary

ACTIVITIES OF DAILY LIVING (ADLs)

Eating, dressing, bathing, toileting, ambulating (walking with or without assistance of a mechanical device), transferring (ability to move from a bed, chair, wheelchair, with or without a mechanical or support device), continence (ability to control bowel or bladder functions, and ability to maintain reasonable level of personal hygiene, with or without the use of medical supplies, protective undergarments, or catheters).

Functional ability can be measured by the type and number of ADLs which a patient can perform. Knowing about ADLs is important for a very practical reason: Most insurance policies base their payments for long-term care upon an elderly person's inability to perform 2 or 3 activities of daily living. In order to put in a claim, a doctor must verify this.

In the beginning stages of dementia, patients can usually perform ADLs, but often patients cannot adequately perform IADLs (see: INSTRUMENTAL ACTIVITIES OF DAILY LIVING).

ACUTE CARE

Usually short-term medical care at a hospital for a patient with an acute disease or trauma.

ACUTE DISEASE

A disease which has a rapid onset and severe symptoms, but is not prolonged. (The opposite of CHRONIC DISEASE.)

ADULT FOSTER CARE

Long-term care in a group or private facility that is more like a residence, than a nursing home. Such facilities may be subject to fewer licensing regulations than nursing homes.

ADVANCE MEDICAL DIRECTIVES

(Declaration under the Natural Death Act, the Patient Self-Determination Act, Health Care Proxy, "Living Will"). Such directives should be signed when the patient is competent. They permit a patient to specify the kind and extent of medical measures to be given, or to choose to receive no life-saving medical treatment, when they become severely ill or profoundly disabled. *(More on advance medical directives in Chapter 10.)*

AGE-ASSOCIATED MEMORY IMPAIRMENT

(Also known as benign forgetfulness or benign senescence.) Mild memory loss that slowly increases with age, e.g. forgetting where you left your glasses, where you parked the car, or names of acquaintances. While embarrassing, it doesn't greatly interfere with daily living, and eventually, you'll remember. Such minor, temporary memory glitches are completely different than dementia, which is progressive major memory loss that interferes with everyday functioning.

ALEXIA

The inability to read and understand words, not caused by eye problems or illiteracy.

ALZHEIMER'S DISEASE

Alzheimer's disease is not a normal part of aging. It is a progressive, degenerative disease, usually with a gradual onset, which affects an estimated 4 million Americans.

The cause of AD is still unknown, but studies are being done to investigate possible environmental, viral, and genetic factors. No one factor is believed to be the cause of the disease, but rather, a combination of factors, to which individuals react differently.

After proper evaluation of a patient's symptoms and testing by experienced professionals, a diagnosis of "probable" Alzheimer's can correctly be made 80-90% of the time.

However, only an autopsy can definitely prove the existence the disease. A tiny piece of brain tissue showing abnormal clumps (neuritic/senile plaques, amyloid plaques), tangled bundles of fibers (neurofibrillary tangles), and other characteristics directly fibers (neurofibrillary tangles), and other characteristics directly related to AD, allows a 100% determination of Alzheimer's, if analyzed within twelve hours after death.

Alzheimer's is the most common cause of dementia. The disease attacks the brain, resulting in severely impaired memory, reasoning and behavior. Approximately 3% of men and women ages 65 to 74 have Alzheimer's disease, 10% of those between ages 75-84 have AD, which rises steeply to 47% of people over age 85.

The life span of an Alzheimer's victim usually ranges between 8-20 years. The disease is the fourth leading cause of death in the U.S. At this time, there is no cure and the disease is always fatal.

At this time, only one drug, Cognex® (generic: tachrine HCl capsules), may help alleviate some of the cognitive symptoms of Alzheimer's. It must be closely monitored by a doctor experienced with the medication, because of possible side-effects which can damage the liver.

Other medications may help control symptoms such as depression, wandering, sleeplessness, anxiety, and agitation. In addition, you and your EFM may wish to participate in clinical trials which are being done on experimental drugs.

Some typical signs of early Alzheimer's may include: memory loss, problems finding the right words and completing thoughts which hamper communication, confusion about times and dates, loss of a sense of direction, misplacing objects, difficulty doing everyday tasks, impaired judgment, shifts in mood, changes in personality and behavior, and depression.

Since these possible indications of Alzheimer's may also have other causes which might be treatable, the person should get a complete work-up (a series of physical, psychiatric, and neurological evaluations), done by physicians who are experienced in treating the elderly.

(Also see: DEMENTIA)

ALZHEIMER'S UNIT
(See: DEMENTIA UNIT)

APHASIA

The impairment or absence of the ability to communicate by speaking or writing, due to brain dysfunction.

APRAXIA

A growing inability to do movements or use objects properly, although there are no physical problems which cause the condition.

ARTERIOSCLEROSIS

(Also called Hardening of the Arteries.) Dementia symptoms can be associated with this condition, but only when multiple strokes have occurred.

ASSESSMENT

The cornerstone of a comprehensive care plan developed by a Geriatric Care Manager.

ASSIGNMENT

When a physician or health supplier agrees to accept Medicare's fee rate as payment in full (except when the patient has co-insurance and a deductible). Medicare usually pays far less than the professional's normal fee.

ASSISTED LIVING

A wide-range of facilities and programs that an elderly family member and their caregiving family can choose from, including: retirement hotels, and board and care homes. Services may include 24-hour supervision, companionship, help with dressing and toileting, bathing, personal care, transportation, giving medications, and nursing care (see Appendix C).

BENEFIT PERIOD

The length of time an insurance policy will pay for a specific illness or hospitalization.

BENIGN FORGETFULNESS / BENIGN SENESCENCE

(See: AGE-ASSOCIATED MEMORY IMPAIRMENT)

BOARD AND CARE HOME

A small facility, frequently 6-12 beds, which cares for elderly people who need extra assistance on a more personal basis. It is less expensive than a nursing home (although Medicaid may cover the cost of a nursing home, but most often will not cover the cost of a small board and care home). Licensed by many, but not all states.

BOARD AND CARE HOTEL

(See: RETIREMENT HOTEL)

CAPITATION

A fixed amount of money per patient, per month, that a health plan pays to a provider of medical services. This fee is the final, total amount that a doctor or medical group receives to render all care, no matter how extensive it may be. If less medical care is needed and, thus, billing is lower, the provider can keep the difference. Such a pre-payment system puts pressure on a doctor to keep medical costs as low as possible, by switching the financial risk from the insurer to the doctor.

This potentially places a doctor in a "conflict of interest" position, since the "least" care he gives a patient, the more money he gets to keep.

CAREGIVER

The person, whether adult child, relative, friend, or hired help, who takes care of an elderly person in need. Doing the job properly requires enormous time, energy, patience, and courage. Ideally, caregiving also takes love, but not all caregivers love their elderly charges, and vice-versa.

The consequences can be peace-of-mind, guilt, moral imperative, anger, intimacy, stress, personal satisfaction, physical deterioration, deep fulfillment, a sense of imprisonment, renewed closeness, martyrdom, confrontation with one's future, a deeper reverence for life, or a combination of all of these. Those who caretake as well as they can are blessed, and so are the recipients of their kindness.

CARRIER
(See: INTERMEDIARY)

CHRONIC CARE
Long-term health care, such as at an assisted living facility or nursing home.

CHRONIC DISEASE
A disease which shows little change and usually progresses very slowly over a longer period of time. Since the disease doesn't go away, a patient has to learn to cope and live with it. (The opposite of ACUTE DISEASE.)

CLINICAL DIAGNOSIS
Based upon actual observations, tests, and responses to treatment, rather than pathological facts. It is the only practical way to diagnose Alzheimer's disease.

COGNITION
Normal awareness and insight, using reasoning, judgment, intuition, knowledge, and intellectual functioning.

COLAs
Cost of living adjustments ("inflation protection") which either increases your EFM's daily benefit by a fixed percentage each year, or by an amount tied to the Consumer Price Index. You can purchase a COLA rider to a health policy, but it is expensive. COLAs are continuously being used as a bargaining chip in Congress' never-ending, futile fight to balance the budget, so they will probably be decreased or even eliminated in the future.

COMMUNITY CARE FACILITY
(See: BOARD AND CARE HOME)

CONGREGATE HOUSING / CONGREGATE LIVING
(See: LIFE-CARE HOME)

CONTINUING CARE RETIREMENT COMMUNITY
(See: LIFE-CARE HOME)

CONVALESCENCE HOME
(See: NURSING HOME)

CUSTODIAL CARE
Assistance that is not skilled nursing care. A worker helps an elderly person with the activities of daily living which are not medically necessary, but necessary for functioning, such as bathing, feeding, toileting, and dressing. This is the type of care that most elderly people need in order to remain living at home, yet it usually is not covered by insurance or Medicare. Long-term health insurance may cover custodial care.

DELIRIUM
A serious, though transient and treatable condition of mental disorientation. Delirium can be caused by simple intoxication, medications, infection, or more complex metabolic deficiencies, electrolyte imbalance, and/or hypoxia (deficiency of oxygen). Symptoms may wax and wane. The patient becomes disoriented, over-excited, and might experience hallucinations, illusions, or paranoia. Speech is often incoherent, as the mind wanders.

DEMENTIA
(Previously labeled"senility.')
Dementia is a global term for impaired cognitive functioning. It is not a disease, but a group of symptoms reflecting a serious disease or medical condition that disrupts the way the brain works. Symptoms gradually become so severe as to interfere with an aging person's ability to perform routine activities, their social life, and their very existence. Dementia can be reversible or irreversible.

Reversible dementia, or dementia-like symptoms, may result from many other causes, such as: TIAs (transient ischemic attacks, i.e. temporary interference with blood supply to the brain), thyroid or metabolic imbalance, depression, reactions to medications, fever, nutritional deficiencies, chronic alcoholism, excessive use of drugs, cerebral hemorrhaging or tumors, brain injuries, epilepsy, syphilis, infectious diseases, and long-term dialysis.

Irreversible dementia (primary dementia) is most commonly caused by Alzheimer's disease. Many people confuse Alzheimer's and dementia, but irreversible dementia may be caused by a number of other conditions and diseases, including: Multi-Infarct Dementia (MID), Parkinson's disease, Huntington's (Lou Gehrig's/Woody Guthrie's) disease, Creutzfeldt-Jakob's disease, Pick's disease, and AIDS.

A good work-up and correct diagnosis are essential to determine the type and nature of the dementia, to determine if it can be treated.

DEMENTIA UNIT

(Also known as an Alzheimer's Unit or Special Care Unit.) A special unit established in about 20% of nursing homes and psychiatric hospitals for patients with dementia, generally those who are agitated, confused, or wanderers. The unit costs more and isn't necessarily better for your EFM, who may or may not need the special care. Opinions vary on the benefit of such units and special care programs. Investigate to see if the staff in the unit have any specific training in working with dementia, and if the facilities are specifically geared to such patients.

DENIAL

The defensive, protective quality in the human psyche which initially rejects facing tremendously stressful and painful situations, such as caring for a demented elderly family member. With professional supportive help and personal courage, a caregiver can confront the truth and deal with it.

EFM

Elderly family member, usually cared for by a spouse, adult child, or other close relative.

ELDER LAW ATTORNEY

An attorney who specializes and is experienced in financial preparation for long-term care, estate planning, asset conservation, and the special legal needs of seniors.

This includes preservation and transfer of assets to avoid spousal impoverishment when one spouse enters a nursing home; Medicaid, Medicare, Social Security, and disability claims and appeals; supplemental and long-term health insurance; Durable Powers of Attorney, Living Wills, Conservatorships, and Guardianships; living trusts, probate, pensions, retirement and survivor benefits; patients' rights, elder abuse, fraud recovery, age and housing discrimination; home equity conversions; health and mental health law.

Often a member of the National Academy of Elder Law Attorneys (*see Appendix G*).

ELIMINATION PERIOD

(Also known as the deductible period.) The number of days a patient must pay for their medical care, before an insurance policy kicks in. The longer the elimination period, the lower the premium.

EXCLUSIVE PROVIDER ORGANIZATION (EPO)

A variation of a PPO managed care plan. Patients must use specified medical and health providers in order to receive insurance coverage. (See: PREFERRED PROVIDER ORGANIZATION)

FEE-FOR-SERVICE

The traditional form of medical care. A patient goes to any doctor or hospital of their choice, and pays whatever is charged. If the patient has good private health insurance, the policy will pay all or part of the bill.

GERIATRIC CARE MANAGER

A professional who has extensive training and experience working with older people and their families who need help with caregiving. The geriatric care manager, often a gerontologist, social worker, psychotherapist, or nurse, offers understanding and compassion, information, assistance, moral support, and referrals, which may make the difference between a successful old age and a traumatic one.

Vital services which a geriatric care manager can provide include: crisis intervention, counseling, assessment of an elderly individual's status and needs, matching needs to services, useful information on community and government assistance programs, planning for future financial demands, and coordination of a professional team of caregiving helpers from various specializations. When an elderly family member needs assistance, families suddenly have to confront the difficult, time-consuming job of negotiating through a vast array of services and agencies, which may have complex requirements and long waiting lists. At this point, the adult children or grandchildren, who are trying to juggle careers and family responsibilities in addition to caregiving, often seek assistance from a qualified private care manager.

Some family members who want to remain fully involved with their caregiving roles use a geriatric care manager for the initial assessment, and for periodic consultations. Others, especially those who live far from their elderly family member, hire a geriatric care manager to oversee a long-term care plan, assuring that a high-level of professional care standards is maintained.

Many care managers are members of the National Association of Professional Geriatric Care Managers (*see Appendix G*).

GERIATRIC PSYCHIATRIC UNIT

(Also known as a Psych Unit.) Separate area of a hospital, with a specially trained psychiatric staff, used for evaluation and treatment of older patients with mental diseases and dementia. The unit must be secured for patients who wander.

GERIATRIC PSYCHIATRIST

A psychiatrist who specializes in the mental diseases of the elderly.

GUILT

An unnecessary, unproductive accumulation of blame from the past (usually childhood), which only serves to render a well-meaning caregiver physically and mentally exhausted. A clear examination of the facts, however traumatic, usually proves there is little cause in reality to feel guilt. Instead, an adult child's focus and energy can be put to better use, caring for themselves, their family, and their elderly family member.

HARDENING OF THE ARTERIES

(See: ARTERIOSCLEROSIS)

HEALTH MAINTENANCE ORGANIZATION (HMO)
A managed care plan which provides a complete range of health services at a fixed monthly rate. The HMO receives the same premium, whether or not a patient needs help. Thus, its motivation is to stress prevention and keep actual medical care under control, often by using the patient's primary care doctor as a "gatekeeper" (or some variation of that title).

HOSPICE
A facility or a caregiving service for terminally ill patients, providing relief and support for their physical, social, financial, and spiritual needs as they are dying. Supportive services may also be given to the patients' families.

INCONTINENCE
The inability to retain urine or feces, because of loss of sphincter control or brain lesions. There are many possible causes for incontinence, but most cases can be controlled, corrected, or cured. Only 1 in 10 elderly people have incontinence, but despite the fact that the condition is fairly common, it frequently is a source of great embarrassment and even recrimination. Incontinence is often a medical problem and should be discussed with your EFM's physician.

INDEPENDENT PRACTICE ASSOCIATION (IPA)
A managed care plan in which a patient sees specialists who are all associated with a specific medical office. The doctors agree to see the patient on a pre-negotiated fee scale.

INSIDIOUS
The onset of a disease, without noticeable symptoms, which leaves a patient and their family initially unaware of what is taking place. With Alzheimer's disease, the onset is slow, with no obvious symptoms. Only upon looking back, does a family realize that beginning mild symptoms were indeed evident, perhaps causing some suspicion, but they were overlooked or emotionally denied.

INSTRUMENTAL ACTIVITIES OF DAILY LIVING (IADLs)

Preparing meals, shopping, ability to use the telephone and TV, doing housework and laundry, managing money and paying bills, using transportation, and taking medications. (In contrast to "ACTIVITIES OF DAILY LIVING.")

INSURANCE

It is important to look for the hidden exclusions and barriers, buried in pages of verbiage in most insurance policies. Some key terms to identify include: ADLs, Bed Reservation Benefit, Benefit Period, COLAs, Elimination Period, Maximum Daily Benefit, Medical Necessity, Non-Forfeiture, Waiver of Premium. Compare the definitions and conditions with those of policies from other companies.

INTEGRATED MODEL

A managed care plan established by a physician group or hospital, which provides all in-patient and out-patient health needs, including in-home and nursing home care. This type of plan both pays for and delivers the medical services, since it frequently owns the hospital, facilities, agencies, and even the hospitals that service the patient.

INTERGENERATIONAL PROGRAMS

Brings together young and old people in regularly planned activities which benefit both age groups, and the community as a whole. Participants support each other, sharing their different perspectives, talents, and abilities. These programs attempt to substitute for the traditional extended family that is vanishing in our fast-paced society, where so many would-be family caregivers live a long distance away.

INTERMEDIARY

(Also known as a Carrier.) A private insurance company which contracts with the U.S. government to handle billing claims for Medicare Part A and/or Part B. The function of these insurance companies is rapidly being replaced by managed care plans.

LIFE-CARE HOME

(Also known as Continuing Care Retirement Community or Congregate Housing.) A combination of health care housing and insurance for seniors, often expensive. The EFM signs a contract, which remains in effect as long as the person lives. There is an entrance fee and regular monthly charges, as well as additional charges for added services. Various levels of long-term care are offered, often including catastrophic nursing care. Starting with almost independent living, according to their condition, the patient may be moved to an intermediate care facility, or if necessary, the home's skilled nursing center.

LOCKED NURSING HOME

(See: SECURED NURSING HOME)

MANAGED CARE

The philosophy which is rapidly taking over the cost of medical care for the 21st Century, based on the need to provide medical services, while reducing and controlling costs. Under managed care, these costs (which are considered financial losses by insurance companies and governmental plans like Medicare and Medicaid), are spread between the payee (you) and the provider. In this way, everyone shares both the responsibility and the incentive to contain costs. Ideally, managed care will provide health and medical services efficiently and effectively, without a decrease in the quality or humaneness of care.

There is a growing consumer concern, sparked by investigative reports from Ralph Nader, "Consumers Reports," TV's 60 Minutes, and daily newspaper articles, that there are weak links in the managed care concept. Of course, there are also weak links in Medicare use and abuse. Time will tell whether or not the current managed care system, a modified version of it, or some completely new approach, will emerge as the best solution to providing quality health care for the elderly.

Among the types of managed care plans now in operation are: Health Maintenance Organizations (HMOs), Medicare Risk Contracts (with HMOs), Point of Service Plans (POSs), Preferred Provider Organizations (PPOs), Exclusive Provider Organizations (EPOs), Independent Practice Associations (IPAs), and Integrated

Models. Alternative names and variations of these plans are also being promoted.

MEDICAID

A program to provide medical care for the poor, jointly funded by the federal and state governments, administered by the states. (Called Medi-Cal in California.) This vital program, like Medicare, is under attack and subject to continuing major revisions.

MEDI-CAL

The term used for the Medicaid program in California.

MEDICARE

Federally-funded medical and hospital care for the elderly.

"Part A" hospital insurance usually pays for inpatient hospital care and medically necessary inpatient care in a skilled nursing facility, as well as some home health care and hospice care.

"Part B" medical insurance pays predetermined amounts for doctors' fees, outpatient hospital bills, certain diagnostic tests, necessary permanent medical equipment, ambulance service, and also for some services and supplies which Part A does not cover.

The rules for Medicare are currently under contention in Washington, and are subject to major changes in the future. The major push now by government and private corporations is to convince the elderly to voluntarily switch to managed health care plans, such as HMOs. In the future, this may become mandatory.

To avoid potentially costly wrong decisions, be sure to find out the very latest information on Medicare, keep abreast of politics and the news, and research the "experts' " future projections.

MEDICARE RISK CONTRACT

A way for financially-strapped Medicare to get out from under the burden of paying the high costs of medical help. Medicare contracts with one of many licensed HMOs to provide health care to an elderly recipient. The HMO gets a per capita amount, based upon a complex formula, which costs the government much less. Upon enrolling, a patient must now abide by the rules of the particular HMO, not the previous Medicare policy. If it is up to Congress, and it seems to be, all Medicare patients will have to be enrolled in such HMOs in the not-too-distant future.

NEUROLOGIST
A specialist in the diseases of the nervous system.

NEUROPHARMACOLOGIST
A pharmacologist concerned with the effects of medications on the nervous system.

NEUROPSYCHIATRIST
A psychiatrist who deals with the physical and chemical aspects of brain dysfunction that affect behavior.*

NEUROPSYCHOPHAMACOLOGY
The study of how medications effect mental illness.

NURSING HOME
(See: SKILLED NURSING FACILITY)

OSTEOPOROSIS
A disease resulting in the reduction of bone mass, so a bone cannot support the weight put upon it. It has been reported that the danger of osteoporosis can be of greater risk than cancer for older women and people on steroids, as well as for the sedentary. About 20% of elderly people who fall and suffer hip fractures die within a year, another 25% lose their independence and may end up in nursing homes.

Frequently, a compression fracture of a bone comes first, then the fall. Even a "safe" environment cannot guarantee that bone breakage will not occur, which is the reason why prevention is so important.

Prevention should begin way prior to bone loss, since attempts

---

*Definition by psychiatrist **Mike Frankel, MD**.

to restore bone are only in the early stage. Prevention and treatment may include: bone density scans, taking supplemental calcium and Vitamin D, estrogen (for menopausal women), quitting smoking, and regular exercise, which can decrease the risk of hip fracture by about half.

An elderly patient should see a doctor who is really knowledgeable about the newest research.

PALLIATIVE
Medical services intended to relieve and alleviate, keeping patients comfortable, rather than curing them.

PARKINSON'S DISEASE
A chronic disease of the nervous system resulting in tremors, muscle weakness, contortion, and rigidity (often lack of facial expression), slow speech, falling, and awkward movements. The onset is generally insidious, although it may be abrupt, duration is indefinite, and recovery virtually non-existent. Approximately 50% of Parkinson's patients may develop dementia. (*See Parkinson's question in Chapter 10.*)

PATHOLOGICAL
Diseased or caused by disease, or behavioral disorder.

POINT OF SERVICE PLAN (POS)
A variation of managed care, combining the benefits of lower health costs with freedom of choice. A patient is permitted to receive medical services from "outside" doctors and providers who are not members of the plan, but must pay part of the fees.

PRE-EXISTING CONDITION
Any medical or psychological problem for which a patient received medical advice, treatment, or drugs. Insurance companies and managed care plans usually will not cover such a condition, if it occurred within a specified amount of time prior to coverage. The policies' fine print tries to eliminate coverage of such conditions.

PREFERRED PROVIDER ORGANIZATION (PPO)

A group of physicians or institutional providers who service a group of patients on a fixed, lower-cost fee-for-service basis. Everyone seems to benefit: Patients pay less and have the choice of any doctors within the PPO, while the doctors are guaranteed volume. Problems in scheduling enough time may arise if the PPO accepts too many patients.

PROGRESSIVE DISEASE

A disease, or symptoms of a disease, which grow worse over time.

PSEUDO-DEMENTIA

Major depression, which is normally treatable, but which is left untreated because of misdiagnosis as dementia.

PSYCH UNIT

(See: GERIATRIC PSYCHIATRIC UNIT)

PSYCHOTROPIC DRUGS

Drugs which, intentionally or unintentionally, affect the functioning of a person's mind, behavior, or experiences. These include antidepressants, anti-anxiety drugs, and anti-psychotic drugs for hallucinations, delusions, paranoia, extreme agitation.

QUALITY OF LIFE

The type of experience which a concerned adult child (and staff members) can gift to an elderly family member, that goes way beyond simple existence. By investing a little more time, sensitivity, concern, and educated awareness, the waning days of an aging human being can be made more joyful and meaningful. In return, such generosity of the spirit usually comes back to the caregiver as love and a sense of deep inner-satisfaction.

REVERSE MORTGAGE

Quick cash for house-rich/cash-poor seniors. Allows an elderly homeowner over age 62 to convert the equity in their home to cash, without needing to sell it. If the mortgage is nearly or completely paid off, your EFM can borrow against the equity, getting regular payments, one large sum of money, or a line of credit. The loan is paid off only after the borrower moves out or dies.

The Federal program, Fannie Mae, is entering the reverse mortgage market, which will make more dollars available. Such loans can be quite costly in the end, and fees to lenders are high. Get the opinion of a good financial advisor before making a decision, compare the figures to a non-Fannie Mae loan, then shop-around for the best deal. When immediate cash is needed, this is a method to consider, although many advisors do not recommended it for short-term emergencies, unless your EFM is terminally ill.

RESIDENTIAL CARE FACILITY

(Also known as a Board and Care Home, Retirement Hotel, or Community Care Facility.) An alternative living facility for elderly people who cannot live alone or with a family caregiver, but don't need a skilled nursing facility.

RESPITE CARE

A service which gives an adult caregiver relief, allowing for independence, freedom, and much-deserved time to get away from the pressures of caring for their elderly family member. In the service, during wartime, it was known as R&R (rest and recovery). The stress of caregiving, especially when an EFM is demented, can emotionally resemble the shell-shocked effects of wartime. Types of respite include short-term care of the patient, such as in-home help, adult day-care programs, and other group care programs, as well as overnight and weekend retreats for the caregiver.

RETIREMENT COMMUNITY

Designed primarily for people who are totally or nearly independent and wish to live in a community with other seniors. Recreational activities, organized social programs, meal service, transportation to doctors, banks, and shopping are usually offered, but not nursing services, although such in-home help can be hired privately.

RETIREMENT HOTEL

(Also known as a Large Board and Care.) A larger facility, ranging from an unlicensed hotel for independent seniors (which provides only room, meals, and housekeeping), to a similar-looking licensed facility for people who need assistance (which provides a range of care and services, adding to the cost). Such a hotel is for elderly people who may use canes, walkers, or even wheelchairs, but are not bed-ridden, and do not have advanced dementia or severe medical problems that require a skilled nursing facility.

SECURED NURSING HOME

(Also known as a Locked Nursing Home.) A facility which has been built and set-up for the safety of dementia patients who wander, so they cannot get out clandestinely. There is some form of electronic monitoring system installed, such as "Wander Guard." Better facilities also have a protected garden area so patients can get visual stimulation, exercise, fresh air, and satisfy their need to move.

Some elderly people, such as Alzheimer's patients with severe wandering needs, actually feel more free in a well-run secured nursing facility than in a small home-like board and care.

SENILITY

(See: DEMENTIA)

SKILLED NURSING FACILITY (SNF)

(Also referred to as a Convalescent Home or Nursing Home.)

A nursing home, licensed for skilled care, which has specially trained staff, as well as the necessary equipment to provide 24-hour nursing and rehabilitation care. Many patients are confined to a bed or wheelchair, and are incontinent. Medical treatment is supervised by a registered nurse, at least during the day.

Many such nursing homes are a part of chains owned by corporations, some of which are more concerned about the patients than others. If possible, investigate the record of the corporate owner.

Ultimately, however, the high quality of any nursing facility is dependent more upon the individual administrator, director, and nurses. They are the ones who really care, or do not care, about the patients and staff. Since the people in these positions are subject to change, the quality of the nursing home may rise and fall, so keep tabs on it.

SPECIAL CARE UNIT
(See: DEMENTIA UNIT)

SSI
(Supplemental Security Income.) A federal program for the elderly poor who do not have Social Security or any other retirement income. It provides limited monthly income at the poverty level. Previously, the small amount has been increased to offset rises in the cost of living, but this policy may change in the near future.

SUBACUTE CARE
An alternative to hospitals or nursing homes, for patients who have severe illness or injury, but don't need such intense care. Patients ready for subacute care need about 4-7 hours of skilled nursing care/day (compared with over 8 hours in hospitals, and more than 4 hours in nursing homes).

SUPPORT GROUP
A family support group consists of caregivers, family members, strangers (soon to be friends), and health care professionals. Groups meet at private homes, senior centers, hospitals, libraries, churches, and care facilities.

Many organizations, including the Alzheimer's Association, sponsor support groups nationwide. Attending your first support group can be one of the most rewarding decisions you will make, because of all the practical information, encouragement, warmth, and morale support members give each other.

TLC
Tender loving care. That which we all need...especially our elderly family members. They are going through changes in life we cannot begin to imagine, at the worst possible time when they are least able to deal with such momentous challenges.

WANDERER

A dementia patient who, for reasons we do not yet understand, has an irresistible need to walk. The patient manages to disappear from the premises, and with good fortune, is often found far away, with no awareness about their dangerous, epic journey. There seem to be two kinds of wanderers: those who are easily distracted from the urge, and those who, like Houdini, always manage to escape. Only in a properly secured facility is there any chance of containing this latter type. One patient who couldn't resist the instinct to get out, jumped through a plate glass window.

WORK-UP

A series of medical and psychological tests used to obtain all necessary information for the correct diagnosis and treatment of an elderly patient. To be most accurate, the tests which are administered by various specialists, should be carefully given in the proper sequence, so that no clues are overlooked. This is especially important for a patient who exhibits symptoms of dementia and is suspected of having Alzheimer's disease, in order to rule out pseudo-dementia and treatable diseases.

Index

Testimonials

"A philosophy that Nancy and I share is that geriatric patients are underserved psychiatrically in our community, and yet, respond remarkably well to even short-term treatment."

Oscar Pakier, MD
Medical Director, Geriatric Services
Northridge Hospital, CA

"If we could only clone the energy and expertise of Nancy Wexler, our elderly population and their families would be greatly helped."

Burt Liebross, MD
Valley Internal Medicine, Van Nuys, CA

"...your contributions to the field through your writing, speaking, referrals and overall participation are unparalleled."

Peter S. Belson, FAMILY LOGISTICS.
(former President of the National Association
for Professional Geriatric Care Managers)

"A comprehensive layperson's guide on how to handle the complicated issues of parent care."

Storm Rogers, MSW, LCSW, Gerontologist

"A formidable work for consumers, very well written and informative. It will have a special place on my shelf."

Peter J. Strauss, Esq.
Author, AGING AND THE LAW

"It was especially good to learn more about the range of expertise that Geriatric Care Managers, in general, and you in particular, can offer to older and middle-age clients...with your insights and experience. My mother became so impressed with (your book) that she insisted I leave it with her."

Neal E. Cutler, Director
Boettner Center of Financial Gerontology

"I wanted to vanish off the face of the earth, but you gave me hope that I could cope with both caregiving and my family."

Sandy Berman, Northridge, CA

"It saved my sanity and perhaps my life. Your book is my bible. My children thank you, and so do I."

Anna Renetsky, Westlake Village, CA

"You gave us the strength to face problems and the courage to make decisions without doubts and fears. Nancy, your insights, thoughts, and love remain with us always."

Maggie Carter and Family, Canyon Country, CA

"I read your book again cover-to-cover before coming in to see you! My emotions are like a Baskin-Robbins' flavor...love and guilt all swirled together."

Sharon Kreiser, Client

"In the darkness of worry, you were the guiding light..."

Janet and Randy Ballin, Los Angeles, CA

"You guys are doing a marvelous job. Hard work with a joyful heart truly pays. Thank you for your help and service to the community."

Marnie and Agnes Lacsamana, Woodland Hills, CA

"You were very helpful to me in a time of crisis. You are a very special person and a joy to have met.

Fran Farrand, West Hills, CA

"I want to thank you for the guidance you provided my sister and me regarding our mother... As a result, her health is improved, and she just celebrated her 88th birthday"

Sandy Wolber, Granada Hills, CA

"(Please) send me order forms, so I can recommend it to families."

Pam Erickson
Professional Geriatric Care Manager
Denver, CO

"It's reassuring to know that I can call on you to help out."

Roberta R. Weissglass
Professional Geriatric Care Manager
Santa Barbara, CA

"I especially appreciate Nancy Wexler's unique ability to provide emotional and problem-solving support to adult 'sandwiched' children and their elderly parents, as part of the geriatric planning process."

Barry S. Siegel, MBA, CLU, ChFC
Woodland Hills, CA

"Thank you so much for all your professional services and personal concern during these last few difficult months...the most difficult time in my life. I really appreciated your help in my time of crisis."

Linda Bratkovich, Beverly Hills, CA

"I recently purchased Mama Can't Remember Anymore and found it a wonderful book for anyone with aging parents - regardless of whether the parent has dementia or not! The resources in the back are outstanding. Thank you - and thank you for the work you do."

Caroline L. Fenton, Glendale, CA

"...I was thoroughly able to relax and enjoy (my trip), knowing that we will be able to gain some control to manage Mom's affairs."

Lynn Blumberg, Northridge, CA

"We have been taking care of my in-laws for the last seven months, and your book has been a great help. I've loaned it to others in similar situations, who also found it very helpful."

Sharon Frost, La Canada, CA

"(We) still talk about how grateful we were to come into contact with you. We couldn't have done it without you."

Arlene Minovitz, Studio City, CA

Biographies

NANCY WEXLER, MA, MFCC, is Director of Gerontology Associates, Alzheimer's Case Management Associates, and Professional Nursing Home Placement Services, located in Los Angeles. She has worked in the profession of gerontology since 1975, and has been licensed in the State of California since 1981.

A gerontologist, licensed in private practice for over 15 years, Nancy Wexler specializes in the problems of middle-aged and older adults who are caring for their aging parents. She has helped thousands of aging parents and adult children find their way through the complex maze of medical, psychological, legal, and custodial care options.

Ms. Wexler is currently on the staffs of UCLA-Neuropsychiatric Institute, Encino-Tarzana Regional Medical Center, Northridge Hospital Medical Center, and has been a consultant at other California medical centers.

After graduating from Cornell University, majoring in Child Development, Ms. Wexler began her first career, which focused on children. She taught kindergarten to second grade. Her drive to help the elderly, as well as the young, led her to help found the first adult day-care center (OPICA), and to support the first intergenerational day-care center, the Mark Taper J.O.Y. (Joining Older & Younger) Program in Los Angeles, where she currently serves on the Steering Committee.

Nancy Wexler did her graduate training at Azusa-Pacific California Family Study Center, and the University of Southern California, Andrus Gerontology Center. She holds a Marriage, Family and Child Counselor License from California, and a New York City Teaching Credential.

Ms. Wexler's work has been written up in *Forbes Magazine, Los Angeles Times, Daily News,* and other publications. She has appeared on CBS, other television and radio programs, given seminars at the Beverly Hills Bar Association, lectured extensively, taught at Chapman College and other schools, and has been a columnist in national magazines.

A pioneer in the field of geriatric care management, Nancy Wexler was a founding member of the National Association of Professional Geriatric Care Managers. She served on the first National Board of Directors for five years, and was on the Association's first Standards Committee. Ms. Wexler helped form the Western Regional Chapter and served on its Board of Directors as well. In addition, she founded the San Fernando Chapter of the Older Women's League (OWL) and served as its first President.

Mama Can't Remember Anymore: Care Management of Elders and their Families was the book that introduced the profession of private geriatric care management to the public.

Nancy Wexler has two children, her daughter, an attorney, and her son, a physician. She lives in Tarzana, California, a suburb of Los Angeles, with her husband of 31 years who is a radiologist, two cats, a dog, and thirty rose bushes.

WESLEY J. SMITH has written numerous well-reviewed books to help consumers: *The Lawyer Book, The Doctor Book, The Senior Citizens' Handbook, Winning the Insurance Game* (co-authored with Ralph Nader), *The Frugal Shopper* (co-authored with Ralph Nader), and *Collision Course* (co-authored with Ralph Nader).

Wesley Smith's latest book, *Slippery Slope*, is an exposé of euthanasia (Times Books), which will be followed by *No Contest* (co-authored with Ralph Nader).

RON NORMAN is a Renaissance man in an era of infinite specialization and computer-generated thought. He has worked professionally as a: book and magazine editor, journalist, ghostwriter, critic, scriptwriter, poet; still photographer; abstract expressionist artist; film director, editor, producer, documentarian; and alternative school teacher. His passions are world cultures, young people, nature, politically-incorrect truth, justice, and peace.

Ron Norman is author of *Cinematic Passion - Fred Tan, Director*, and a children's book, *The Boy Who Had Nothing and Was Very, Very Happy*. Currently, he is writing, *VALUES: A Revolutionary Old Way to Make Society Work and Discover Personal Freedom*.